APR - - 2003

You Can't Be President

DISCARD

Also by John R. MacArthur

SECOND FRONT:
CENSORSHIP AND PROPAGANDA
IN THE 1991 GULF WAR

THE SELLING OF "FREE TRADE":
NAFTA, WASHINGTON, AND
THE SUBVERSION OF AMERICAN
DEMOCRACY

You Can't Be President
The Outrageous Barriers to Democracy in America

John R. MacArthur

MELVILLEHOUSE
BROOKLYN, NEW YORK

Copyright © John R. MacArthur 2008

FIRST MELVILLE HOUSE PRINTING. AUGUST 2008

Melville House Publishing
145 Plymouth Street
Brooklyn, NY 11201
www.mhpbooks.com

ISBN: 978-1-933633-60-2

Library of Congress Cataloging-in-Publication Data

MacArthur, John R.
  You can't be president : the outrageous barriers to
democracy in America / John R. MacArthur
      p. cm.
  Includes index.
  ISBN 978-1-933633-60-2
  1. Democracy--United States.
  2. Political participation--United States.
  3. Two-party systems--United States.
  4. Campaign funds--United States.
  5. Oligarchy--United States.
  6. Presidents--United States--Election.
  7. Presidents--United States--History.
  8. United States--Politics and government.
  9. Political culture--United States.
  I. Title.
  JK1726.M33 2008
  320.973--dc22

                                    2008024449

For Emme

Contents

In the late spring of 2007, when I was first seriously thinking about writing this book, I found myself in a Manhattan playground in the midst of what can only be described as a children's riot. Moving to protect my younger daughter from the mob, I wound up surrounded by kids firing squirt guns and hurling water balloons at a boy who appeared to be the target of an organized attack. The wild intensity of the conflict made me curious, enough to ask the boy, while he fended off his assailants from the upper platform of a jungle gym, to explain his plight. He shouted his reply: "They're rebelling against me because I'm the dictator!"

So far so good, I thought. At least *these* 11- and 12-year-old Americans still understood the spirit of democracy. Unfortunately, I wasn't so sure about their parents. Granted, there were lots of prominent adults, ranging from political right to left, who continued to profess their faith in America as a functioning democracy committed to its Constitution. However, there was plenty of evidence to contradict their optimism. Some pessimists might, for example, cite the disputed 2000 presidential vote count in Florida.

Others could point to the Bush Administration's frequent resort to torture and "rendition" of terrorist suspects, warrantless domestic spying, and presidential "signing statements" intended to nullify the will of Congress as evidence of a decline in U.S. democracy—and a commensurate rise in an imperial presidency. They might also mention the decidedly undemocratic result of the 2006 congressional elections, in which the Democratic Party's retaking of Congress on a surge of antiwar sentiment was followed by an *escalation* of U.S. troops in Iraq.

But these skeptical voices, while significant, still formed a distinct minority. Most established commentators remained insistently upbeat about what they viewed as a fundamental, almost genetically coded American devotion to self-government and freedom—a profound faith that any damage caused by President George W. Bush to the constitutional system was somehow automatically self-correcting. Typical was the introduction to an admiring 2005 book about Thomas Paine by the liberal political historian Harvey Kaye. "Paine's new popularity left and, especially, right has been astonishing," Kaye remarked. Regardless of their ideology, he claimed, pundits and politicians continued to associate themselves with the great theorist of popular government and freedom because Americans so dearly loved their democracy:

> However conservative the times appear, we
> Americans remain—with all our faults and
> failings—resolutely democratic in bearing and
> aspiration. When we rummage through our
> revolutionary heritage, we instinctively look for
> democratic hopes and possibilities.

Certainly the group of juvenile rebels I encountered in my neighborhood playground would agree with Kaye's thesis. So too would the editors of *Junior Scholastic* magazine. In a September 3, 2007, article titled "Could *You* Be President?" the magazine's editors outlined what they said were the basic requirements for the job of "President/Chief Executive," presumably with the aim of educating and inspiring their junior high school readers about the obligations and responsibilities attached to the nation's highest political office. According to *Junior Scholastic*, "The presidency has been called the world's toughest job," in part because of the "immense responsibility" of being "the leader of the free world."

But as hard as it is to *be* President, the editors clearly wanted to suggest that virtually anyone could *become* President. Employing the format of a help-wanted advertisement, the article asked, "Before you decide whether or not to run, let's take a closer look at our ad—and the Constitution." True, as *Junior Scholastic* writer Kathy Wilmore explained, "you might get" the idea "looking at the Presidents we've had so far" that the Oval Office was off limits to vast sectors of the population: "All but one have been white male Protestants. (The exception, John F. Kennedy, was Catholic.)" But, according to Ms. Wilmore, this was no reason to be discouraged, since the wide-open eligibility rules under the Constitution had caused the current presidential campaign to be "more diverse than ever before." Just consider the candidates: a woman, Hillary Clinton, "the first woman to be a frontrunner and taken seriously as a presidential candidate"; an Italian-American Catholic, Rudy Giuliani, a leading Republican contender; an African-American, Barack Obama, the first black "presidential candidate with broad acceptance and appeal across racial, cultural, and class lines"; and Mitt Romney, the "first Mormon presidential candidate." (The leading white male Protestant candidate, Senator John McCain, appears in a photograph on the following page, but in keeping with McCain's then low poll numbers the caption didn't bother to say he was running for president.) To underscore this multicultural melting pot of presidential potential, *Junior Scholastic*'s report included a photograph depicting a young black female student with long braids, right hand raised above a lectern affixed with the Presidential seal, as she "finds out how it feels to take the oath of office."

Wilmore and her editors aren't blind to practical political reality, and it's in this vein that they mention the existence of political parties ("which did not exist in 1787") and put forth the notion that "speeches, fund-raiser appearances, and participation in debates" are something akin to "job interviews" for the presidency. Still, while I don't doubt that the people at *Junior Scholastic* mean well, their cheerful discussion about access to the highest office in the land only reinforces what is increasingly a destructive national delusion—that widespread, up-from-the-ground, truly popular democracy, both political and economic, really exists in America. I suppose we can be grateful that such a deep and abiding faith in the possibility of equality and self-government survives against such great odds. At the same time, however, we should be alarmed by political propaganda that exploits the sort of naive assumptions promoted by both popular magazines and university professors. I'm all for hope, audacious or otherwise, but I'm opposed to wishful thinking in dire times. Saying that anyone can be president—or that Americans remain "resolutely democratic in bearing and aspiration"—is a bit like expressing a belief in the literal existence of Santa Claus.

Broadly speaking, you *can't* be president—any more than you can be a billionaire CEO if you were born poor, or well educated if you went to a segregated inner-city public school, or a member of Congress if you buck your local two-party duopoly. Not that miracles never occur, or that brilliant poor boys don't sometimes make good. But one Abraham Lincoln does not a democracy make.

The latest Pollyannaish narrative about the triumph of popular democracy has focused on the savage duel between Hillary Clinton and Barack Obama, finally won by Obama in early June, on the night of the South Dakota and Montana primaries. Since the "Could *You* Be President?" issue of *Junior Scholastic* was published, Obama, with overt reference to Lincoln's own life, seemed to revive the hopes of authentic democratic choice. As the primary season wore on, the junior senator from Illinois was increasingly portrayed in the media as the "people's choice," versus the junior senator from New York, who was, at least at the outset, clearly favored by the majority of state and national party bosses, foremost among them her husband. But Obama's experience as a community organizer among the poor, mixed with his carefully blended rhetoric of populism and national unity, belied his impeccable establishment credentials as well as his own sponsorship by the Daley machine of Chicago. I will address the Obama-Clinton contest in greater detail at the end of this book, but for now it's sufficient to examine their fierce competition for money to understand why Obama's idealistic-sounding campaign slogan, "Yes we can!," rings so hollow when contrasted with the political facts of life. "Yes we can!"—a softer, blander version of Howard Dean's 2004 campaign slogan, "You have the power!"—implies that ordinary people can determine their own political fate. Certainly Obama's early success at raising money in sums of $200 or less (an estimated 625,000 such contributions compared with 210,000 for Clinton through January 2008, according to the Campaign Finance Institute) supported the argument that his was the more popular candidacy. Clinton's relentless attacks on Obama's supposed "lack of experience" for holding the office of president—even going to the extraordinary length of praising their presumptive Republican opponent John McCain's allegedly *superior* qualifications—reinforced the image of Obama as a popular tribune pitted against a political oligarchy.

But Clinton's criticism unfairly, and inaccurately, slighted Obama's genuine experience as an organization man who posed little threat to business as usual in Washington. Just a cursory look at the top twenty contributors to both campaigns was enough to rattle the bones of that authentic partisan of popular sovereignty Thomas Paine. To read Obama's list of prominent bank, media, law-firm, and corporate contributors—eleven of which were also in Clinton's top twenty—was to see a man already deeply compromised by the exigencies of power politics. Every time Clinton replied to "Yes we can!" with "No you can't!" Obama found himself unable, or unwilling, to reply with an obvious question: "Who says we can't?" In part this could be chalked up to Obama's own upbringing, despite the modest finances of the white mother who raised him, in the top echelon of the nation's education system: the most elite private high school in Honolulu; Occidental and Columbia colleges; and Harvard Law School. Such a background generally makes for polite conversationalists, and Obama was nothing if not well mannered.

But the money was even more important than the degrees or, for that matter, Obama's rhetoric of racial reconciliation: in his book *The Audacity of Hope*, Obama acknowledges that a successful campaign proclaiming "Yes we can!" simply isn't feasible in modern American politics without a huge amount of money to pay for the amplifiers. He couldn't very well point out that Clinton's "No you can't" was a message paid for in large measure by Obama's very own sponsors—the wealthy individuals and institutions with the most to lose from authentically popular government. Such a cold understanding of political reality is what enabled Obama to outspend his rival on television advertising by an estimated $75 million to $46 million. In his speech announcing his candidacy for president in Springfield, Illinois, Obama alluded to Lincoln's famous "House Divided" speech—which highlighted the toxic split between slaveholding states and free states—to buttress his call for the country to "stand together." But if one looked at the millions pouring into his campaign coffers from Wall Street and K Street, it was hard to know what sort of house Obama wanted to live in and on which side of town. Was it the house down the street or the house of J. P. Morgan?

And what of the people themselves, so alienated from their government that barely half of them could be stirred to vote in any presidential election? From what I can see, the passion for "homeland security" seems inexorably to be replacing the passion for a self-governing homeland. In this observation I find support, though not comfort, from Joseph Schumpeter, the celebrated economist and darling of so many right-wing ideologues. I'm no admirer of Schumpeter's free-market theories (for example, he views capitalism as "creative destruction"), but his brutally pessimistic analysis of American democratic practice is hard to refute in the twilight of the second Bush Administration. It was Schumpeter who, in his classic 1942 book, *Capitalism, Socialism and Democracy*, posed the critically important question: "How is it technically possible for 'people' to rule?" In reply, the Moravian-born scholar bluntly argued that some ideal system of "Rule by the People" was neither practical nor necessarily desirable. Better to accept this impossibility, he advised, and "drop government by the people and substitute for it government approved by the people," since "democracy means only that the people have the opportunity of accepting or refusing the men who are to rule them." Unlike Jefferson and Lincoln, Schumpeter thought that in the short term, at least, manipulative political elites very often fooled "the people" into accepting things "they do not really want" and that "no amount of retrospective common sense will alter the fact that in reality they [the people] neither raise nor decide issues but that the issues that shape their fate are normally raised and decided for them."

While acknowledging that "beyond direct democracy" there were other outlets through "which the 'people' may partake in the business of ruling," Schumpeter understood better than many of his American-born contemporaries how the American system really worked:

> A [political] party is not, as classical doctrine (or
> Edmund Burke) would have us believe, a group of
> men who intend to promote public welfare "upon
> some principle on which they are all agreed." This
> rationalization is so dangerous because it is so tempting.
> For all parties will of course, at any given time, provide
> themselves with a stock of principles or planks and
> these principles or planks may be as characteristic of
> the party that adopts them and as important for its
> success as the brands of goods a department store sells
> are characteristic of it and important for its success.
> But the department store cannot be defined in terms
> of its brands and a party cannot be defined in terms
> of its principles. A party is a group whose members
> propose to act in concert in the competitive struggle
> for political power. If that were not so it would be
> impossible for different parties to adopt exactly or
> almost exactly the same program. Yet this happens as
> everyone knows. Party and machine politicians are
> simply the response to the fact that the electoral mass
> is incapable of action other than a stampede, and they
> constitute an attempt to regulate political competition
> exactly similar to the corresponding practices of a trade
> association. The psycho-technics of party management
> and party advertising, slogans and marching tunes, are
> not accessories. They are the essence of politics. So is
> the political boss.

Moreover, says Schumpeter, the people were not as fitted to self-government, as the classical theorists might believe:

> Newspaper readers, radio audiences, members of a
> party even if not physically gathered together
> are terribly easy to work up into a psychological crowd
> and into a state of frenzy in which attempt at
> rational argument only spurs the animal spirits.

Thus, Schumpeter also warned against conflating civil liberties and democracy, for he well understood that the democratic endorsement by the "rabble" in places like Hitler's Germany or Mussolini's Italy could easily destroy freedom and justice in a working (if only temporarily so) democracy.[1]

In his employment of the term "Manufactured Will," Schumpeter shares more in common with the left-wing linguist Noam Chomsky than with the right-wing economist Milton Friedman. So do I, though I confess that Chomsky's bleak brilliance sometimes wears me out. Despite my own pessimism, my heroes and guides are still the idealistic optimists of democracy: Benjamin Franklin, Thomas Jefferson and Jefferson's greatest student, Abraham Lincoln. I try to keep Jefferson's dictum, expressed in a letter to James Madison, somewhere close to my heart: "We are never permitted to despair of the Commonwealth." And I'm ashamed when I think I haven't taken enough to heart Franklin's exquisite aphorism, so perfect for the post-9/11 era: "Those who would give up essential liberty, to purchase a little temporary safety, deserve neither liberty

---

1 Schumpeter encouraged his readers to imagine "a hypothetical country that, in a democratic way, practices the persecution of Christians, the burning of witches, and the slaughtering of Jews," and asked, "Would we approve of the democratic constitution itself that produced such results in preference to a non-democratic one that would avoid them?"

nor safety." In this, I suppose, I'm guilty of the same arrogant and inflated sense of American "exceptionalism" that Alexis de Tocqueville identified in 1831—the notion that America is so different, so special, that it deserves to be judged by a different set of standards than the rest of the world. I don't pretend it's logical, but I can't help feeling that America should be held accountable to its own high-flown principles of conduct and morality—principles that were best exemplified by the deeds and writings of Jefferson and Lincoln—rather than to, say, international law. For this reason, I don't attempt to analyze the health of American democracy by measuring it against an abstract or universal standard, and I have avoided making explicit comparisons with foreign countries.

However, in my reading of Tocqueville's *Democracy in America* I'm struck by the fact that this foreign visitor never hesitated to make comparisons between Jacksonian America and Europe, with special attention to England and his native, then undemocratic France. To this day, Tocqueville's celebrated generalizations about the United States, based on nine months of highly subjective interviews, are often—even excessively—quoted to support the pro-American precepts of the true believers in our democratic system. Of course, there's nothing wrong with quoting someone selectively to make a point, but when I finished the second volume of *Democracy in America* (published in 1840, five years after the first), I wondered whether the American enthusiasts of Tocqueville had read much beyond the passages that are enshrined in *Bartlett's Familiar Quotations*. The young aristocrat's fundamental admiration for the youthful republic is well known, but some of his most daring criticisms are not.

Tocqueville expressed an aristocrat's conventional mistrust of enforced equality (enhanced by the near execution of his father during the French Revolution), for he instinctively feared a society without rank. But his analysis of the possible consequences of such a system seems to me quite unconventional and even original. "I had remarked during my stay in the United States, that a democratic state of society, similar to that of the Americans, might offer singular facilities for the establishment of despotism," he wrote near the end of the second volume in a chapter titled "What Sort of Despotism Democratic Nations Have to Fear." He noted that despite the tyranny practiced by emperors in ancient republican Rome, "the different nations of the empire still preserved manners and customs of great diversity . . . the details of social life and private occupations lay for the most part beyond [the emperor's] control." Roman tyrants controlled "the whole strength of the State" and "abused that power arbitrarily to deprive their subjects of property or of life," but "their tyranny was extremely onerous to the few" and "did not reach the greater number; it was fixed to some few main objects, and neglected the rest; it was violent, but its range was limited." Liberal countries in Tocqueville's era, like England and America, possessed some of the same tendencies, but "if despotism were to be established amongst the democratic nations of our days, it might assume a different character; it would be more extensive and more mild; it would degrade men without tormenting them." Under such soft tyranny, the government would seek to keep the people "in perpetual childhood," in such a manner that it "every day renders the exercise of the free agency of man less useful and less frequent." Under this form of "democratic despotism,"

> The will of man is not shattered, but softened, bent, and
> guided: men are seldom forced by it to act, but they
> are constantly restrained from acting: such a power does
> not destroy, but it prevents existence; it does not tyran-
> nize, but it compresses, enervates, extinguishes, and
> stupefies a people, till each nation is reduced to be
> nothing better than a flock of timid and industrious
> animals, of which the government is the shepherd.

I have always thought that servitude of the regular, quiet, and gentle kind which I have just described, might be combined more easily than is commonly believed with some of the outward forms of freedom; and that it might even establish itself under the wing of the sovereignty of the people. . . .

By this system the people shake off their state of dependence just long enough to select their master, and then relapse into it again. A great many persons at the present day are quite contented with this sort of compromise between administrative despotism and the sovereignty of the people; and they think they have done enough for the protection of individual freedom when they have surrendered it to the power of the nation at large. This does not satisfy me: the nature of him I am to obey signifies less to me than the fact of extorted obedience.

When I survey the political landscape of contemporary America, I fear that the worst of Tocqueville's hypotheses have come true. We now have a reckless, authoritarian President impervious to the will of Congress, and, more important, the will of the people; a Congress unwilling to defy the President; candidates in collusion with the money interests; an apathetic, consumption-obsessed citizenry that has lost the habit of exercising power. Some would say that the best treatment for such a weakness in the body politic is an election, but as the next one approaches I find myself returning to Tocqueville's darkest reflections: "It is in vain to summon a people, which has been rendered so dependent on the central power, to choose from time to time the representatives of that power; this rare and brief exercise of their free choice, however important it may be, will not prevent them from gradually losing the faculties of thinking, feeling, and acting for themselves, and thus gradually falling below the level of humanity." We might add, falling below the level of self-governing adulthood. In 1777, Thomas Paine issued a rhetorical challenge to colonists anxious about the wisdom of separation from England: "To know whether it be the interest of the continent to be independent, we need only ask this easy, simple question: Is it the interest of a man to be a boy all his life?" Without reference to gender, we would do well to pose the same question to today's electorate. Do they really want to run their own government?

—

I started the reporting for this book in a playground on Manhattan's Upper West Side. Symbolically, I ended it in Virginia more than five months later with my wife, my two daughters, and my sister at Monticello, Thomas Jefferson's magnificent architectural obsession and the physical manifestation of so many of the Enlightenment principles that animated his life. After writing so much bad news about American democracy, I needed inspiration and hoped that visiting Jefferson's citadel would provide me with it.

It was unseasonably warm for a late October afternoon, though at 867 feet above sea level some leaves were turning lovely reds and yellows at the summit of Jefferson's "little mountain." I wasn't surprised by what appeared to be the uniformly white faces that crowded onto the shuttle bus at the bottom of the hill and unloaded to line up for the house tour when they reached the top. Jefferson's great hypocrisy—advocating equality for "all men" while owning hundreds of slaves—is known far and wide, and I presume that African-Americans are more comfortable making pilgrimages to Lincoln's home in Springfield, Illinois, or to the Lincoln Memorial in Washington, D.C. What did surprise me was the upward rush of excitement I felt when I stood in front of the east portico of Jefferson's neoclassical dream house for the first time.

I can't bring myself to dislike Jefferson for owning slaves, cling-
ing as I do to La Rochefoucauld's insight that "hypocrisy is the
compliment vice pays to virtue." This patrician plantation-owner
turned civil-rights lawyer vigorously, but unsuccessfully, advocated
emancipation of the slaves, whereas Lincoln, the poor boy turned
corporation lawyer, actually abolished slavery. But while I'm certain
there would have been an American revolution without Jefferson, I
don't think that without Jefferson there could have been a President
Lincoln, for Jefferson's influence on Lincoln was profound. In an
open letter in 1859 written for the occasion of Jefferson's birthday,
Lincoln wrote, "The principles of Jefferson are the definitions and
axioms of free society," although in the context of slavery "they are
denied and evaded, with no small show of success." It is not a coincidence that both men were principal founders of new political parties
that revived American democracy—Jefferson in order to combat the
authoritarian tendencies of John Adams, Alexander Hamilton, and
the Federalist Party; Lincoln, in order to put an end to what he
called the "monstrous injustice" of slavery. Indeed, Lincoln not only
found inspiration in Jefferson but also cleverly put his egalitarian
forebear to work in the service of Republican Party politics. When
he spoke out against the Democrat-sponsored Kansas-Nebraska Act
of 1854, which permitted settlers to adopt slavery in vast new areas
in the West, Lincoln invoked the slave-owning Democrat Jefferson
to advance the anti-slavery cause. In a speech in Peoria, Illinois, he
called Jefferson "the most distinguished politician of our history."
More to the point, he reminded his audience that as a congressman,
Jefferson had successfully pushed for the adoption of the Ordinance
of 1784, which, three years later, in a different form, banned slavery in what was then the Northwest Territory (the future states of
Ohio, Indiana, Illinois, Michigan, Wisconsin, and Minnesota). For
Lincoln, the principle expressed in Jefferson's Declaration of Independence that, in Lincoln's paraphrase, "no man is good enough to

govern another man, without that other's consent" constituted the "sheet anchor of American republicanism."

But as we drove back down the hill past the Jefferson family graveyard, I couldn't help feeling a little of the dreaded despair forbidden by Jefferson. Our excellent tour guide, Patricia Abbitt, had urged us to "think about Thomas Jefferson and liberty" after she pointed out the decorative engraving of the Declaration, by John Binns, that hangs on the wall of Monticello's first-floor sitting room. Instead, my thoughts turned to the two-party system and the feeble opposition mounted in response to George W. Bush's assault against liberty, honest vote counting, and the rule of law.

Earlier that day, while we waited at the airport in New York for the flight to Richmond (where we would rent a car for the drive to Monticello), I happened to glance at the lead editorial in the *New York Times*. Since the fall and winter of 2002-03, the *Times* had contributed so much to Bush's Iraq disaster, by spreading disinformation and administration propaganda, that I was surprised to find myself reading one of its institutional declarations with such interest. Headlined "With Democrats Like These . . . ," the editorial criticized the opposition party's weak-kneed response to Bush's unconstitutional violation of the 1978 Foreign Intelligence Surveillance Act. Under FISA the government was required to obtain a judge's warrant before it could eavesdrop on phone conversations between people in the United States, whether citizens or not, and any resident of a foreign country. The Democrats, with a two-house congressional majority since January 2007, had responded to Bush's program of warrantless wiretapping by simply giving in and permitting what had previously been forbidden. Instead of cutting back the President's brazen overreach of his executive authority, the new Democrat-controlled Congress had amended FISA to legalize the previously illegal wiretaps of phone calls and emails and then expanded the President's power, as the *Times* put it, to "authorize warrantless surveillance of Americans' homes, offices and phone records; permit surveillance of Americans abroad without probable cause; and sharply limit the power of the court that controls electronic spying." Now, after promising to revisit their "revision" of the President's power to spy, the Democrats had once again backed down in the face of White House and Republican pressure.

With uncharacteristic clarity, the *Times* editorialist wrote:

> Every now and then, we are tempted to double-check
> that the Democrats actually won control of Congress
> last year. It was particularly hard to tell this week.
> Democratic leaders were cowed, once again,
> by propaganda from the White House and failed, once
> again, to modernize the law on electronic spying in
> a way that permits robust intelligence gathering on
> terrorists without undermining the Constitution. . . .
> It was bad enough having a one-party government
> when Republicans controlled the White House and
> both houses of Congress. But the Democrats took
> over, and still the one-party system continues.

As readers will better understand in Chapter Nine, I'm reluctant to cite the *New York Times* in support of my underlying thesis: that democracy in America is frozen by a two-party oligarchy and a campaign finance system that have raised the barriers of entry to our political process to nearly insurmountable heights. But when the establishment's paper of record decries one-party government, we should take note, for things must be very bad to rouse the *New York Times* from its own deep slumber.

Indeed, waking up is what this book is all about; I wrote it in the hope of contributing to a democratic revival, to help thaw what has become an American political ice age. While much of what I describe is disturbing, it's also of practical use—at the very least in understanding the formidable odds facing any citizen who wants to participate in his or her self-governance. Moreover, I don't intend to leave readers feeling hopeless. Quite the contrary. If you are dismayed and angered by the dominance of party bosses and the big money that guarantees their hold on power, by an economic and education system that increasingly underwrites inherited privilege, by the seemingly inexorable expansion of Wal-Mart and Wall Street, by a war that the Democratic majority refuses to end, then already you have the knowledge necessary to fight back. But everybody needs inspiration and I find mine among the several authentic democrats who appear in these pages, some of them living and others very much alive in our national memory: Conni Harding of Portsmouth, Rhode Island; Ned Lamont of Greenwich, Connecticut; George McGovern of Mitchell, South Dakota; Eugene McCarthy of Watkins, Minnesota; I. F. Stone of Haddonfield, New Jersey; Ralph Nader of Winsted, Connecticut; and Joe Moore of Chicago, Illinois. These are people who have exhibited a powerful sense of American entitlement—the good democratic kind, not the kind you encounter in gated communities like Washington, D.C. There are many different ways to cause change in American society, but every important movement starts with just one person who believes he or she has a citizen's right and obligation to do something. To restore the business of government to the people—to wrest it from oligarchic control—you generally need a large number of allies. But to establish a certain democratic integrity in your town or neighborhood, it sometimes only takes a few. But one person has to start somewhere.

Despite what you learn in school or in *Junior Scholastic* magazine, you can't be president. But even if you could, chances are you wouldn't know what kind of government you would lead. Americans often have difficulty appreciating their democratic rights and privileges, and one reason might be because so many don't understand what American democracy means. Poll after poll illustrates a disturbing lack of understanding among a substantial portion of the world's "freest" citizens about the origins of their republic and its written guarantees of liberty and self-government. "A republic, if you can keep it," Benjamin Franklin famously, and ominously, remarked at the close of the Constitutional Convention in 1787. I suspect he feared that blindness to the letter and intent of constitutional democracy, combined with indifference, would kill popular sovereignty as surely as counterrevolution.

Statistics about the formal teaching of the United States Constitution, and the Bill of Rights that comprise its first ten amendments, are hard to come by, but it is clear that what's being taught is inadequate. According to the First Amendment Center at Vanderbilt University, most Americans do not even know this most famous amendment to the Constitution. In ten polls conducted from 1997 to 2007, the center found that no more than 16 percent of Americans could identify freedom of the press as a right guaranteed in the First Amendment. Freedom of religion was known to 22 percent at most, though in 1999 only 13 percent could identify it as a specified constitutional right. Just 11 percent, in 2006, noted the right of assembly, and no more than 3 percent in any poll mentioned the right to petition for redress of grievances. As for knowledge of the guarantee of freedom of speech, the numbers were somewhat less distressing—44 percent in 1999; 64 percent in 2007—but one had to wonder about the 40 to 50 percent of Americans who consistently failed to note that this right existed under the First Amendment. The other nine, much less celebrated amendments in the Bill of Rights would no doubt score even lower on a scale of recognition.[1]

More alarming are the surveys that show how Americans actually feel about their birthright of freedom. For example, a 2006 poll conducted by the Knight Foundation found that 45 percent of American high school students (an increase of 10 percent from their 2004 survey) thought the First Amendment protections of religion, speech, press, assembly, and petition go "too far," while only 54 percent thought that "newspapers should be allowed to publish freely without government approval of a story." Adults were no more protective of their civil rights than their children, according to a 1989 *Washington Post*-ABC News poll that found that 62 percent of Americans "would be willing to give up a few of the freedoms we have" to help fight the dubious "war on drugs" conceived by President Richard Nixon and revived by President George H.W. Bush.

---

1 As to the right to vote itself, scholars disagree on whether the Constitution actually, explicitly guarantees such a thing. This is why Rep. Jesse Jackson Jr., a Democratic congressman from Illinois, advocates a constitutional amendment specifying voting as a right of citizenship.

I hesitate to lean too hard on these depressing figures, however, since it is unfair for the educated elite in America to blame the less-educated for failing in their constitutional duty. The "mob" as well as the young have always been maligned by people who consider themselves to be their betters. Moreover, membership in a democratic elite implies responsibility for setting a good example, and time and again I find myself astonished by the sheer ignorance of some of our leading citizens about the origins of American democracy.[2] As the constitutional scholar Michael Kammen notes, "Even the so-called experts (judges, lawyers, political leaders, and teachers of constitutional law) have been unable to agree in critical instances about the proper application of key provisions of the Constitution, or about the intentions of those who wrote and approved it."

The lack of basic comprehension of the Constitution and its antecedents by America's political and media leaders is a crippling defect in a country that habitually vaunts its superiority over undemocratic cultures it considers woefully unenlightened. In the spring of 2005, I participated in a *Providence Journal*/Brown University conference on the "possibility" of democracy in the Middle East. The condescending premise of the forum troubled me, since American democracy, in the wake of George W. Bush's fraudulent presidential "victory" in 2000, was hardly anything to brag about. Nevertheless, I welcome any discussion with academics who know more than I do. Unfortunately, instead of meeting genuine scholars, I found myself debating Joshua Muravchik, a "resident scholar" at the American Enterprise Institute, a wealthy "think tank" funded by right-wing

---

2 Apparently, the problem starts young. In 2006, the nonprofit Intercollegiate Studies Institute tested about 7,000 college seniors on their "American civic literacy." The ISI graded the students from 50 private and public universities, including Harvard, Princeton, and Yale; they found that the students scored an overall 54.2 percent, which the ISI said was the equivalent of an "F." According to the survey, only 45.9 percent of the students knew that the phrase "We hold these truths to be self-evident, that all men are created equal" comes from the Declaration of Independence.

corporations and individuals with little pretense of thoughtfulness but very high standards for propaganda. At a certain point, Muravchik began musing about the origins of democracy: "We know that democracy developed first, historically, in Protestant countries. And we know that, from then to now, there have been questions about the compatibility of democracy with different kinds of cultures, with different religious beliefs."[3]

Muravchik's historical gaffe went unremarked by the largely academic audience until I expressed astonishment at the news that ancient Greece and Rome were Protestant cultures. But this hardly made up for the innumerable times that pseudohistorians like Muravchik are permitted to masquerade as scholars on American television and radio.

Similarly, in the right-wing media, interest in the Constitution and the history of democracy often seems superficial at best. Not long after 9/11, I was invited to appear on *The O'Reilly Factor*, then the most popular talk show on Rupert Murdoch's Fox News Network, to discuss Fox's permanent display of an American flag on the corner of the television screen. As a media critic, I saw the flag brandishing for what it was: an advertisement intended to demonstrate Fox's single-minded patriotism, as well as its alignment with

---

3 Alexis de Tocqueville believed that Catholics, contrary to popular prejudices current in 1831, were at least as well-suited as Protestants to self-government and the doctrine of equal rights under law. Himself a Roman Catholic, he wrote: "On doctrinal points the Catholic faith places all human capacities upon the same level; it subjects the wise and the ignorant, the man of genius and the vulgar crowd, to the details of the same creed; it imposes the same observances upon the rich and the needy, it inflicts the same austerities upon the strong and the weak, it listens to no compromise with mortal man, but reducing all the human race to the same standard, it confounds all the distinctions of society at the foot of the same altar, even as they are confounded in the sight of God. If Catholicism predisposes the faithful to obedience, it certainly does not prepare them for inequality: but the contrary may be said of Protestantism, which generally tends to make men independent, more than to render them equal."

the Bush Administration. Blind, pro-government jingoism, I felt, should always be discouraged in journalism, but especially in times of national hysteria and war.

Host Bill O'Reilly, a graduate of Harvard's Kennedy School of Government, disagreed and pressed me on whether I considered it "harmful and inappropriate for the media to display signs of patriotism, for example an American flag." When I suggested that Fox display the actual Bill of Rights instead of posting a symbol (since presumably it was the freedoms embodied in the literal text of the Constitution that we were fighting to defend against terrorists), O'Reilly bridled and waved away my idea:

> Let me disagree with you and tell you in a gentle way why you are wrong. The symbol of the flag, all that connotates [sic] to me—and I'm looking at it now as an employee of the Fox News Channel but also as a viewer—is that we are proud of our country.... That in this time of need not only are we journalists but we're also Americans. That we have a bond with the viewer, a bond with the people who watch us. So that's an easy way to get that message across. It's a very utilitarian way to tell the viewer, "We're with you on this."

Of course, American ignorance and indifference regarding the Constitution, and our particular form of democracy, is by no means a right-wing phenomenon. In the wake of the failed effort by a substantial number of Democratic congressmen in the spring of 2007 to force a troop withdrawal from Iraq, National Public Radio's Robert Siegel interviewed "policy experts," including Peter Rodman, a senior fellow in foreign policy studies at the Brookings Institution, the somewhat liberal counterpart to the right-wing Heritage Foundation. Siegel—a mildly liberal voice on an occasionally liberal radio network—was having difficulty explaining to his audience why, with popular opinion running heavily against the war and Congress having dramatically changed hands in November to a Democratic majority in both houses, antiwar members of Congress seemed incapable of influencing President Bush's war policy. Furthermore, absent congressional action, he wanted to know when the Bush Administration might respond to public opinion.

> **Siegel:** There's yet another poll out today [May 24, 2007] that shows public dissatisfaction with the war as it's going now and with the original decision to get into the war in Iraq—dissatisfaction is rising still.[4] How can a policy continue with such a lack of public support? And neither of you has described anything that might happen in the near future that would give people cause to support it more. Peter Rodman, at some point, as the rubber hits the road, [when do] you say the public is not with us?"

> **Rodman:** No, I think there's an objective reality out there, namely, the vital American interest in the Middle East and the catastrophic consequences of an American collapse in Iraq. And I think it's a responsibility of our political leaders to respond to the real challenge and the real requirements for American policy and not to decide things by public opinion polls.

> **Siegel:** Or by elections, for that matter?

---

4 A CBS News/*New York Times* poll released that week had found that 63 percent of Americans favored a "timetable for Iraq withdrawal in 2008"; 69 percent said that current funding of the war should include "benchmarks" for improvement by the Iraqi government; and 61 percent thought the United States "should have stayed out" of Iraq in the first place. Nevertheless, on May 24 Congress appropriated new money for the war without a timetable for withdrawal but with the so-called benchmarks.

Rodman did not respond to Siegel's trenchant question, but neither did the cautious newsman press the matter. Siegel had already failed to identify Rodman as a pro-war, pro-occupation partisan who until joining Brookings six months earlier had been an assistant secretary of defense in the Bush Administration; it was too much, perhaps, to expect him to explain how the Constitution, by granting Congress the power of the purse, empowers it to stop a war.

Siegel could have also mentioned that a large portion of the Democratic congressional caucus still—and in spite of the popular will—supported the basic Bush Administration war premises ("democratizing" the Middle East; controlling oil resources; fighting "terrorism"; maintaining military bases to facilitate an attack on Iran or the defense of Israel and Saudi Arabia; etc.), either openly or tacitly. He could have noted that the Constitution requires a two-thirds majority in the Senate (67 votes, if all members are present) and in the House (290 votes) to override the presidential veto of a bill and that the Democratic antiwar faction in the Senate (where the Democratic caucus held a bare majority of 51 to 49, thanks to the hawkish "independent" Joseph Lieberman caucusing with the Democrats) numbered at most 29 firm members.

Fundamentally, what Siegel would not, or could not, say to a national radio audience was that despite Americans' turn against the war, a great deal of policy and politics in the United States had little to do with Abraham Lincoln's concept of "government of the people, by the people, for the people." American "democracy" was by design, and by a series of pragmatic compromises, a limited form of self-government—that America was only intermittently a democracy in the most genuine sense. Thomas Paine's "Common Sense" (1776) and Thomas Jefferson's Declaration of Independence (1776) promoted the genuinely radical idea of rule by the many and the ordinary, but by the time the Constitution was ratified in 1788, a powerful competing notion, the more conservative idea of rule by the few and the elite, had become well established. As Michael Kammen writes:

> The concept of consent, so sacred and popular in constitution-making between 1776 and 1785, began to receive less emphasis during the later 1780s. The founders became increasingly persuaded that once consent had been given by the citizens, and once authority had been entrusted, the people should not vary the terms of their trust so long as those to whom it had been delegated exercised authority in accordance with the terms on which it had been granted. . . . The desire for energetic and stable government persuaded the advocates of a new national constitution to be less populistic and more legalistic, to rely more heavily upon institutions than upon individuals for restraint in public affairs . . .

This push toward creating a distance between the people and their governmental institutions was summed up by John Adams, the most pessimistic and reactionary of the founding fathers, in a 1789 letter to his more radical cousin, Samuel Adams: "Whenever I use the word republic with approbation, I mean a government in which the people have collectively, or by representation, an essential share in the sovereignty." Adams was at odds with the prevailing opinion, held by James Madison and the other federalists—indeed, held by most Americans—that, as the historian Gordon Wood has written, "All governmental power was derived from the people" and that this power was "lent out to the various government officials, so to speak, on a short-term, always recallable loan." This crucial disagreement about the nature of popular sovereignty has never really been resolved. But it's safe to say that by the early twenty-first century, the John Adams position—and its fundamental mistrust of popular government—was very much in the ascendancy.

With this contentious history in mind, it should never be surprising that Congress responds so slowly to the popular will. I, for one, wasn't shocked by the obvious foot-dragging of major Democratic politicians after their party recaptured the House and Senate on a wave of popular disgust over the war. I encountered one of the foot-draggers just a few weeks after the 2006 election, at a reception in Washington following a memorial service for a prominent Washington lawyer. In the backyard of a gracious home not far from the chapel of the ultra-establishment St. Albans School, I was introduced to the newly re-empowered Senator John D. Rockefeller IV, Democrat of West Virginia, who was soon to become chairman of the Senate Intelligence Committee in the new Congress. Given the shift in congressional control and the majority antiwar feeling in the country, I asked Rockefeller, the great-grandson of the oil billionaire John D. Rockefeller, how we might exit Iraq. I assumed that Rockefeller favored withdrawal, not only because of the disastrous military situation but also out of anger and shame, since he himself had been the victim of the massive intelligence lies that preceded the invasion. As a member of the Intelligence Committee during the debate on Iraq in the fall of 2002, Rockefeller had firmly endorsed Bush's war plan against Saddam Hussein's regime. Before voting for the Joint Resolution to Authorize the Use of United States Armed Forces Against Iraq, on October 10, 2002, Rockefeller declared, "There is unmistakable evidence that Saddam Hussein is working aggressively to develop nuclear weapons and will likely have nuclear weapons within the next five years."

But there was little convincing evidence that Saddam was building nuclear weapons; indeed, there was a great deal of evidence from the International Atomic Energy Agency and other sources that he wasn't. Like so many others in politics and the media, Rockefeller had signed on to the central premise of the Bush propaganda campaign: "Saddam Hussein represents a grave threat to the United States, and I have concluded we must use force to deal with him if all other means fail."

On the occasion of our meeting, Rockefeller, who is known by the nickname Jay, showed no embarrassment when he replied to my question about exiting Iraq: "The only person who can get us out of Iraq," he said, "is the President." But what about Congress's power of the purse, as specified under the Constitution? I asked. Couldn't the legislative branch cut off funding for the military occupation of Iraq? As though scripted, Rockefeller promptly replied, "We couldn't get the votes to override the President's veto."

Rockefeller was being somewhat disingenuous. Granted, it is difficult for Congress to overcome a president's veto. For example, when in the spring of 2007, Congress attached a deadline for troop withdrawal from Iraq to the main Pentagon appropriations bill, Bush rejected it and antiwar Democrats could not muster the votes for an override. But nothing in the Constitution requires the House or the Senate to appropriate money for a war just because the President desires it. A simple majority in either house can defeat any spending bill favored by the White House and sponsored by the President's congressional supporters. If Rockefeller and the other Democratic leaders in Congress really wanted to get out of Iraq, they could, with 51 votes in the Senate and 218 in the House (assuming that all members are present), vote down every military appropriations bill that comes before them until the President agreed to withdraw the troops or the Pentagon could not meet its payroll. Rockefeller's exaggerated deference to the executive was never intended by the founding fathers, most of whom envisioned a fairly weak executive. So it seems likely that the junior senator from West Virginia, unlike his eloquent senior colleague, Robert Byrd, the other Democratic senator from his state, agreed tacitly with Peter Rodman's manifestly undemocratic view of "objective reality" in the Middle East. The will of the people be damned.[5]

Congressional reluctance to stop the war in Iraq illustrates what is so confusing and paradoxical about American democracy. Time and again in American history, figures rise up from the citizenry, riding a wave of popular sentiment, only to be rebuffed by the professional political class, including elected officials (typically trained as lawyers), senior political appointees, and prosecutors and judges (not always independent and often indebted to the politicians who sponsored them). Among the legal profession generally, Tocqueville found what he described as an elitist "jurist's temperament"—a mind-set, he said, that was born of lawyers' specialized knowledge and "a notion of their superiority" that tended "to separate it [the legal profession] more and more from the people, and to place it in a distinct class" that "formed the most powerful, if not the only counterpoise to the democratic element." According to Tocqueville, "A portion of the tastes and of the habits of the aristocracy may consequently be discovered in the characters of men in the profession of

---

5 Rockefeller's voting record in 2006-2007 revealed a decidedly ambiguous position on the war. In June 2006, he was not present to vote on a resolution offered by Senators John Kerry and Russ Feingold, which called for a deadline for troop withdrawal in 2007. In April 2007, Rockefeller, now in the majority, voted for an emergency funding bill that gave President Bush the defense money he asked for but required troops to begin withdrawing within four months if the Iraqi government satisfied certain benchmarks. President Bush vetoed the bill on May 1. Two weeks later, Feingold introduced an amendment similar to his 2006 resolution, now attached to a water-resources bill. This time, Rockefeller voted to prevent Feingold's antiwar amendment from reaching the Senate floor for a vote. In the final draft of the emergency defense authorization bill, any reference to troop withdrawal had been removed and supplanted by non-binding "benchmarks" requiring improved military, economic, and political performance by the Iraqi government. Rockefeller voted for this bill, which passed the Senate by a vote of 80-14 (and the House by a vote of 280-142) and was signed by President Bush.

the law. They participate in the same instinctive love of order and of formalities; and they entertain the same repugnance to the actions of the multitude, and the same secret contempt of the government of the people." The same could be said of many congressmen. In his 1880 novel of Washington politics, *Democracy*, Henry Adams (great-grandson of one president, John Adams, and grandson of another, John Quincy Adams) was explicit in his characterization of privileged and haughty politicians: "A certain secret jealousy of the British Minister [ambassador] is always lurking in the breast of every American Senator, if he is truly democratic; for democracy, rightly understood, is the government of the people, by the people, for the benefit of senators . . ." [6]

Thus, when Cindy Sheehan, the mother of a soldier killed in Iraq, decided to protest against the war, she found to her dismay that "American democracy" could be as unresponsive to popular opinion as an embedded aristocracy. In their formulations of the Constitution, James Madison and his colleagues had done their utmost to protect against not only the "tyranny of the majority" but also the narrowly dangerous interests of political factions. But their astute separation of constitutional powers in 1787—among the legislative, executive, and judiciary branches—did not anticipate what Sheehan described in 2007 when she bitterly renounced her position as the "face" of the antiwar movement. Frustrated by congressional inaction on the war, Sheehan expressed perplexity similar to that of NPR's Robert Siegel, but her "heartbreaking conclusions" about the political system were far bolder than Siegel could ever have permitted himself on the public airwaves:

---

6 In September 1970, during the Vietnam War, the Democrats controlled the Senate 57-43. But here again, an unresponsive majority party refused to pass legislation that would have ended an unpopular war directed by a Republican president, Richard Nixon. A bipartisan amendment to cut off war funding co-sponsored by a Democrat, George McGovern, and a Republican, Mark Hatfield, was defeated 55-39.

I was the darling of the so-called "left" as long as I limited
my protests to George Bush and the Republican Party. Of
course, I was slandered and libeled by the right as a "tool" of
the Democratic Party. . . . However, when I started to hold
the Democratic Party to the same standards that I held the
Republican Party, support for my cause started to erode and
the "left" started labeling me with the same slurs that the
right used. . . . I am deemed a radical because I believe that
partisan politics should be left to the wayside when hundreds of thousands of people are dying for a war based on
lies that is supported by Democrats and Republicans alike. It
amazes me that people who are sharp on the issues and can
zero in like a laser beam on lies, misrepresentations and political expediency when it comes to one party refuse to recognize it in their own party. Blind party loyalty is dangerous
whatever side it occurs on. People of the world look on us
Americans as jokes because we allow our political leaders so
much murderous latitude, and if we don't find alternatives to
this corrupt "two" party system our Representative Republic
will die and be replaced with what we are rapidly descending
into with nary a check or balance: a fascist corporate waste-
land. I am demonized because I don't see party affiliation or
nationality when I look at a person, I see that person's heart.
If someone looks, dresses, acts, talks and votes like a Republican, then why do they deserve support just because he/she
calls him/herself a Democrat?

Sheehan's *cri de coeur* might have seemed exaggerated to some—the
complaint of a self-styled martyr—but then most Americans have
never met a professional politician. When I met Senator Rockefeller,
and I confronted his defeatism about the possibility of withdrawal
from Iraq, I tried to be diplomatic, and constructive. Had he read

the cover article of a recent issue of *Harper's Magazine*, I asked, in which former Senator George McGovern and a former state department official, William Polk, presented a detailed and practical plan for withdrawal from Iraq? No, said Rockefeller, but he would be happy to read it if I sent it to his home. I did, and about a month later I received a handwritten note from the patrician politician. "To be honest," he said, "I haven't read the article yet—with all the Christmas clutter. But I obviously will. I am so skeptical about the whole mess, I'm looking for any good idea (much less a workable one)."

That Rockefeller did not share Cindy Sheehan's sense of urgency was disheartening. Worse was Sheehan's newly acquired despair: "The most devastating conclusion that I reached this morning . . . was that [my son] did indeed die for nothing. . . . Our brave young men and women in Iraq have been abandoned there indefinitely by their cowardly leaders who move them around like pawns on a chessboard of destruction. . . . This system forcefully resists being helped and eats up the people who try to help it."

On May 28, 2007, the day Sheehan said she was renouncing politics, it seemed that the tyranny of the majority so feared by James Madison had been supplanted by the tyranny of a determined minority made up of professional politicians, policy experts, and a hard-core faction of Republican Party loyalists. If so, was this tyranny, as Sheehan put it, "carved in immovable, unbendable and rigidly mendacious marble"? [7]

---

7 Not long after her "renunciation" of politics, Sheehan seemed to change her mind. She decided to run for Congress in 2008 as an independent candidate against Democratic House Speaker Nancy Pelosi in her San Francisco district because Pelosi hadn't moved to impeach Bush. As of this writing, Sheehan needed to gather 10,198 signatures from district residents (about 3 percent of its registered voters in 2006) by August 8 to get her name on the ballot.

The editors at *Junior Scholastic* magazine are not altogether wrong in promoting the idea that virtually anyone can be president, or at the very least state senator or city alderman. Assuming that America is a true democracy—representative, popular, and constitutional—political office should, in theory, be open to those with the ability—through persuasiveness, intelligence, charisma, or sheer determination—to win a lot of votes. Surely the candidate with the most popular appeal is the sort of person who tends to get elected to high office, including president.[1]

If all this is true, then how is it that George W. Bush was elected president in 2000 with a minority of the popular vote? Some Americans will cite spoiled ballots in Palm Beach County, Florida (which should have gone to Al Gore), Ralph Nader's third-party candidacy (which took votes away from Gore), or the U.S. Supreme Court's aggressive and constitutionally questionable overruling of the Florida Supreme Court's order for a statewide recount.

---

1 The U.S. Supreme Court's appointment, in effect, of Bush as president—rather than allowing a recount or leaving the question to the House of Representatives—is all the more galling when one considers what Michael Kammen calls the "mystery" of "why the federal Constitution never explicitly mentions judicial review." Kammen notes that "With the passage of time that power has been broadly accepted; yet it remains an assumed power, and could be curtailed by Congress with respect to particular categories of legislation."

A small number of better informed, perhaps more sophisticated citizens will blame the broadly undemocratic Electoral College enshrined in Article II Section I of the Constitution. Beyond the technical and legal controversies surrounding the counting of the Florida vote, they will express outrage that the voters of just one state chose the president of their great American republic. Bush's victory in the electoral college (271 to 266) and defeat in the popular vote was the fourth time in American history that the more popular candidate lost the presidential election, although in the other cases—John Quincy Adams's minority victory over Andrew Jackson, in 1824, Rutherford B. Hayes's over Samuel Tilden, in 1876, and Benjamin Harrison's over Grover Cleveland, in 1888—Congress or the Electoral College determined the winner, not the Supreme Court.[2]

To be sure, the Electoral College is a pox on the presidential selection process. The Constitution requires that the legislature of each state "appoint, in such Manner as the Legislature thereof may direct, a Number" of presidential electors equaling the total of U.S. representatives and senators in that state; it is these 535 people, plus three electors from the District of Columbia, who select the president and vice-president. The Constitution says nothing about conducting a popular vote for president, and it wasn't until 1832, during Andrew Jackson's populist administration, that it became customary for electors to be chosen directly by the people in nearly all states. In theory, Americans are voting not for a candidate per se but for a slate of electors named by the major parties who have pledged to vote for a particular candidate. Nevertheless, once selected, nothing in the Constitution or federal law binds the electors to vote for a candidate, and, in fact, there have been eight electors since World War II who have defied their party and declined to vote for the designated nominee. The winner-take-all understanding, however,

---

2 The official 2000 popular vote tally was Gore 50,999,897, Bush 50,456,002.

prevails in all but two states, Nebraska and Maine, which award one elector to the winner in each congressional district and two to the winner of the overall popular vote in the state.

Why the other 48 states insist on a winner-take-all formula has more to do with the power of political parties than with any sense of proportional fairness. The Electoral College resulted, like so many other elements of the Constitution, from a compromise designed to protect the interests of less populous states in the new union. As with their several compromises on slavery (among other things, the slaveholding states were permitted to count a slave as three-fifths of a person for the purpose of increasing their populations and thus their representation in Congress and the Electoral College), the federalists understood they could not get agreement on a draft constitution without the consent of the smaller states in the North and the rural slave states in the South. But what a compromise was wrought! Today, the state with the fewest people, Wyoming, has three electors, one for every 171,668 people, whereas the most populous state, California, has 55 electors, one for every 662,865 people. Thus, the vote of an individual in California, which in 2000 went for Gore, has proportionally less value than a vote in Wyoming, which went for Bush.

But as manifestly undemocratic as the Electoral College has been, it doesn't fully explain Bush's sullied "victory." To understand elections in America, as opposed to democracy, one must first learn about the two-party duopoly that decides the rules of the game. There is great irony in duopoly, since the founding fathers, as the historian Richard Hofstadter explained in *The Idea of a Party System*, "had a keen terror of party spirit and its evil consequences." Parties, he said, were viewed as "sores on the body politic," little more than factions. Indeed, even Thomas Jefferson, the founder of what became the modern Democratic Party, and his arch political rival John Adams agreed in principle that parties were a bad idea.

To James Madison, often called the father of the Constitution, a faction is "a number of citizens, whether amounting to a majority or a minority of the whole, who are united and actuated by some common impulse of passion, or of interest, adverse to the rights of other citizens, or to the permanent and aggregate interests of the community." Since "the latent causes of faction are thus sown in the nature of man," the only way to "check the inducements to sacrifice the weaker party or an obnoxious individual"—short of curtailing liberty—was to avoid "pure democracy" and establish republican institutions that would guarantee the rights of people outside a domineering faction.

Madison was amazingly farsighted, but I don't think he could have envisioned Katherine Harris, Florida's secretary of state during the 2000 election, or Kenneth Blackwell, Ohio's secretary of state in the 2004 election. No doubt he would have been distressed by a system in which the state official in charge of supervising the fairness of an election was also a prominent member of a faction whose primary interest was in winning that election.

In America, each of the 50 states has its own election laws, and in many states, election customs and practices under state law vary widely from county to county. Thus, despite federal legislation passed in 2002 (the Help America Vote Act) to encourage uniform voting procedures, in the more than 3,000 counties, parishes, and independent cities, voter registration and precinct polling places are still controlled by party functionaries answerable to elected state officials whose loyalty resides with the leaders of their particular faction, rather than with the people.[3]

"Have you never refused to go with your party?" Henry Adams's fictional Washington hostess, Madeleine, inquires of her star guest

---

3 Only eight states permit "same day registration." Elsewhere a voter must register ahead of time to vote on Election Day.

and suitor, the powerful Senator Silas Ratcliffe of Illinois. "'Never!' was Ratcliffe's firm reply . . . 'Is nothing more powerful than party allegiance?'

"'Nothing except national allegiance,' replied Ratcliffe, still more firmly."

In 2000, in addition to her duties as administrator of the election, Ms. Harris worked as the co-chair of George Bush's state presidential election campaign, under the close supervision of the Republican nominee's brother, Florida Governor Jeb Bush. This dual work was an obvious conflict of interest, but Harris never let her governmental obligations interfere with her political ones. Among the other inconsistencies in state election laws in 2000 was the fact that 15 states, including Florida, forbade ex-felons from voting. Between May 1999 and Election Day, November 7, 2000, Harris and her predecessor as secretary of state, Sandra Mortham, ordered 57,700 of these supposed former convicts taken off the voter rolls. There was a political logic to this aggressive vigilance, since in the 35 states that permit ex-felons to vote, historically about 90 percent have voted Democratic, in keeping with their likely race (black) and economic status (poor). However, the so-called scrub lists were compiled in a methodologically curious way.

Thousands of voters with the same or similar names as ex-felons were purged from the voter registration rolls, and many were turned away when they went to vote. The more common the name, such as Johnny Jackson Jr., the greater the likelihood of a legitimate voter being purged. According to the U.S. Commission on Civil Rights, an estimated 8,000 "matches" with the Florida felons lists were false, but in settling an ensuing lawsuit brought by the NAACP and other groups, the state of Florida later agreed to stricter criteria that would reinstate approximately 20,000 disenfranchised voters. In Leon County alone, elections supervisor Ion Sancho could verify only 33 actual felons out of a list of 697 provided by Harris's office.

Assuming the 2000 statewide average turnout of 70 percent (African Americans flocked to the Florida polls in record numbers that year) among these 8,000 to 20,000 citizens, with the great majority probably voting for Gore, this class of disenfranchised voters could easily have erased Bush's official 537-vote margin of victory in Florida.

Katherine Harris's suppression of potential, mostly minority Democratic votes amounts to a kind of preemptive vote fraud. But old-fashioned vote stealing on Election Day is an old American story. In 1960, Chicago Mayor Richard J. Daley, the boss of the Chicago and Cook County Democratic machine, very likely stole the state of Illinois for the Democratic candidate, John F. Kennedy, from the Republican Richard Nixon. Unlike Florida in 2000, Illinois in 1960 was not the one state that decided Kennedy's victory in the Electoral College—Kennedy could have still won without it—but given his narrow margin in the overall popular vote (about 100,000) and in Illinois (8,858), the extraordinary vote total driven by Daley in his county fief remains a potent emblem of party power versus popular power in American elections.

Kennedy apologists have long minimized the importance of Illinois in 1960, but as Seymour Hersh argued in *The Dark Side of Camelot*, "Illinois was essential to Kennedy's victory." This election was an anomaly in modern times because many segregationist southern Democratic electors had refused to pledge their votes to Kennedy, a senator from liberal Massachusetts, if he won the popular vote in their states. "Without [Illinois's] 27 electoral votes," Hersh wrote,

> Kennedy would have had a plurality of only 7 votes
> over Nixon in the electoral college, with 26 unpledged
> Democratic electors in Mississippi, Georgia, and Ala-

bama threatening to bolt unless they received significant concessions on federal civil rights policy from the
Democratic Party. A loss in Illinois would have given
those unpledged electors——fourteen of whom eventually did choose to cast their votes for Democratic
Senator Harry F. Byrd, of Virginia—a huge increase in
leverage. They had the power, if Kennedy lost Illinois,
to throw the election into the House of Representatives
for the first time in the twentieth century.[4]

---

4 Another writer who has studied the question of fraud in Illinois, Edmund Kallina
Jr., wrote in *Courthouse over White House* that "It was within the realm of possibility
that Kennedy's total of 297 [electoral votes] could be driven below the necessary
269, but it would have meant [Nixon] cutting a deal with southern electors who were
less interested in helping Nixon than in gaining leverage over Kennedy. If Kennedy
had been denied the necessary electoral votes and the election had been thrown
into the House of Representatives, not only would Nixon have been subjected to
considerable criticism but there was little chance that he could have emerged the
victor." Daley was not a bookish man, but one wonders if he had read Henry Adams's
Democracy. In it, Senator Ratcliffe of Illinois boasts of how he stole a presidential
election by withholding the vote totals in northern Illinois until he knew exactly how
many were needed to win the state. Kallina concluded that Daley's larger purpose
in stealing votes for Kennedy might well have been to help defeat the incumbent
Republican state's attorney, Benjamin Adamowski, a former Democratic Party rival
who had ambitions to become mayor himself. Using two different methods, Kallina
estimated that while Daley may have stolen a minimum of either 4,674 or 7,968
votes from Nixon, he likely stole at least 31,284 or 32,391 votes from Adamowski.
As Kallina writes, "It appeared that in Chicago, Nixon was cheated out of several
thousand votes, at a minimum, but this estimate was not so overwhelming that one
can assert with confidence that Nixon was swindled out of Illinois's electoral votes." I
think that Kallina may have underestimated the statewide reach of the Cook County
Democratic machine. Kennedy's 8,858-vote "victory" is suspiciously close to Kallina's top minimum of stolen votes. Historically, before computerized vote-counting,
political bosses watched statewide election returns and waited until the last minute
to steal what they needed. It seems clear, however, that Adamowski was robbed of
his re-election, since he lost by only 26,000 votes. "The conclusion that Adamowski
was cheated out of the election is inescapable," Kallina writes.

More recently, suspicion of vote fraud has centered on Ohio, where in 2004 the Republican secretary of state, Kenneth Blackwell, like Katherine Harris before him, moonlighted as "honorary" co-chair of Bush's reelection campaign. Here, the official victory margin for Bush of more than 100,000 made it more difficult for critics to challenge Ohio's decisive contribution to Bush's Electoral College victory. But evidence compiled after the election by Rep. John Conyers Jr., the ranking Democrat on the House Judiciary Committee, found many irregularities in many localities. These problems ranged from lack of voting machines in Democratic-dominated precincts, to preposterous overcounts of Bush and third-party totals in certain precincts (more votes than there were voters), to the use of a technique known as "caging." As the Conyers report described it, the Ohio Republican Party sent registered letters requiring a signature of receipt to newly registered voters in minority and urban areas (many of whom had decided to vote for the first time out of enthusiasm for voting against Bush), "then sought to challenge 35,000 individuals who refused to sign for the letters," including "voters who were homeless, serving abroad, or simply did not want to sign for something concerning the Republican Party." Caging dovetailed nicely with other techniques of vote suppression, such as Blackwell's sudden insistence in early September on strict adherence to a state bylaw that county boards of elections reject new voter registrations not "printed on white, uncoated paper of not less than 80 lb. text weight." Since the Cleveland *Plain Dealer* had printed voter registration forms in its flimsy newsprint pages—and because the newspaper had a large black readership in its mostly urban circulation area—Blackwell's intention seems to have been to discourage voter registration, particularly by blacks, in order to reduce the turnout for Kerry. In Ohio, as in Florida, blacks vote overwhelmingly Democratic—an estimated 84 percent went for Kerry in 2004. As Mark

Crispin Miller recounted in an August 2005 article for *Harper's Magazine,* "under public pressure [Blackwell] reversed the order three weeks later, by which time unknown numbers of Ohioans had been disenfranchised."

With a patchwork system of electronic, mechanical, paper, and optic-scan technology used to record and count votes around the country, nothing much has been done since 2000 to lessen the likelihood, or the expectation, of vote fraud or vote suppression. But technical issues, such as the greater possibility of vote fraud with electronic voting machines as opposed to paper ballots, obscure the larger reality about American elections: the fundamental lack of choice imposed on the people by two parties that collude when it suits their interests. If fraud is common in the counting of votes in American elections, then there is a more profound fraud in the selection of candidates before the votes are ever cast.

It is a fact of American political life that intra-party control is paramount in the minds of party politicians. Membership in a party commits a politician to a life of regimentation under internal party rules. If you play by the rules, you can rise to some measure of power; if you don't, you will likely be dismissed to the outer reaches of political life. Party loyalty even can take precedence over winning elections, so an insurgent candidate—one who not only seeks office without permission but also challenges the power of the party leadership—invites ferocious attack, even if the insurgent seems more likely to win the popular vote than the party's candidate for office.

The two major parties decide together on so much in the state legislatures and in Washington—budget, patronage appointments, election laws—that it would be strange if they did not find common ground on matters concerning power over their own members. As the political historian Walter Karp wrote:

> National party collusion means that neither party will
> raise issues or initiate policies or launch partisan attacks
> which would weaken the other party's organization. . . .
> The abiding principle of action of the party organizations,
> the principle which necessitates their collusion, is their
> constant and unremitting effort to remain party organiza-
> tions and thereby control elected officials.

Political scientists and conventional journalists will scoff at the notion that a party would rather lose an election than empower an insurgent. So, too, would professional politicians, because such an admission would scandalize the electorate. What can't be said out loud
in public, however, is stated plainly in popular American fiction. In
Sinclair Lewis's iconic novel *Babbitt*, the protagonist embodies all
that was small-minded and fearful in the provincial Middle West
of the 1920s. Babbitt is a modestly successful businessman who,
on occasion, is drawn into the periphery of civic life and politics
(to boost development schemes for his own profit). When a pro-
labor candidate for mayor arises on the left, the local Democratic
and Republican parties unite behind an ultra-respectable mattress
manufacturer named Lucas Prout in order to defeat the representative of "whining laziness" among the working class: "Mr. Prout was
supported by the banks, the Chamber of Commerce, all the decent
newspapers, and George F. Babbitt." Since Prout is almost certainly
a Republican (Lewis doesn't specify), the putatively pro-labor Democrats have conceded city hall in the name of stopping a genuine
pro-labor candidate.

The political landscape in America is littered with the dashed
careers of reformers and rebels who tried to buck the system; unfortunately, only a few are willing to speak out about the secret of party

power in America. One such rebel was Senator Eugene McCarthy, the Democrat from Minnesota whose insurgent, anti-Vietnam War candidacy for the presidency in 1968 caused the incumbent president, Lyndon Johnson, to forgo a reelection campaign for the White House. By driving the leader of his own party from office, McCarthy had violated the iron rule of party loyalty, and the consequences were severe, both for the man and for the nation. Not only would McCarthy be denied his party's nomination for the presidency but the Democrats would ultimately present a weaker candidate, Vice President Hubert Humphrey, to face the Republican Richard Nixon in the general election. Humphrey, saddled with Johnson's unpopular war policy, would lose narrowly to Nixon. Although Humphrey enjoyed a late surge in the polls beginning with a September 30 speech in Salt Lake City distancing himself from the president on the war, it was too little independence too late. Nixon's version of Vietnam would drag on for another five years at the cost of nearly 21,000 U.S. soldiers' lives, more than a third of the total American war dead.

McCarthy was a reformer by instinct, though he often ridiculed the pieties of "innocents" and reformers. But he was no radical and during his career had functioned well enough within the strictures of the regular party organization.[5] Indeed, in 1964 Johnson had seriously considered McCarthy as a vice-presidential running mate, instead of his eventual choice of Humphrey. But after his defeat at the hands of the party machine at the fractious 1968 convention, an alienated McCarthy chose not to seek reelection to his Senate seat

---

5 At the 1960 Democratic Convention in Los Angeles, McCarthy had made what some considered a quixotic, if brilliant nomination speech for the hopeless candidacy of Adlai Stevenson. This had offended loyalists of the eventual nominee, John F. Kennedy, but hardly constituted an act of outright rebellion.

and receded to the fringes of politics, preferring life as a critic and a poet rather than as what he called "a vote-getter." [6]

Writing in 1998, after two independent bids for the presidency, McCarthy had become convinced that the only salvation for American democracy was a third party, agreeing with John Adams that, as McCarthy paraphrased, "the worst possible development would be politics controlled by two strong factions." In his book *No-Fault Politics*, McCarthy contended that "Today free and effective participation in the process of choosing a government, especially the president of the United States, is limited and controlled by two parties: the Republicans and the Democrats. Not only is effective participation in the political process denied to new parties and independent candidates, but recent restrictive laws and practices have had the effect of suppressing limited movements of protest or division within the two major parties."

As McCarthy correctly noted, this was not always the case in American history:

> The moves to control politics in the interest of the
> Republican and Democratic parties did not begin until
> early in this century. When the Republican Party was
> born in 1854 as a party of protest against the extension
> of slavery into territories, it combined various dissident

---

6 Putting aside Robert F. Kennedy's assassination-shortened candidacy in the spring of 1968, the odds were stacked against McCarthy, because in those days only about 39 percent of the 2,622 total delegates to the nominating convention came from states with primaries. The rest were selected by state Democratic officials beholden to President Johnson. Moreover, even in primary states, such party bureaucrats did not feel obligated to allocate delegates according to the results. For example, McCarthy won Pennsylvania with 72 percent of the vote but received less than 20 percent of its delegates. By mid-June of 1968, according to the *New York Times*, Vice President Humphrey was able to win the support of 1,600 delegates (or 288 more than the 1,312 needed to win) without having entered a primary.

Whigs, Free-Soilers, Anti-Slavery Democrats, and fringe groups, including Know-Nothings and Barnburners. In [the twentieth century], following the success of [former Republican president] Teddy Roosevelt and his Bull Moose Party in the 1912 campaign (in which Teddy ran ahead of the official Republican nominee [William Howard Taft]), Republican Party initiatives were undertaken to restrict third-party activities.

Although many Americans decry the corrupt system of private campaign financing in America, McCarthy viewed the 1974 legislation amending the Federal Election Campaign Act, which created taxpayer-supported campaigns, as just another impediment to independent candidacies, since, with this act, "for the first time in our history" Congress "gave federal preferential status to the two established parties." He goes on to say that "the 'two-party system' came to be accepted, not only as a condition to effective government in the United States but also as an article of public faith, accepted by politicians, professors, and the press."

The dearth of successful independent candidacies in recent U.S. history tends to support McCarthy's view, but he understates the problem of the two-party monopoly. Without proportional allocation of presidential electors, independent candidates are easily marginalized, even when they have a significant popular following, as had the left-wing Progressive Party candidate Henry Wallace in 1948 and his racist Dixiecrat counterpart Strom Thurmond, both of whom had left the Democratic Party. Even with these important defections, the beleaguered Democratic nominee Harry Truman was able to win election over a strong Republican candidate, Thomas Dewey. But McCarthy only touches on the more brutal system of internal party control and the crushing of insurgencies. For many years, open

primaries—that is, truly competitive and democratic contests to select nominees—were a rallying cry for reformers. Until 1972, when
George McGovern was able to profit from the new rules dictated
by his own reform commission, most state Democratic Party central
committees selected substantial numbers of delegates to the party's
presidential convention, or tightly controlled who got to run for delegate. In certain states like Illinois, the popular vote in the primary
was merely symbolic and had no relation to the number of delegates
awarded to a presidential candidate. In this way, a candidate could
win the popular vote but gain no delegates.

In recent years, two genuine reform Democrats have been
nominated for president, the antiwar McGovern in 1972 and the
Georgia farmer turned politician Jimmy Carter in 1976. Of the two,
McGovern was punished for his anti-organization tendencies and
abandoned by large segments of his party before the general election. McGovern's cardinal sin at the 1972 convention in Miami was
to permit the unseating of the regular party delegation from Illinois,
replacing it with delegates whose first loyalty was to him, not Mayor
Daley. Afterward, John Connally, the former governor of Texas and
a close ally of Lyndon Johnson, formed a group called Democrats
for Nixon to oppose McGovern's supposedly radical/pacifist platform.[7] More dramatically, the nation's principal labor federation, the
AFL-CIO (which usually functioned as an affiliate of the Democratic Party), declared its neutrality in the 1972 presidential race,
declining to endorse the Democratic candidate for the only time
in the federation's history. The AFL-CIO's non-endorsement cost
McGovern millions of votes from union members who ordinarily
would have voted Democratic. Other large unions, like the Teamsters, endorsed Nixon outright, and McGovern was defeated in one

---

7 Like McCain, McGovern was a decorated combat pilot, who flew 35 bomber missions, the maximum allowed, in World War II.

of the worst landslides in history, winning only 17 votes in the Electoral College.

In the wake of Watergate and Nixon's forced resignation, Carter's anti-Washington, outsider candidacy in the 1976 election was impossible to halt, though Democratic Party oligarchs like Sen. Henry Jackson and Hubert Humphrey, who had returned to the Senate, tried to stop him. The party's revenge came later, when Sen. Edward Kennedy, the youngest brother of the martyred president, challenged Carter's reelection in the 1980 primaries. This was an extraordinary move, for there was no compelling reason like Vietnam for Kennedy to challenge the incumbent president from inside his own party. [8]

. Carter prevailed and was re-nominated, but then was dropped by large portions of the party establishment. Years later, in answer to a question by PBS's Charlie Rose about Kennedy's refusal to shake hands publicly with the re-nominated president at the 1980 convention, Carter said:

> Well I was happy having gotten the nomination,
> but I was kind of peeved about it. And then after that,
> there was no reconciliation. . . . They didn't support me
> ever. I mean the Kennedy wing of the Democratic
> Party never supported me. They supported [independent, former Republican presidential candidate] John
> Anderson . . . and he picked up an enormous amount of
> support from the liberal wing of the Democratic
> Party, who abandoned me.

---

8 Kennedy was famously unable to provide a clear reason for running in a nationally televised interview with Roger Mudd of CBS. The episode marked the beginning of the end of his campaign.

If Carter had substituted "establishment" for "liberal" he would have been closer to the truth, for Kennedy's run was more about competing factions than competing ideas. In any event, he weakened Carter badly and helped paved the way for the landslide election of Ronald Reagan, by far a greater threat to Kennedy's liberal values than Carter.

More recently we see reform candidates like the Republican John McCain and the Democrat Howard Dean neutralized or virtually destroyed by their own parties, despite their demonstrated appeal to voters. McCain, a senator from Arizona with a famously courageous record as a prisoner of war in Vietnam, shocked the Republican Party establishment by winning the New Hampshire primary in February 2000. Even before the primary season, though, George W. Bush had already been anointed the nominee by his party's managers, and McCain, with his "Straight Talk Express" and pledge to drive special-interest money out of politics, was clearly a threat to the party leadership, including Bush's father.

In the crucial South Carolina primary that followed New Hampshire's, McCain was subjected to a savage assault on his character and record. Even his suffering as a POW was called into question by a Bush supporter and Vietnam veteran named J. Thomas Burch Jr., who accused McCain of letting down his fellow POWs and Vietnam comrades. "Senator McCain has abandoned the veterans," Burch declared in Sumter, South Carolina, with Bush at his side (Five U.S. senators—all Vietnam veterans—defended McCain in a joint statement directed at George W. Bush, noting that, ironically, "Mr. Burch was a leading critic of President Reagan's and your father's policies on POW/MIA issues.") McCain, himself a Navy pilot who was shot down over Hanoi, had actually refused on principle a North Vietnamese offer of liberation ahead of other POWs who had been imprisoned longer. But his heroism was not enough to counter the Bush-inspired attacks. So-called push polling also left its mark: phone operators would call potential Republican primary voters and ask leading questions, implying that McCain had sired an illegitimate daughter with a black woman (he and his wife had an adopted daughter from Bangladesh). McCain ended up losing badly to Bush in South Carolina, and his campaign never really recovered.

In 2004, Howard Dean, the former governor of Vermont, ran a campaign strikingly similar to McCain's in its emphasis on campaign-finance reform and unscripted "town meetings" in which the candidate would field questions from ordinary citizens for as long as two hours. To be sure, Dean was to the "left" of McCain on many issues, including the invasion and occupation of Iraq, but both candidates aggressively sought to purify their respective parties of corruption and special-interest lawmaking. Both wanted to eliminate so-called soft money contributions to the major parties. The post-Watergate 1974 election reforms had limited direct contributions to federal candidates to $2,000 but placed no limits on contributions to the parties. This "soft money," whether it comes from rich individuals or political action committees (PACs), inevitably winds up aiding individual candidates once they secure their party's nomination. (The two crusaders did not, however, decry the practice of "bundling"—another method of circumventing the 1974 and 2002 reforms—whereby an individual contributor solicits his family, friends, and employees to match his donation and then gets credit from the campaign for having raised far more than the legal limit.[9])

---

9 Through May of the 2008 presidential campaign, McCain led all candidates, with 507 bundlers, 70 of whom were federal lobbyists, according to Public Citizen, a Washington-based nonprofit consumer-advocacy organization. Obama had 361 bundlers (17 lobbyists), and Clinton could boast of 322 (22 lobbyists). Clinton's numbers, however, were underreported, since her campaign only released the names of those who "bundled" at least $100,000.

McCain's and Dean's cries for reform were a direct assault on the power of the party leaders, not only in Congress but also in every state capital dependent on federal largesse and patronage. More importantly, the party leaders derived much of their status from the leverage they could place on donors, particularly wealthy individuals and corporations that sought favors through new legislation and reduced regulation.

Any limit on campaign contributions interferes with the reward system in Washington: if sitting politicians couldn't extract money in exchange for political access, how would they fund their reelection campaigns? Without the built-in fund-raising advantage of incumbents, challengers would be emboldened to raise money in smaller amounts from ordinary citizens. And, indeed, this was how McCain and Dean were able to get as far as they did: with modest contributions from people who had little access to official political power. According to the Campaign Finance Institute, 41 percent of McCain's total fund-raising haul from individuals came from those donating less than $200, compared with only 16 percent of Bush's total. For Dean, this number rose to 60 percent. In all, Dean raised an astonishing $51 million, most of it before he, too, was shot down in the early primaries.

Thus do "popular" candidates lose elections, sacrificed to the imperatives of internal party control. In 1968, a July 20 Harris poll found that if the election had been held that day, Eugene McCarthy would beat Richard Nixon 42 to 34 percent, whereas the eventual nominee, Humphrey, led Nixon by only two points, 37 to 35 percent.

On February 7, 2000, following his surprise victory in New Hampshire, a CNN/*USA Today*/Gallup poll found that John McCain would beat the presumptive Democratic nominee, Al Gore, by 58 percent to 36 percent, compared with a margin for Bush of 53 to 44 percent. Moreover, the poll found that 64 percent of Republicans preferred a candidate "not tied to your party's leaders" compared with 30 percent who wanted a candidate "who is loyal to your party."

On December 13, 2003, just after the front-runner Dean received the high-profile endorsement of Al Gore, a *Newsweek* poll found Dean trailing Bush 49 to 42 percent: the eventual nominee, John Kerry, was not even recorded. In January, after Dean, under relentless assault similar to what McCain had endured, faded into third place in Iowa behind Kerry and John Edwards (26 to 23 to 20 percent), according to a *Des Moines Register* poll, the same poll still found that 48 percent of the state's Democrats felt that Dean's leading strength was his "ability to defeat Bush."[10] Despite the constant references to Kerry's so-called electability by pundits everywhere, only 35 percent thought Kerry's ability to defeat Bush was his leading strength.

This is not to say that the people have no role in selecting presidents, only that the people's choice is often different from the party's choice. In 2004, just 7.2 percent of the total American electorate voted in presidential primaries. With such low participation in the selection process (political professionals typically pick candidates for state and local office, a practice they call "slating"), it's no wonder that party officials, along with the rich and well-organized pressure groups, have a vastly disproportionate say about who occupies the White House. Party leaders and the elites that support them always tend to favor incumbents, if for no other reason than that an incumbent is a known loyalist with a built-in fund-raising advantage that benefits the whole party.

In Congress and the state legislatures, this top-down party domination of the nomination process—that is, who gets to be on

---

10 At the beginning of the 2008 Democratic primary season, it appeared that Hillary Clinton was the choice of the party managers to be their nominee for president, this despite her pro-Iraq War stance in the Senate and persistently high "negative" poll ratings.

the ballot—is reflected in America's almost Soviet-like reelection rates. According to researchers at Emory University, the 99 percent reelection rate in the House in 2002 and 2004 was the highest in the post-World War II era. The story was the same in the Senate in 2004: in only one of 26 contested races did an incumbent (Tom Daschle, the Democratic majority leader) lose his seat. To beat Daschle, the Republican challenger in sparsely populated South Dakota spent $14.7 million, or $74 for every vote he received. Even in years of supposed seismic shifts, such as the 1994 Republican takeover of the House after 40 unbroken years of Democratic control, 90 percent of incumbents held on to their seats. In 2006, when Democrats retook control of the House, 95 percent of incumbents remained in office. The state legislatures are similarly impermeable to change. Between 1990 and 2002, incumbent state legislators won their reelection bids at a nationwide average of 93 percent, according to Thomas Carsey, a professor of political science at the University of North Carolina. In New York State, losses by incumbents are almost as rare as sightings of the Florida panther. Since 1982, only 35 incumbents have lost reelection bids for the 150 Assembly and 62 Senate seats.

It is, therefore, no wonder that the rate of participation in American elections is among the lowest in the Western world. According to the International Institute for Democracy and Electoral Assistance (IDEA), the U.S. average of 48.3 percent from 1945 through 1998 was far below the average of 77 percent in Western Europe. Presumably this is because many Americans believe that their vote doesn't count, that the doctrine of "one man, one vote" decreed by the Supreme Court in 1964 is unsupported by political reality. But is money corruption the main cause of this disaffection?

If Barack Obama's presidential campaign has proven anything, it is that you need a vast amount of money to become president, especially if you want to dislodge a party favorite like Hillary Clinton. The notion that a person of modest means and common education can, Lincoln-like, gain access to the nation's highest office—absent major corporate backing, regular party support, or a galvanizing national crisis like slavery—has become increasingly preposterous as the 2008 campaign sets new fund-raising records with each successive month.

Not everyone agrees that money constitutes an insurmountable barrier to the presidency or other elected federal office. Eugene McCarthy, for one, minimized the problem of money in politics, calling public funding of campaigns a "gimmick" that had become "a deus ex machina—a magic key to resolve the conflicts of values and interests inherent in our democracy." McCarthy believed there should be no individual limits on campaign contributions, half-joking to me in conversation that "it's better to be owned by three millionaires than by all millionaires."

But as the major candidates of the two parties continued to pile up enormous sums of money for the 2008 presidential campaign, it was hard not to conclude that politics was a rich man's luxury, since there are no limits on what an individual candidate can spend on his or her own campaign.[1] Certainly, it was difficult to conceive of a serious presidential candidacy by a non-wealthy politician lacking formal party support. Indeed, of the three major independent presidential candidates since 1980, by far the most successful has been the billionaire Ross Perot, who ran in 1992 and 1996. The eccentric Texan's opposition to free trade agreements, coupled with his McCain/Dean-like attacks on special interests, garnered about 19.7 million votes, or 19 percent of the total number cast, in 1992. But Perot needed to spend $65 million of his own money to get on the ballot in all 50 states, as well as for campaign publicity.

Ralph Nader also ran independent, anti-party campaigns in 2000 and 2004.[2] In 2000, Nader raised $8.4 million and was able to

---

1 In 1976, the election after Watergate-era campaign-finance reform was made into law, 15 Democratic and Republican presidential candidates raised $44 million in private contributions during the primaries, to which $25 million in matching public funding was added. For the general election, Jimmy Carter and Gerald Ford each received a public grant of $22 million. By 2004, these figures had exploded: George W. Bush and John Kerry alone, through a combination of individual donors, PACs, and other sources such as loans, raised over $500 million in private money. Bush and Kerry refused public financing in the primaries in order to be allowed to raise more money privately, but were required to accept $75 million each in public money for the general election. In June 2008, the cash-rich Barack Obama angered John McCain and some reformers by announcing that he would refuse public financing for the general election.

2 Even as independents, Perot and Nader felt obliged to run under the banner of a party. However, neither candidate seemed to take his party responsibilities very seriously. Perot's Reform Party, founded in 1995 after his first, strictly independent run for president, was largely a creature of his personal ambition. The Green Party existed before Nader became its nominee, but no one would call Nader a "Green" politician. His affiliation with the Greens appeared to be more convenience than conviction.

get on the ballot in just 43 states. A man of modest means, Nader could not afford to advertise and litigate on a level with Perot and received only 2.9 million votes, or 2.7 percent of the total votes cast. Four years later, facing immense hostility from regular Democrats for his "spoiler" role in 2000, Nader raised only about $5 million, and he got on the ballot in just 34 states. Nader's vote totals suffered commensurately: he received 465,650 votes, or just .4 percent of the total ballots cast. According to Nader's campaign manager, Theresa Amato, the Nader campaign spent 75 percent of its funds defending itself against Democratic Party legal efforts to prevent Nader from appearing on ballots in states where he posed the greatest threat to John Kerry. In Oregon, for example, Nader's supporters submitted more than 28,000 signatures to get him on the ballot, but county officials disqualified 10,000 of them. Then, Democratic Secretary of State Bill Bradbury struck 3,082 more, because sheets weren't sequentially numbered and—even more galling to the Nader forces—the petitioners supposedly didn't sign and date them correctly. Nader's campaign fell 218 signatures short of the required 15,306 to make the ballot and ultimately lost its legal challenge in Oregon's Supreme Court.

The playing field of the Senate is less expensive, but the barriers to running, and winning, are similarly high. In 2006, a very wealthy businessman, Ned Lamont, challenged the incumbent Democratic senator in Connecticut, Joe Lieberman, over his steadfast support of George W. Bush's policy in Iraq. In the state's Democratic primary in August, Lamont shocked the party professionals by decisively defeating Lieberman, a pillar of the Democratic establishment and Al Gore's vice-presidential running mate in 2000, forcing Lieberman to run as an independent in the general election for senator.

Lamont succeeded despite pronounced support for Lieberman from the party's leader and chief fund-raiser, former President

Clinton, who addressed a packed Lieberman campaign rally in Waterbury two weeks before the primary. But money can't buy everything in American politics. Even as Lamont rode a groundswell of antiwar sentiment and Bush hatred, his $15 million in personal campaign expenditures couldn't overcome Lieberman's "independent" candidacy—in part because Lieberman wasn't a genuine independent. Having lost his party's primary by 52 to 48 percent, the angry incumbent reorganized under the banner of "Connecticut for Lieberman." In this he enjoyed the open support of key members of the state's Democratic Party establishment, such as Waterbury Mayor Michael J. Jarjura, as well as the tacit backing of Democratic officials who feared the consequences of public disloyalty to the party's nominee. But Lieberman also benefited from two-party collusion to crush the parvenu Lamont. The state's Republican Party, not wanting to lose a pro-Bush voice in the Senate, nominated Alan Schlesinger, a three-time failed congressional candidate who had been caught in a gambling casino using the alias "Alan Gold."[3] With Lamont's victory, the state's Republican establishment virtually abandoned the hapless Schlesinger and rallied around Lieberman, who insisted that he was still a Democrat.

After Lieberman lost the primary, Lamont recalled in November 2007, the incumbent senator "fired everybody, and he got wall to wall carpeting from [New York City Republican] Mayor [Michael] Bloomberg. Bloomberg's entire campaign apparatus came [to Connecticut.]" Collusion also occurred on a national level. "There's

3 Schlesinger, an admitted card counter who nevertheless lost money playing blackjack and had been sued twice by casinos seeking to recover gambling debts, defended his deception by claiming that he wished to protect himself from identity theft. According to the Associated Press, Schlesinger said that he provided a fake name to a casino owned by the Mashantucket Pequot tribe to obtain a "wampum card"—a rewards program based upon how much money patrons gamble—because "They're a sovereign nation, so you never know what they can do with the information . . . I didn't know what they were going to do." Schlesinger also said he wanted to avoid accusations of bias, since he voted on gaming issues as a state representative.

no question that Joe's campaign was in regular contact with [Bush adviser] Karl Rove and had access to the Republican donor files," Lamont said. "That was explicit . . . and that was explicit here in Fairfield County . . . Joe's campaign and [Republican Congressman] Chris Shays worked together hand in glove."

Carrying 70 percent of the Republican vote, and 33 percent of Democrats, Lieberman easily held on to his seat, 50 to 40 percent, with Schlesinger receiving 10 percent. True to his values, Lieberman remained inside the Democratic caucus in the 110th Congress and continued to vote for every pro-war measure and against every anti-war initiative.

Such is the power of an organized state or national political party—thus do the professional politicians overcome amateur challengers. For all his money and popularity, Ross Perot never won an electoral vote and wasn't able to repeat his 1992 success in his 1996 bid for the presidency. That year, his vote total fell steeply, to about 8 million, or 8.4 percent of the total.

Yet money does count in American politics. Any candidate would rather have a large war chest than a small one. But party loyalty trumps money time and again, for loyalty to the leader usually brings important returns. In the case of the centrist Dean, his greatest disloyalty was to raise money entirely on his own, without the sanction of the party leadership, dominated by Bill and Hillary Clinton. He had begun to form a kind of party outside the party that in the end totaled more than 300,000 donors, many of whom contributed through the Internet. The Clintons were not pleased by this.[4] As one Hillary biographer, Edward Klein, wrote, the first

---

4 In 1972, George McGovern evidently posed a similar threat to the Democratic party leadership. McGovern's antiwar reform candidacy foreshadowed Dean's in its ability to raise large sums of money in small amounts from a great many people. According to Jeff Smith, a McGovern campaign aide, the South Dakota senator's direct-mail efforts collected about $30 million from 1.2 million donors who gave an average of $25 apiece. "After the '72 election, I personally hand-delivered a

couple didn't fear a Dean victory over Bush (which would have delayed or destroyed Hillary's drive to become president) so much as they feared his newfound power within the party due to his bottom-up fund-raising prowess:

> In [Hillary's] view, Howard Dean's very *nomination* posed a major threat to her power over the Democratic Party. Unlike John Kerry and the other candidates, Dean was not dependent on the traditional Democratic money pool controlled by Bill and Hillary Clinton . . . If Hillary was going to hold on to the reins of the Democratic Party for the next four years, she had to stop Dean and his army of young, Internet-savvy volunteers from capturing the nomination. With that in mind, she huddled with Bill Clinton and her other top advisers and devised a two-pronged strategy. . . . On the one hand, she would do everything in her power to prop up John Kerry or some other Democrat as an alternative to Dean. At the same time, she would position herself as representing a broad spectrum in the party—from left to right.

With Dean's collapse and Kerry's surge to the nomination, Clinton's priorities shifted, for, as Klein baldly put it, "Hillary's future depended on George W. Bush remaining in the White House." The Il-

---

computer tape to Bob Strauss, then chairman of the DNC," containing the names of the more than one million small donors, Smith said in an email. "McGovern did this in a heartfelt gesture. He wanted the tape used to raise money to strengthen the DNC. According to my sources at the DNC and in the direct-mail business (Roger Craver), Strauss let the tape sit on the shelf for nearly two and a half years because he didn't want to mail 'to all those damn issue people.' Roger estimated that Strauss's pique and short-sightedness cost the Democratic Party . . . about $40-50 million dollars." The McGovern direct-mail campaign was engineered by the team of Stan Rapp, Tom Collins, and Morris Dees.

linois-born Hillary, whose husband had, in effect, appointed her the Democratic nominee for Senate in New York in 2000, now "had to *appear* as though she was doing everything in her power to advance the cause of John Kerry" while actually doing very little. At the same time, as with Dean, she also needed "to prevent Kerry from taking over the Democratic Party," Klein wrote. "A key part of her strategy was to strengthen her hold on the party's fund-raising machinery through Terry McAuliffe, the Clintons' handpicked chairman of the Democratic National Committee." As the one-time Clinton political adviser Dick Morris wrote,

> McAuliffe dominates the party's fund-raising efforts. Democratic fat cats give when they are told, and to whom they are instructed by the smoothly oiled national fund-raising operation. Despite Howard Dean's now-legendary Internet-driven fund-raising success, the big checks still do the talking—and the Clintons control the process.

The destruction of Howard Dean is illustrative not only because of its ruthlessness but because it represented the perfect marriage of money and mutual political interest between the two major parties. And Dean was not so easy to target. A centrist, good-government, teetotaling physician raised on Park Avenue by a wealthy (and Republican) Wall Street broker and his patrician wife, he was hard to tear down—at least at first. Indeed, a left-wing Vermont radio host testified to Dean's impeccably moderate and establishment credentials when he joked to me that Dean "was the best Republican governor we've ever had." He meant that Dean was an old-fashioned Republican in the fiscally conservative, honest Abe Lincoln, Connecticut Yankee sense.

What distinguished Dean centrism from Clinton centrism was that nearly everything the Clintons do smacks of political tactics and fund-raising. They have made their mark in politics by eschewing the leftish politics of their youth, dating from Bill's antiwar activity at Oxford in 1969 and their work for the McGovern presidential campaign, and embracing "business-friendly" initiatives inspired by the Democratic Leadership Council, a party within the party. Like Tony Blair aping Margaret Thatcher, the Clintons have poached on traditionally Republican turf—with pro-corporate, pro-Wall Street trade deals like the North American Free Trade Agreement (NAFTA) and Permanent Normal Trade Relations (PNTR) with China; welfare cuts, masquerading as reform, that removed 8 million people from the welfare rolls; and lots of "Third Way" economic rhetoric (another name for financial deregulation) that won them the praise of Wall Street and the Fortune 500 alike.

Machine politicians at heart, Bill and Hillary last hinted at idealism during the summer of 1993, when Hillary wanted to present health care reform as the administration's first great legislative initiative. Her spouse insisted on pushing the former President Bush's already negotiated, but not legislatively approved, NAFTA accord, leaving Hillary's socially progressive health care program for later. Against the wishes of his party's core constituencies of organized labor and the working poor, Clinton rammed NAFTA through Congress—with the able assistance of the Business Roundtable, the country's premier CEO lobby, and his sometime Republican rival Newt Gingrich—and Hillary's health care plan, a threat to the insurance and pharmaceutical industries, was defeated.

Bill Clinton's signal political achievement in the White House would be his own reelection in 1996; his signal contribution to the "party of the people"—the party of Thomas Jefferson and Andrew Jackson—was to achieve fund-raising parity with the party of business, the Republican Party, at the highest levels of American corporate finance. As James Robinson, the Republican, pro-free trade former chairman of American Express, said: "NAFTA happened because of the drive Bill Clinton gave it. He stood up against his two prime constituents, labor and environment, to drive it home over their dead bodies."

In part because of NAFTA and failed health care reform, the Democrats lost their 40-year hold on the House in 1994, and relinquished their majority in the Senate as well. But the Clintons were making a great many new friends in the financial and corporate world.[5] With the normalization of U.S.-China trade in May 2000 (a top priority for businesses seeking cheap labor and cross-border investment deals) and with Hillary installed as senator from New York, it seemed the Clintons' party leadership was impregnable, even in Bill's "retirement."

Until Howard Dean came along. On February 21, 2003, when he stunned a DNC meeting in Washington by announcing his arrival from the "Democratic wing of the Democratic Party," as well as his opposition to the impending invasion of Iraq (a war supported by the party leadership and the Clintons), Dean became a threat to the Clintons' and the party's carefully constructed power structure. Nothing threatens a party oligarchy more than mass participation, and Dean's 280,000 contributors in 2003, averaging $143 each, spelled trouble.

Dean echoed McCain, who in 2000 denounced the "iron triangle [of] special interests, money, and legislation" and talked of restoring "the people's sovereignty over government" by reforming campaign fund-raising and "trying to change this party." As Dean put it in his 2003 campaign autobiography, "I know we need to lessen the influence of big money." A year later, after his defeat, he was

---

5 McAuliffe had many perks in his arsenal of fund-raising come-ons, including the offer of overnight stays in the White House Lincoln Bedroom, as well as invitations to "coffee klatches" with the Clintons, Vice President Gore and his wife, Tipper, and assorted cabinet secretaries. In all, McAuliffe could claim credit for having raised more than $300 million for his party over six years as chairman. He stepped down as DNC chairman in February 2005.

blunter: "The Democratic Party, just like the Republicans, emerged from the 1990s pretty much the captive of big-money interests."

But it wasn't just Dean's Internet fund-raising that frightened the party professionals. It was the hugely enthusiastic crowds he was drawing in 2003, more than a year before the general election. Worse still, if Dean could win the Democratic nomination, his fiscally conservative, anti-deficit platform might draw disaffected Republicans—traditionalists horrified by Bush's reckless war spending and the ballooning federal deficit—into the Democratic camp.

And Dean looked like he was all but in the winner's circle. A national Gallup poll taken from December 11 to 14, 2003, found Dean leading the crowded field of nine candidates with 28 percent to Joe Lieberman's 12 percent and John Kerry's 10 percent. In hotly contested Iowa, scene of the first major presidential primary, Dean had led the field since August, with 23 percent of Democrats polled to Dick Gephardt's 21 percent and Kerry's 14 percent, according to the *Des Moines Register*/Iowa poll. As late as January 8-10, the Zogby poll showed Dean rising in Iowa to 25 percent over Gephardt's 23, with Kerry at 15 percent and Lieberman not even contesting Iowa. Things looked even better for Dean in New Hampshire, the big primary following Iowa. In early December, Zogby gave Dean a commanding 42 percent in New Hampshire, with Kerry at 12 percent. On January 9, Iowa's best-known Democrat, Senator Tom Harkin, endorsed Dean, saying with unwitting irony, "He is the Harry Truman of our time." (Truman was the most hidebound of organization Democrats.) So inevitable did Dean's victory appear that the same day, Iowa's Republican Senator Charles Grassley declared, "I think, without a doubt, [Harkin] is endorsing the winner of the Democratic nomination."

But the Clintons and the party hadn't yet spoken. In November 2003, a secretive new "527" group calling itself Americans for Jobs, Health Care, and Progressive Values and organized by Democratic Party operatives appeared on the scene. 527s are tax-exempt political organizations that report to the IRS under Section 527 of the Internal Revenue Code. Because 527s are not legally allowed to coordinate with a specific candidate's campaign, they are not required to report to the Federal Election Commission and are thus not regulated by the McCain-Feingold Bipartisan Campaign Reform Act of 2002. In December, Americans for Jobs, Health Care, and Progressive Values advertised on television in Iowa, New Hampshire, and South Carolina. The ads trumpeted Dean's endorsements from the National Rifle Association and questioned his commitment to Medicare. But the most effective and devious message was also the cheapest: running on one day, December 13, for $15,000, the commercial depicted Osama bin Laden looming large in the background while an anonymous announcer questioned Dean's lack of experience in foreign policy. The cable-news networks picked up the controversial ad and replayed it repeatedly nationwide. Not required to report its donors until January 31, 2004—after the Iowa Caucuses—the group's founders, Democratic Party operatives David Jones and Tim Raftis, remained mute on their sources of support or their motives. When the group's donors were made public, the list included a corrupt former senator from New Jersey, Robert Torricelli, a Clinton ally who gave $50,000 from his defunct campaign fund, which had folded when Torricelli was forced to resign his seat. But the bigger donations came from rich individuals and unions associated with the Clintons and the party, most prominently S. Daniel Abraham, the billionaire founder of Slim-Fast, a diet-drink company. Americans for Jobs, Health Care, and Progressive Values eventually reported having raised $1 million between November and January (nearly $700,000 of it before the end of December), and by the time it had finished its dirty work Abraham had contributed $200,000.[6]

---

6 After Iowa, the group contributed much of its leftover money, $225,445, to the National Progress Fund, a 527 organized to fight Ralph Nader's independent candidacy.

Abraham was no ordinary Friend of Bill, having made the maximum hard money contributions to Hillary's Senate campaign in 1999 and 2003, and her political action committee in 2001. His gifts to McAuliffe's DNC, the Democratic Congressional Campaign Committee, and the Democratic Senatorial Campaign Committee totaled more than $3 million in 1997-2003. But his biggest contributions to the Clintons supported the softest of soft money—events, like the Clinton's privately financed New Year's Eve 2000 millennial extravaganza on the Mall in Washington, D.C. According to McAuliffe, who co-chaired the celebration with Americans for Jobs co-founder David Jones, Abraham donated $1 million to defray the first couple's expenses. In exchange for the contribution, Abraham was duly acknowledged at the festivities: guests arriving at the party enclosure on the Mall were greeted with a gigantic illuminated sign announcing, "Thank You Slim-Fast."

Abraham, who sold Slim-Fast to Unilever in 2000 for $2.3 billion, was so close to the Clintons during their two terms in the White House that he frequently conducted private diplomatic missions between Israeli politicians and Yasir Arafat when the president needed back-channel messages delivered. He was a frequent guest at the White House, with almost carte blanche access. His special interest was Israel, but his passion was for the Clintons themselves and for their "faction" of the Democratic Party.

Another contributor to the anti-Dean 527 ($15,000) was Bernard Schwartz, the chairman of Loral, a defense contractor that had benefited greatly from President Clinton's largesse. Meanwhile, the YES Network, a sports-television channel devoted to the New York Yankees, one of Hillary's adopted home teams, donated $125,000 to the anti-Dean propaganda. The then chief executive of YES, Leo Hindery, was a Democratic loyalist of long standing, having given large sums of soft money to the Democratic Party as well as the legal maximum to all of Hillary's various campaign funds in New York.

To this day, "new" Democrats and upscale liberals recoil at the suggestion that the Clintons are political "bosses" and that they run the Democratic Party with as much ruthlessness and cunning as their cruder, less elegantly educated predecessors, Lyndon Johnson, William M. ("Boss") Tweed of New York, and Richard J. Daley of Chicago. For the most part, Bill Clinton plays the book-learned sophisticate who persuades rather than intimidates. Occasionally, however, he will slip into the language of a boss, as he did at the annual Harkin Steak Fry (hosted by Senator Tom Harkin) in Indianola, Iowa, in the late summer of 2003. Speaking to party loyalists, including the nine Democratic presidential candidates, Clinton reminded his audience that while at first they would "fall in love" with a candidate, ultimately they must "fall in line."

Similarly, mainstream journalists and ordinary Americans find it difficult to believe that the two parties would collude to destroy an insurgent in one party. They assume that the two parties are always competitive and that they place winning elections ahead of all other priorities. But tacit two-party collusion occurred in the effort to stop Dean. Around the same time that Americans for Jobs, Health Care, and Progressive Values began airing its attack ads, a Republican political action committee, the Club for Growth, made an unusual entry into a Democratic primary, by launching its own media assault against Dean.[7] The centerpiece of the estimated $100,000 campaign was a television commercial that depicted a folksy, married-looking couple of Iowa seniors outside a barbershop while an off-screen announcer asks them how they feel about Howard Dean's "plan to raise taxes." The husband responds, "What do I think? Well I think Howard Dean should take his tax-hiking,

---

7 The Club for Growth may have been inspired by the Committee to Re-Elect Richard Nixon, whose operatives harassed Democratic presidential primary candidate Sen. Edmund Muskie with a dirty-tricks campaign that contributed to his downfall.

government-expanding, latte-drinking, sushi-eating, Volvo-driving, *New York Times*-reading...," to which his wife adds, "body-piercing, Hollywood-loving, left-wing freak show back to Vermont where it belongs."

Jeani Murray, Dean's Iowa campaign manager, told me that she and her staff at first laughed at the ad. And well she might have, since Dean's determined centrism on subjects ranging from the federal budget (he wanted it balanced), to gun control (which he mostly opposed), to universal health care (which he only partially endorsed), to the death penalty (which he mostly supported) annoyed many left-wing Democrats. And the characterization of Dean's supporters was preposterous; as anyone who attended a Dean rally could attest, the typical Dean supporter was a modestly attired type living in the slower lane of society. Dean himself was the picture of personal probity.

But Murray said she realized later that it was the beginning of the end. "It was just the pile-on," she said. "When Vice President Gore endorsed us [on December 9] that was the catalyst." The word went out, "We've definitely got to kill this guy." Dean's national campaign manager, Joe Trippi, put it similarly: "The campaign alarms said, *we've got to kill this guy now, or he's going to be the nominee.*" While the Club for Growth ran its "Go Back to Vermont" ads, all Dean's Democratic rivals remained silent, both on the Republican origins of the group (founded by Stephen Moore, a flat-tax advocate and associate of former Republican House Majority Leader Dick Armey) and its tactics.

Why would a Republican hit squad jump into the first Democratic primary and attack only one candidate? It would have seemed that for the right in late 2003 Howard Dean was the dream opponent for Bush, a veritable left-wing radical. A prominent Senate Democrat and chairman of the Democratic Leadership Council, Indiana's Evan Bayh, had earlier warned that in Dean's success, the "Democratic Party is in danger of being taken over by the far left." But a more persuasive analysis is that Bush and the Republicans feared Dean's antiwar and anti-deficit message—feared that he would make a stronger opponent than the ambivalent and tortured John Kerry, who voted for the Iraq War resolution. In addition, Dean was a phenomenal fund-raiser. "One of the fears, I suppose, on their side was that this is a guy who can raise more money than anybody in Democratic politics ever has because of the Internet," Tim Raftis told me in an interview in 2007. "And maybe we [Republicans] really ought to think seriously about it. Plus he's untainted by the war." As former Iowa State Democratic Chair Sheila Riggs told me, the advantage of Dean would have been that "we would've just had a clear delineation on the war; that would've been the big difference [from Kerry]." Thus did a confluence of Democratic and Republican party interests destroy the antiwar reform candidate, very possibly the candidate with the best chance of beating Bush.

In 2008, as I write, American party politics still aren't ready for any significant kind of reform. The Democratic presidential candidates jockeying for position behind the party leader's consort, Senator Hillary Clinton, were all watching the money. In mid-July 2007, the chief executive of the investment bank Morgan Stanley, John Mack, made news when he hosted a fund-raiser for Hillary. This event was notable, for Mack, a Wall Street plutocrat, had in the past quite logically supported George W. Bush and other Republicans. But Mack was just following the example of other multinational titans: the previous year, Rupert Murdoch had hosted a fund-raising breakfast for Hillary at Fox News headquarters in New York City.

In mid July 2007, it was also revealed that the maverick John McCain's campaign had foundered, as Republican money sought other opportunities within the party. McCain's difficulties could be traced to his disloyalty to Bush and his party's establishment in 2000, but one can't be sure. Reporting on McCain's dilemma, the *Wall Street Journal*'s Jackie Calmes consulted two longtime Clinton loyalists, James Carville and Congressman Rahm Emanuel, a Chicago Democrat. Carville and Emmanuel noted that their leader had also appeared to have been beaten early in 1992, after the sensational emergence of an old mistress and the story of how Clinton had dodged the Vietnam draft. According to Calmes's article, they recalled "that on the weekend after the worst week, Mr. Clinton held a hugely successful fund-raiser in New York," which "sent a crucial signal . . . that political investors still saw Mr. Clinton as a viable stock." Clinton hung on through New Hampshire, finishing second, and eventually captured the nomination and the presidency. The stock pickers and money people had bet correctly about American "democracy" that year. But where did that leave the individual voter, the one without even $100 to spare?

In January 2005, I went to Iowa to conduct some interviews in an effort to understand how Howard Dean had lost his grip on the nation's crucial first "primary." Jimmy Carter had broken through here from near total obscurity in 1976, so it seemed an advantageous terrain for another Democratic governor from a largely rural state. In Iowa, a voter goes to a meeting in his or her home precinct and caucuses with other voters, trying to persuade them to support a given candidate. A candidate with a strong precinct organization can win simply by turning out a disproportionately high number of voters, who then can dominate a caucus and pressure others to join them. There is no secret ballot, and voters must publicly declare their support for a candidate for their vote to count. In the end, a proportional number of delegates committed to a given candidate are sent to the county convention, which in turn sends delegates to the state convention, where the delegates to the national party convention are selected. With no secret ballot, all sorts of subtle and not so subtle pressure can be brought to bear on minority-candidate supporters who don't shift to the majority as the evening wears on. Thus, a daughter might find herself in public conflict with her father, or an employee with his or her boss. And there's another catch: typically, if a candidate's support drops below 15 percent, a vote for that person is not recorded in the caucus. The choice is between switching to another candidate or leaving. Such an atmosphere can be intimidating for an ordinary citizen, which may explain why turnout for the Iowa Caucuses is so low: in 2000, 6.8 percent of the state's eligible voters attended a caucus; in 2004, just 6.1 percent participated. Consequently, some people, including Dean, have criticized the Iowa Caucuses as less than pure democracy, and certainly not the best system for picking a future president.

On the way to my hotel from the Des Moines airport I struck up a conversation with my cab driver, Darrell Leroy Walldorff, then 72 and a native of Des Moines. Walldorff told me he decided to attend his local caucus for the first time in his life to vote for Howard Dean in 2004. "I listened to him," Walldorff recalled, "and I liked that he was a doctor and had a little more compassion for people."

Walldorff had driven to the David W. Smouse Opportunity School, where the Democratic caucus of the 3rd Ward, 66th precinct was meeting. "I liked it when we had the primary [the pre-1972 direct election primary]," he said. "This other stuff is corrupt. First they try to talk you into voting for their guy and then they don't want to fool with you. What happens [in the caucus] isn't the opinion of the public or of Des Moines; it's the opinion of the people in the room. They group you off." Walldorff estimated there were about 40 people in the room among whom was "this old gal, a hard-nosed thing, who insisted that everyone vote for Kerry. I said I just came to vote for my candidate. She said we're all majority for

Kerry. She just walked away." Feeling outnumbered, and with Dean nowhere near the 15 percent minimum, "after 15 or 20 minutes I just left." Of the caucuses, Walldorff commented, "so many people are swayed so easily, it's unbelievable. They have no backbone. It's not the voice of the people."

On American democracy in general, Walldorff said, "we don't even know if our vote counts anymore."

N ear the end of the 1972 film *The Candidate*, the lead character, played by Robert Redford, discovers to his astonishment that he is the winner of a seat in the United States Senate. Having devoted himself for so long to the practical, and often cynical, process of winning an election, the candidate finds himself at a loss. In all innocence, he pulls his chief campaign adviser (played by Peter Boyle) into a room, away from the throng of noisy supporters and journalists, and inquires: "Marvin . . . what do we do now?" Of course, this is a question that politicians in any country in any era might be prone to pose on election night. For so many of them, ambition drives out reason and principle, and the idealist of yesterday will frequently become the cynical man of power tomorrow.[1]

---

1 In Henry Adams's *Democracy*, Senator Silas Ratcliffe of Illinois lays out the brutal parameters of his political life when Madeleine, the woman he courts, presses him to consider his role in Congress and society at large. Madeleine, tempted by power but wary of its moral and emotional consequences, has already concluded that politicians were inordinately practical and "had no great problems of thought to settle, no questions that rose above the ordinary rules of common morals and homely duty." . . .

"She discussed the subject with Ratcliffe, who told her frankly that the pleasure of politics lay in the possession of power. He agreed that the country would do very well without him. 'But here I am,' said he, 'and here I mean to stay.' He had very little sympathy for thin moralizing, and a statesmanlike contempt for philosophical politics. He loved power, and he meant to be President. That was enough."

Power wasn't enough for Abraham Lincoln, but Lincoln was one of the great exceptions in American history. And Lincoln was nevertheless enormously ambitious, and frustrated, as a politician. His law partner, William Herndon, famously commented that "his ambition was a little engine that knew no rest," and well before his accession to the White House, Lincoln had experienced a disappointing and short-lived legislative career in Washington. So exploited is Lincoln for so many corrupt political reasons (by President Bush among others) that contemporary Americans know little about his principled, and politically self-destructive, stand against the American war with Mexico in 1846—a stand that very likely cost the first-term congressman a chance at reelection to his seat in the House of Representatives.

This is not to say that in American history there have not been great legislators and principled presidents who have swayed the U.S. Congress, reflected the will of the people, and enacted laws that benefited the many as opposed to the few. "Exceptions there were," wrote Thurman W. Arnold in *The Folklore of Capitalism*, "such as Jefferson and [Theodore] Roosevelt, who combined political technique with aristocratic background." Arnold, a prominent New Deal lawyer, could have included Franklin D. Roosevelt as a further anomaly. "Such men incurred the bitter enmity of their friends as traitors to their class," Arnold noted.

To be sure, America has enjoyed periods of great legislative achievement and constitutional virtue. If we take the era of Lincoln and the Radical Republicans alone, the record of legislation favoring the common man and former slaves is significant. Beginning in 1861, Congress passed a series of laws that progressively improved the legal status of blacks, slave, fugitive, and free, including the Confiscation Acts (1861, 1862), which freed slaves employed by rebel forces; the Act Prohibiting the Return of Slaves (1862), which forbade Union troops from returning fugitive slaves to their former owners; the abolition of slavery in the District of Columbia and the territories (1862); the Militia Act (1862), which permitted blacks to serve in the Union army; the equalization of pay for black and white soldiers (1864); the Thirteenth Amendment to the Constitution (1865), which formally abolished slavery; the Fourteenth Amendment (1868), which established the supremacy of the federal constitution over all state constitutions, thus guaranteeing equal protection and due process for freed slaves and anyone else in the former rebel states; and the Fifteenth Amendment (1870), which guaranteed the right to vote to all American males. That the Fourteenth and Fifteenth amendments were subverted for generations by Southern racism and Northern indifference does not subtract from their glory. But these amendments had little impact on American democracy until the 1950s, when the civil-rights movement successfully attacked the panoply of state laws that had kept blacks segregated from whites and excluded them from full citizenship since the end of Reconstruction.

Too little is known, however, about the socialistic Homestead Act or the Morrill Land-Grant Colleges Act, both passed in 1862, the second year of the Lincoln Administration and the Civil War. For these two pieces of legislation also contributed immensely to democratizing the country. The Homestead Act was radical in its redistributive effects: it offered 160 free acres of undeveloped public land to any head of a family at least 21 years of age and a U.S. citizen who hadn't supported the secessionist cause. All a settler had to do was live on the land for five years before he was granted title, and veterans of the military could deduct from those five years their time of service. Settlers in a hurry could buy the land for $1.25 an acre after six months. In all, the Homestead Act distributed land to a million and half people, most of whom would otherwise not have been able to afford such independence. As late as 1976 an American could still homestead anywhere public land was available, and homesteading remained legal in Alaska until 1986.

The Morrill Land-Grant Colleges Act, named for its sponsor, Vermont Republican Congressman Justin Smith Morrill, was equally grandiose in its public scope and ambition. Like the Homestead Act, the Morrill Act distributed free federal land, but the land was to be used for the establishment of colleges and universities that would remain under public control and cost less than a private college for in-state residents. A foreign visitor to the United States can justifiably stand in awe of major research universities like Rutgers in New Jersey and Cornell in New York, of the universities of California, Minnesota, Illinois, and Wisconsin, without any notion of Justin Morrill's (or Abraham Lincoln's [2]) legislative contribution to truly democratic higher education. This was a system that genuinely encouraged upward social mobility among those of low and modest incomes, extending even to disenfranchised blacks during the worst of the Jim Crow era, with its systematic oppression.

These ambitious laws, however, were passed during a national emergency, the Civil War, and it's fair to say that most of the other outstandingly popular congressional legislation in American history took place during times of national upheaval, when the normal political order could not resist change. If we consider the labor-capital conflicts of the Progressive Era, the Great Depression, World War II and its immediate aftermath, and the civil-rights upheavals of the 1950s and urban race riots of the 1960s, we see laws being promulgated under times of great national stress, when Congress could not avoid taking action. Industrial strife and mass immigration from Europe in the 1880s and 1890s led to the first wage and hour laws; the growth of monopolies and trusts sparked the Sherman Antitrust Act (1890); the horrors and filth of mass production in the Chicago meatpacking plants (publicized by Upton Sinclair's *The Jungle*) led to passage of the Pure Food and Drug Act (1906); stark plutocratic

---

2 The act had been vetoed by Lincoln's predecessor, Democrat James Buchanan.

wealth and corruption contrasted with mass poverty led to the Sixteenth Amendment to the Constitution (1913), which institutionalized and broadened the federal income tax; the immense concentration and control of money and credit by interlocking banks, trust companies, and corporations led to the creation of the Federal Reserve system (1913).

In the wake of the 1929 stock market crash and the ensuing Great Depression, the administration of Franklin D. Roosevelt proposed, and Congress passed, a whole series of what, for America, were radically socialistic programs, including Social Security, the creation of the Securities and Exchange Commission, and all manner of public-works programs to employ the masses of people who lost their jobs in the 1930s. After World War II, the G.I. Bill rivaled the Homestead and Morrill acts in the enormous boost it gave to homeownership and access to college and graduate education. Similarly, the creation of Medicare and Medicaid by the Johnson Administration's Great Society policies brought the health care of millions of people under the umbrella of federal protection. Along with the Civil Rights Acts of 1957 and 1964 and the Voting Rights Act of 1965, Lyndon Johnson and the Democratic majority in Congress contributed immensely toward the creation of a more egalitarian state in America.

But this social-democratic legislation is not typical of the American Congress. The gap between the daily life of a U.S. Representative or a Senator and the noble aspirations of the Declaration of Independence is considerable. We can be certain that the Robert Redford character in *The Candidate* would not have followed up his question "What do we do now?" by rushing to the United States Senate Gift Shop in the east wing of the Capitol building to buy the pamphlet, published by the Government Printing Office, entitled "How Our Laws Are Made." In the pamphlet's introduction, House Parliamentarian Charles W. Johnson innocently explains its mission:

This brochure is intended to provide a basic outline of the numerous steps of our federal lawmaking process from the source of an idea for a legislative proposal through its publication as a statute. The legislative process is a matter about which every person should be well informed in order to understand and appreciate the work of Congress.

It is hoped that this guide will enable readers to gain a greater understanding of the federal legislative process and its role as one of the foundations of our representative system. One of the most practical safeguards of the American democratic way of life is this legislative process with its emphasis on the protection of the minority, allowing ample opportunity to all sides to be heard and make their views known. The fact that a proposal cannot become a law without consideration and approval by both Houses of Congress is an outstanding virtue of our bicameral legislative system. The open and full discussion provided under the Constitution often results in the notable improvement of a bill by amendment before it becomes law or in the eventual defeat of an inadvisable proposal.

Nowhere in "How Our Laws Are Made" is there any reference to the army of 13,595 registered lobbyists who participate in the lawmaking process alongside our elected representatives. These peddlers of influence today wield as much or more power than at any other time in U.S. history—perhaps even more than they did during the Grant Administration (1869-1877), once considered the most corrupt. However, it is a common misperception among journalists and reformers alike that lobbyists, corporations, rich individuals, trade associations, and labor unions in effect bribe politicians with campaign contributions in order to get favorable legislation passed. In fact, more typically a congressman pressures potential contributors by dangling helpful or threatening legislation before them, then asking for their "support" for either the congressman's party or next campaign. As Ned Lamont puts it, businessmen often pay politicians "protection money; you certainly invest in an incumbent."[3] Whereas civil-rights legislation benefits mostly poor minorities who have little money to contribute to candidates running for office, legislation affecting taxes or tariffs is worth billions of dollars to businesses, and thus becomes a powerful tool for fund-raising.

Two cases illustrate the point: In June 2007, an immigration-reform law intended to make it easier for illegal immigrants to acquire U.S. citizenship was defeated in the Senate, despite the official support of President Bush and a good number of politicians from both parties. But illegal immigrants, almost by definition, do not constitute a lobby; only their lawyers (if they can afford one) can pony up for a political campaign. The immigration bar has some influence, but nothing close to that of a powerful corporation or a trade association.

Two years earlier, a bill affecting the credit-card companies and other lenders had a quite different legislative outcome. Since the Reagan Administration came to power in 1981, "private enterprise," in alliance with a resurgent conservative movement, has sought to

---

3 Such fund-raising pressure on businessmen crosses party lines. For example, the plutocrat David Rockefeller, a Republican (and Democratic Senator Jay Rockefeller's uncle), regularly donates to the Democratic Party. In 2000, the retired chairman of the Chase Manhattan Bank gave $2,500 to the Democratic Senatorial Campaign Committee (DSCC); he also gave $1,000 to each of Hillary Clinton's campaigns for Senate in 2000 and 2006. During an April 2006 interview with the French newspaper *Le Figaro*, conducted at his estate in Pocantico Hills, New York, Rockefeller is interrupted by a telephone call from New York Senator Charles Schumer, the chairman of the DSCC. "Later," Rockefeller tells his servant. No doubt the ultra-persistent Schumer wouldn't wait too long for a return phone call.

reverse many of the liberal initiatives of Roosevelt's New Deal and Johnson's Great Society. In Reagan's view, the poor and disadvantaged in America had too good a deal. Thus came into common usage the notion of "welfare queens" and overly pampered "deadbeats," all of them feeding voraciously at the public trough at the expense of honest, hardworking taxpayers.[4] As a result, millions of people were thrown off the welfare rolls from 1981 to 2001 under the Reagan, Bush, and Clinton administrations.

Then, in 2001, profiting from the pro-business climate ushered in with the new Bush Administration, credit-card companies redoubled their campaign to make it harder for "serial abusers" of the bankruptcy laws to protect themselves against creditors. In fact, most of these alleged deadbeats were overstretched borrowers and credit-card holders who had suffered some calamitous financial reverse. The journalist Steve France, writing in the *Washington Post*, noted that only 3 percent of people filing for bankruptcy under Chapter 7 of the old bankruptcy law had the money to "pay back substantial amounts of unsecured debt." As Elizabeth Warren, a Harvard Law professor who testified against the new legislation, put it: "Overwhelmingly, American families file for bankruptcy because they have been driven there—largely by medical and economic catastrophe——not because they want to go there."

Such a bill nevertheless made good business sense to the creditors, who stood to gain more revenue in interest from prolonged debt payment by bankrupts, including the ones who could barely pay. More to the point, it also made good fund-raising sense for congressmen, who could use a new bankruptcy law to raise more

---

4 The most pointed definition I've found of a "Reagan Democrat"—the term for "socially conservative" Democrats who supported the Republican president—appeared in a November 9, 1988, editorial in the *Philadelphia Daily News*: "Most 'Reagan Democrats,' as far as anybody can figure, are resentful rednecks willing to vote against their own interests because somebody black might get a break."

campaign cash while also claiming to restore "the moral stigma" of bankruptcy.

But reducing access to bankruptcy protection was controversial, since America has a long tradition of relative tolerance toward individual debtors. Until 1869, an Englishman might be sent to Coldbath Fields Prison, or Australia, for failing to pay his bills. But in the United States, beginning in 1833, during the populist administration of Andrew Jackson, imprisonment for unpaid debt was abolished on the federal level, and most states eventually followed suit. In 1898, the Bankruptcy Act offered protection for the first time to businesses, with an emphasis placed on reorganization and rehabilitating companies while creditors were held at bay. During the New Deal, a time of mass unemployment and poverty, a series of laws created new protections for individuals that allowed them time to liquidate their assets and pay off only the portion of their debt that they could reasonably afford—beyond that, they were absolved of responsibility. In 1978, during the Carter Administration, a new Bankruptcy Reform Act established Chapters 7, 11, and 13, which formalized protection for businesses and individuals to an even greater extent.

Credit-card companies such as the Delaware-based MBNA had been trying since 1997 to get Congress to make it more difficult for individuals to use Chapter 7, which allowed them to pay what they could and then forgave the remaining debt. The alternative for individuals, Chapter 13, requires a debtor to continue paying creditors out of future earnings under a three- to five-year plan with the hope of paying off as much of the debt as possible. Under the absurdly named Bankruptcy Abuse Prevention and Consumer Protection Act (BAPCPA), passed in 2005, Congress established a "means test" for Chapter 7 applicants that was all but impossible for most bankrupts to pass. With the new rules, only those making less than their home state's median income, and earning less than $166 per month of "disposable income," could have their unpaid debt forgiven. Failure to pass this means test meant that they could not file for bankruptcy protection under Chapter 7 and instead would be forced to file under the more stringent Chapter 13—prolonging the debt and ensuring a regular stream of monthly payments to the creditor. In addition, the new law made it more expensive to file for bankruptcy. Prior to passage of the new law, a Chapter 7 filing cost $600; under the new statute, the price rose to $2,500, a serious barrier to someone in financial distress. As Steve France explained, "If you can squeeze out [$166] a month after paying for peanut butter and bus fare, you are in the abuser category and headed for the purgatory of Chapter 13."

According to parliamentarian Johnson's description of the lawmaking process, "Bills originate in many diverse quarters," but "primary among these is the idea and draft conceived by a Member." Once again, the earnest Mr. Johnson fails to mention that many bills are drafted by lobbyists in the architecturally uniform stretch of the nation's capital known as K Street, which has become synonymous with lobbying firms.

Credit-card companies are among the regular employers of K Street lobbying shops, and they make large contributions to Senate campaigns. BAPCPA's sponsor, Republican Charles Grassley of Iowa, had received $123,300 in 1997–2002 from financial institutions, including banks, credit-card companies, and non-bank mortgage lenders. Senator Joseph Biden, a Delaware Democrat whose state was headquarters for MBNA, America's largest credit-card company, received $147,700 between 1999 and 2004 from MBNA's political action committee, the company's subsidiaries, and its employees. Anticipating eventual passage of the bill, MBNA had also contributed generously to George Bush's 2000 presidential campaign. As one of Bush's so-called Pioneers (a classification of donor requiring a minimum bundling pledge of $100,000), MBNA Chief Executive Officer Charles Cawley had gone above and beyond the call of ordinary lobbying. At the time, Cawley was prohibited by the 1974 election reform law from personally giving more than $2,000 to Bush, so he bundled the contributions of hundreds of MBNA's employees, eventually turning over $240,000 to the Bush campaign committee. Besides winning friends in the White House, Cawley also qualified for the higher honorific of Ranger in the hierarchy of Bush contributors.

With so much corporate largesse directed toward both parties, it was no surprise when BAPCPA passed the Senate on March 10, 2005, by a margin of 74–25 (with 18 Democrats voting in support) and a month later passed the House, by 302 to 126 (with 73 Democrats in support). When President Bush signed the bill into law on April 20, his rhetoric was hardly Jacksonian, but it warmed the hearts of the members of his faction. Besides congratulating Sen. Grassley to jovial laughter ("I think you told me you'd been working on this bill for nine years. That's a long time"), Bush extolled the virtues of paying back creditors. "Our bankruptcy laws are an important part of the safety net of America," he said disingenuously. Echoing the self-help, anti-welfare rhetoric of Reagan, Bush went on:

> They give those who cannot pay their debts a fresh start. Yet bankruptcy should always be a last resort in our legal system. If someone does not pay his or her debts, the rest of society ends up paying them. In recent years, too many people have abused the bankruptcy laws. They've walked away from debts even when they had the ability to repay them. . . . America is a nation of personal responsibility where people are expected to meet their obligations.

CEO Cawley certainly had met his obligation to his shareholders and his political patrons. One financial analyst, Kenneth Posner, had predicted a windfall of $75 million for MBNA in the first year after the bill's passage. Meanwhile, Bush said, the good news for "society" at large was that "debtors seeking to erase all debts will now have to wait eight years from their last bankruptcy before they can file again." This, he added, would prevent "fraud" and "clamp down" on "abusers" who "game the system."

But nobody games the system better than an incumbent congressman. For so many elected officials, the game has less to do with legislation than with simply remaining in office, and raising reelection funds by paying off the needs, desires, and fears of constituents——whether they are individuals or businesses—is common. Together, the Democrats and Republicans raised more than $1.3 billion for the 2006 congressional election. To be sure, the lobby system contributes both to corruption and inaction. Spectacular frauds support the popular image of politicians as corrupt. The Jack Abramoff scandal erupted in 2004 with revelations that he and his partner in crime, Michael Scanlon, had overcharged Indian tribes seeking to preserve their special reservation gambling concessions (he charged the tribes a total of $82 million, in part by persuading them to hire ancillary firms that would then kick back money to him). But it was Abramoff's lavish gifts of free travel to members of Congress that captured the public's attention, for it now seemed as though a golf trip to Scotland or a tropical vacation in the Mariana Islands could buy a vote. When Abramoff pleaded guilty in 2006 to charges of fraud, tax evasion, and conspiracy to bribe public officials, some observers felt that the boil of corruption had been lanced.

But the Abramoff scandal was a symptom, not a cause. When two beneficiaries of Abramoff's favor——Republican representatives Tom DeLay, the former majority leader, and Robert Ney (the congressman responsible for changing the names of "french fries" and "french toast" to "freedom fries" and "freedom toast" on the House cafeteria's menus, after France opposed the Bush Administration's push to invade Iraq)—were themselves forced to resign on corruption charges, Americans believed a fundamental change was in the wind. This was wishful thinking. For a time fewer goodies probably were distributed directly to hungry politicians, but the far more significant corruption, the practice of "earmarking," continued unabated. Accepting a gift from a lobbyist is certainly corrupt; providing millions of dollars in taxpayer money for a useless project in collusion with other congressmen is closer in spirit to conspiracy.

One notable example of contemporary and innovative earmarking was provided by veteran Republican Don Young, Alaska's sole Representative in the House—notable in part because earmarking usually benefits some person or entity in a congressman's district or home state. Young had fallen in with a Florida real estate developer named Daniel J. Aronoff, who hosted a fund-raising event for Young on February 19, 2005, at the Hyatt Regency Coconut Point Resort and Spa in Bonita Springs, Florida—many miles and degrees removed from Young's frigid home district. The event netted $41,750 for Young's campaign coffers. A few days later, Young, as the then chairman of the House Committee on Transportation and Infrastructure, attached an earmark to his own 2006 transportation bill that provided $10 million toward plans for construction of an extension connecting Lee County's Interstate 75 and Coconut Road (the street where the Hyatt Regency is located). Aronoff, as it happened, owned about 4,000 acres of land along Coconut Road and stood to profit from its future development, which would be greatly enhanced by construction of the extension. The transportation bill passed, with Young's earmark intact, alongside 6,374 other earmarks worth $24 billion. By the summer of 2007, Young was in the minority on the transportation committee, but he was still pressuring Lee County authorities to move ahead with the road project, despite local opposition and newspaper revelations pointing out the blatant deal between the congressman and the developer.

None of this was new in American politics, or the American political imagination. Like Aronoff, Sinclair Lewis's fictional character Babbitt was rewarded for his political work on behalf of the incoming mayor of Zenith, a fictional Midwestern city: "Babbitt was offered several minor appointments to distribute among poor relations, but he preferred advance information about the extension of paved highways, and this a grateful administration gave to him." Thus was Babbitt able to purchase land that was sure to increase in value when the road came.

In Washington, earmarks operate on a grander scale and are a crucial form of political patronage. Earmarking is the procedure by which members of Congress insert last-minute allocations of money for local projects into huge, complicated appropriations bills— the better to hide them, for no one has the time to read the final bill, much less object to the details of congressional largesse, more commonly known as "pork." As explained by Ken Silverstein, the Washington editor of *Harper's Magazine*, businessmen like Daniel Aronoff are the beneficiaries of a "process . . . so willfully murky that abuse has become not the exception but the rule. Earmarks are added anonymously, frequently during last-minute, closed-door sessions of the appropriations committees. An especially attractive feature for those private interests seeking earmarks is that they are awarded on a noncompetitive basis and recipients need not meet any performance standards. In other words, applicants need not demonstrate that their project, program, or company actually delivers a useful good or service."

Most journalists view patronage in terms of jobs—cabinet positions, ambassadorships, and membership on federal and presidential commissions—and these jobs remain valuable currency in the brokerage of political favors. The president's appointments for over

6,000 governmental positions are among the most sought-after favors in Washington. At the highest level, especially foreign embassy postings for rich businessmen who were big campaign contributors, these positions flatter the vanity of their recipients. At the lower levels of the cabinet departments, they can lead to lucrative jobs after government service. Aside from congressmen themselves, nothing opens doors to power in Washington like a former government official. The K Street lobbying complex is filled with ex-assistant secretaries, legal counsels, and directors of departments, each with a special expertise in an area of the federal bureaucracy that can lead a client to a better bill and greater riches. It's why in American history texts and historical novels one finds constant reference to office-seekers hounding officeholders and officeholders alternately browbeating and enticing office-seekers and other officeholders under their sway. Here is how Arthur Schlesinger Jr. describes Martin Van Buren's arrival in Washington in 1829 to assume the post of Secretary of State in the new Jackson Administration:

> It was after dark when Van Buren reached Washington. His coach hardly arrived at the hotel before office-seekers surrounded it. They pursued him inside, flocking relentlessly into the room where he lay on a sofa, weary from the journey. The Secretary of State listened to them patiently for an hour, then dismissed them to go to the White House.

In his fictionalized but highly realistic portrait of Washington, *Democracy*, Henry Adams portrays a nearly identical scene in the rooms of Senator Silas Ratcliffe before the inauguration of a new president sometime in the 1870s. Ratcliffe himself, according to his great antagonist, John Carrington, will be offered a choice of patronage jobs by the president, either Secretary of State or Secretary of the Treasury. ("If he takes either it will be the Treasury, for he is a desperate political manager, and will want the patronage for the next national convention.") In Adams's description, an atmosphere of grasping ambition reigns over the capital city as the office-seekers demand their "honestly earned harvest of foreign missions and consulates, department-bureaus, custom-house and revenue offices, postmasterships, Indian agencies, and army and navy contracts . . .":

> This is the moment when the two whited sepulchres at
> either end of the [Pennsylvania] Avenue reek
> with the thick atmosphere of bargain and sale. The old
> is going; the new is coming. Wealth, office, power are
> at auction. Who bids highest? who hates with most
> venom? who intrigues with most skill? who has done
> the dirtiest, the meanest, the darkest, and the most
> political work? He shall have his reward.
>   Senator Ratcliffe was absorbed and ill at ease.
>   A swarm of applicants for office dogged his steps
> and beleaguered his rooms in quest of his endorsement
> of their paper characters.

By 1883, this spoils systems was so rampant that Congress felt obliged to reform the civil service by passing the Pendleton Act, which greatly reduced the number of political appointees. Of course, this act did not eliminate patronage as a way of life in Washington or in what were then 38 state capitals; nor did it halt other forms of political buying and selling. Removing local postmaster positions from political patronage only raised the stakes for higher-level appointments, including judges, U.S. attorneys, and directorships of government information agencies. But then, who in the eighteenth century, or in the nineteenth century for that matter, could have imagined a Secretary of Defense overseeing a 2008 budget of

$624.6 billion or a Department of Homeland Security with nearly 200,000 employees?

Not all earmarking is wasteful—though 15,584 separate earmarks totaling $32.7 billion in 2004 is a considerable figure—and some of it seems harmless in comparison with the vast amounts of money poured down the black hole of moral and policy disasters such as the invasion and occupation of Iraq.[5]

But the most pernicious aspect is its reinforcement of the two-party monopoly on American politics. Virtually no private citizen, no unelected public figure, no executive of a private foundation or trade association, can match the power of an established congressman to bestow favors and money on people and institutions that will in turn strengthen his hold on power. Moreover, local "pork" is often nothing more than a confidence trick—a way to cover inaction on more pressing problems—foisted on the beleaguered constituents of depressed cities like Utica, New York, which I visited twice, in

---

5 Democratic Party stalwart and Clinton lieutenant Rahm Emanuel, a congressman from Chicago, did his best to defend earmarks in a *New York Times* op-ed piece in August 2007: "In my own district, I obtained an earmark to rebuild a bridge that not only was rated as deficient but also was identified by the Department of Homeland Security as a major evacuation route in case of a terrorist attack on Chicago. Does that make me an 'earmark thug' or a congressman who took care of a critical need in his district?" Emanuel is well known for his talents as a political enforcer—indeed, something of a thug—for his party's bosses, including Chicago Mayor Richard M. Daley. Emanuel's key role in pushing the passage of NAFTA, while working on Clinton's White House staff, is the stuff of lobbying legend. Emanuel's justification for the earmark system echoes an iconic character from American fiction, Willie Stark of Robert Penn Warren's *All the King's Men*. Stark, who is based on the long-time political boss of Louisiana, Governor Huey Long, lectures a political rival on what he believes is the false assumption that political progress can take place without corruption: "'Dirt's a funny thing,' the Boss said. 'Come to think of it, there ain't a thing but dirt on this green God's globe except what's under water, and that's dirt, too. It's dirt makes the grass grow. A diamond ain't a thing in the world but a piece of dirt that got awful hot. And God-a-Mighty picked up a handful of dirt and blew on it and made you and me and George Washington and mankind blessed in faculty and apprehension. It all depends on what you do with the dirt. That right?'"

May and August of 2006 and again in 2007. Utica was once a mid-sized industrial powerhouse, but, as with so many other Northern manufacturing centers, its factories began to disappear in the 1970s and '80s as corporations sought cheaper, non-unionized labor in the Southern states, Mexico, and Asia. Utica's decline was matched by the decline of other upstate New York cities, such as Schenectady, Rome, and Buffalo, creating a "rust belt" the length of the 340-mile Eire Canal.

Today, Utica is hollowed out, denuded of its former industrial vibrancy. Beyond its dramatic Beaux Arts train station and other Greek and Classical Revival buildings downtown, little is left of the setting that inspired Theodore Dreiser's great 1925 novel, *An American Tragedy*, the story of a factory manager and the factory girl he seduces and ultimately murders. Utica is now emblematic of a contemporary American tragedy: the destruction of a high-wage unionized working class by "free trade" policies promoted as beneficial to all. At one time Utica was known as the "radio capital of the world," employing 8,000 people at General Electric alone. By the 1990s, with the city's population falling (toward its current 60,000, from over 100,000 in 1960), bumper stickers appeared that read, "Last One Out of Utica, Please Turn Out the Lights."

But Utica was not entirely abandoned, or undefended. When I last visited in August 2007, the Oneida County Airport was closed to all commercial and private aviation, but it was now home to the New York State Preparedness Training Center, established under the auspices of the New York Office of Homeland Security. The only thing more preposterous than the idea of terrorists targeting a cluster of depressed cities in upstate New York was the notion that they would be tempted to attack a defunct airport. Nevertheless, it seemed that U.S. Rep. Sherwood Boehlert, a Republican, had successfully worked in concert with Republican Governor George Pataki to bring $5.5 million in state money to the county to establish a "school" for training 500 to 600 emergency workers at a time in "WMD [Weapons of Mass Destruction], response, prevention and recovery." The airport tarmac itself was to be used for an "emergency vehicle operations course." Meanwhile, Utica's boosters and unemployed alike were hoping that eventually more public money would arrive to build a "state-of-the-art emergency operations center" that would serve as central New York State's command and control headquarters "in the event a catastrophic event or disaster occurs." As Pataki put it at the press conference announcing the creation of the center, "We want to make this a national model for how you train first responders . . . synergistic with Griffiss [Airfield], Rome labs, and everything the Congressman has done to bring a stronger defense department here to the Mohawk Valley." Nearing retirement as chairman of the House Committee on Science, Boehlert was busily preparing his constituents for a hi-tech, military future that would soon include earmarks of $2.5 million for, among other things, development of "warfighter visualization tools" in his district.[6]

Boehlert, it should be noted, had voted for NAFTA in 1993 and Permanent Normal Trade Relations (PNTR) with China in 2000, two tariff-reducing, cheap-labor-ensuring measures that finished off dying industrial cities like Utica. Homeland security, it appeared, was the only growth industry left in town.

In Washington, the spirit of reform disappeared under an ava-

---

6 Utica's mayor, Timothy Julian, also a Republican, was another direct beneficiary of Homeland "pork" designed to rescue his constituents from terrorist attack, if not cheap Chinese labor. Not to be outdone by Boehlert, he proudly announced in August 2005 the receipt of a $250,000 grant from the New York State Office of Homeland Security, money that would, he said, "be used to fund the Utica Police and Fire Departments for projects involving reducing New York's vulnerability to terrorism, minimizing the dangers of potential attacks, and improving the ability of first responders to communicate with each other and coordinate their efforts more effectively."

lanche of earmarking and political fund-raising. These two activities, while having very little to do with the business of the people, had everything to do with the business of reelection and maintaining party control of Congress and the White House. If anyone had any hope of reviving the Dean/McCain crusade against "special interests," he or she was faced with two disturbing political facts. After his defeat in 2004, Howard Dean attempted to resurrect his national political career—as Terry McAuliffe's successor as chairman of the Democratic National Committee, a role that required him to aid and abet his party's fund-raising machine, still dominated by Dean's antagonists, Bill and Hillary Clinton. In 2007, the only reform candidate who emerged in the Democratic Party was former Senator Mike Gravel, a gruff 77-year-old from Alaska too honest to mince words. Gravel had won his seat as an insurgent amid the antiwar furor of 1968 and had never been a party loyalist. Thus, he lost his seat in 1980 when a party regular, Clark Gruening, helped by Republican crossover votes, defeated him in the Democratic primary. Gruening was in turn defeated in the general election by the Republican candidate in the Reagan landslide that also removed Jimmy Carter, another outsider, from the White House.

During an early Democratic presidential debate hosted by CNN in July 2007, it was left to Gravel to tell the truth about money and the American political system. The debate format permitted voters to ask questions in prerecorded videos, and Cris Nolan, a Democratic precinct committeeman from Mundelein, Illinois, cut right to the chase when he queried Hillary Clinton about dynastic party politics:

> With Bush, Clinton, and Bush again serving as the last
> three presidents, how would electing you, a Clinton,
> constitute the type of change in Washington so many
> people in the heartland are yearning for, and what your

campaign has been talking about? I was also wondering
if any of the other candidates had a problem with the
same two families being in charge of the executive branch
of government for 28 consecutive years, if Hillary Clinton
were to potentially be elected and then reelected.

By now a relatively adroit campaigner, Clinton elicited laughter
when she replied, "Well, I think it's a problem that Bush was elected
in 2000. I actually thought somebody else was elected in that election . . ." But she didn't answer Nolan's question about her own candidacy, referring to her pride in "my husband's record as president"
and then resorting to this bromide:

> You know what is great about this is look at this
> stage and look at the diversity you have here in the
> Democratic Party. Any one of us would be a better
> president than our current president or the future
> Republican nominee.

Asked by moderator Anderson Cooper if he had "a problem with"
dynastic politics, Gravel was stunning in his candor:

> Well, yes, I do, a serious problem. The Democratic
> Party used to stand for the ordinary working man. But
> the Clintons and the DLC [Democratic Leadership
> Council] sold out the Democratic Party to Wall Street.
> Look at where the money is being raised right now,
> for Hillary, Obama, and Edwards. It's the hedge funds,
> it's Wall Street bankers. It's the people who brought
> you what you have today. Please wake up. Just look at
> the *New York Times* of the 17th of July that analyzes
> where the money's coming from.

"Time's up," announced Cooper. But Gravel insisted: "It comes from the bankers on Wall Street and of course hedge funds, which is code for bankers on Wall Street. And they're lock, stock, and bar-, rel in their pocket." None of the other candidates responded. Before the next debate, sponsored by the AFL-CIO at Chicago's Soldier Field, Gravel was punished for his rebelliousness. The labor federation, evidently unimpressed by Gravel's protest against big-money influence on politics, refused to let the party's strongest spokesman against Wall Street participate in the debate. This was not surprising, since during election time the AFL-CIO operates almost entirely as a subsidiary of the Democratic Party, and Chicago is home to the most powerful local Democratic monopoly in the country. The excuse for denying Gravel a place on the platform was his alleged failure to respond to a questionnaire on health care (a charge Gravel disputed), but whatever the official reason, the banning was almost certainly a reprisal. Party oligarchs like Hillary Clinton could not have been happy with Gravel's bald statement of political reality.

And where was the avatar of Republican reform, the courageous war hero, Senator John McCain? Two weeks earlier, just outside the hallowed floor of the United States Senate, McCain had been caught making a conference call to his chief fund-raisers, according to the *New York Times*, "to urge them to keep up the fight" for his faltering campaign. This was a blatant violation of Senate ethics rules, which prohibit campaign work either on the floor or inside the Republican cloakroom, where McCain made the call; it also possibly broke a federal law that forbids political fund-raising on government property. It was only ten years since McCain had called for appointment of an independent prosecutor to investigate charges that then vice president, Al Gore, was guilty of similar solicitations.

It seemed that McCain's reformist betrayal of his party in 2000 had finally caught up with him, since the *Times* story revealing his indiscretion was likely leaked by a rival senator or staff member only too delighted to point out McCain's hypocrisy. "For all intents and purposes, McCain's campaign is over," announced Charlie Cook of *The Cook Political Report* on July 14, 2007. "The physicians have pulled up the sheet; the executors of the estate are taking over."

Cook was wrong, of course. As McCain demonstrated with his stunning resurgence in the New Hampshire primary in January 2008, an independent-minded candidate could still revive himself against long odds, at least up to a point.

Could the same thing happen to American democracy?

I f democracy in Washington (in the sense of genuine rule by the people) is little more than a series of symbolic gestures obscuring the real business of government (the processing of political power, patronage, and public money), then what has become of the local democracies in New England so celebrated by Alexis de Tocqueville? Although the Puritan-inspired idea of the town meeting is exceedingly rare south and west of Connecticut, New England has largely maintained its three-centuries-old tradition of direct and universal citizen participation in government in a majority of the 844 towns that make up the region's six states. Depending on the state and the size of the town, citizen power in such locales at least once a year can still determine basic policies for education, road building, zoning, and police and fire protection.

The annual town meeting itself—which is sometimes merely a pro forma affair with low citizen turnout—can be less important than the offshoots of rebellion engendered by the very idea of a town meeting. For when people are accustomed to the principle that government belongs to them, they will occasionally reaffirm their sovereignty in sudden and surprising ways. And if democracy still functions at all in America, it seems to function best in the smaller New England towns, away from the more impersonal, party-dominated atmosphere of big cities.

Such formal citizen assemblies are to be distinguished from the more informal assemblies guaranteed under the First Amendment to the Constitution, such as the street rallies outside a government building that one associates with antiwar demonstrations, the civil-rights movement, or outside abortion clinics. Town meetings, or public hearings conducted under town auspices, can be heated, but they operate under a different assumption than a street action: that power really does reside in the people and not in some remote location inaccessible to the average citizen. This is why Howard Dean, the former governor of a New England state, relied so heavily in his presidential campaign on so-called town meeting-style rallies, where he would answer unscripted questions from voters for what seemed like hours.[1] Thousands of times over the course of his ill-fated crusade, he would end the rally by insisting to the usually enthusiastic audience that "you have the power!" By 2003, dispirited citizens in many towns and cities across the country had good reason to believe that in fact they did not have the power to change anything, much less the sort of candidates who got to run for high office. So Dean's message carried a tremendous punch. When I watched him work a crowd at the middle school auditorium in Keene, New Hampshire, on a frigid January night in 2004, he seemed to be awakening a dormant gene inside the members

---

1 Conversely, George W. Bush has increased the use of "free speech zones"—small areas set up far from a political event designed to corral hostile protesters and keep them off the evening news—by using them for "town meetings" and official presidential visits around the country. The idea for "free speech zones" goes at least as far back as the 1988 Democratic Convention in Atlanta. Unlike the "town meetings" in the McCain and Dean campaigns, Bush's 2004 reelection organization carefully screened people attending his events and ejected anyone who could be identified as having anti-Bush sympathies.

of the audience. They knew instinctively that they were supposed to have the power but had forgotten where to get hold of it.

To better understand this somewhat nostalgic New England notion of people power, I traveled to Portsmouth, Rhode Island, in early August 2007 to find out how democracy works in the way we might like to imagine, with ordinary citizens making significant choices in concert with one another. The setting for this remarkable display of democratic initiative was a very old, colonial-era town, founded in 1638, that spreads across three islands in Narragansett Bay. The largest part of Portsmouth occupies the northern half of Aquidneck Island, which it shares with the far more famous town of Newport, residence of the old American plutocracy and, by coincidence, the port where Alexis de Tocqueville landed when he began his American journey in 1831.

Today, on the southern end of Aquidneck, ritzy old Newport, with its magnificent Gilded Age (pre-income tax) mansions, hosts a gigantic Wal-Mart. To the north, along Route 114, adjacent Middletown, situated between Newport and Portsmouth, has any number of ugly strip malls packed with large, discount retail establishments and motels. Somehow, more rural Portsmouth had been spared the "anywhere U.S.A." sprawl that now blights so much of the country. Except for the CVS (a chain pharmacy) and Clements' Marketplace across the road, there wasn't anything you could call "big" retail in Portsmouth. Moreover, Clements', a locally owned and family-operated supermarket, is, by American standards, a modest 32,000 square feet and has the feel of a much smaller neighborhood store. Because Portsmouth has no downtown, Clements' serves as an unofficial town center and meeting place for the population of about 17,000. The only genuinely big commercial presence in Portsmouth is the defense contractor Raytheon, which manufactures high-tech equipment for the U.S. Navy and sits quietly, if ominously, out of the way, south of Clements', on West Main Road.

So when word got out in March that Target, a national "big box" retail chain, was applying to the town government for permission to build a 136,500-square-foot store and six-acre parking lot at the corner of West Main and Union, an empty lot abutting a residential neighborhood and the islands' only reservoir, alarms sounded. It was then that an authentic democrat (as opposed to a partisan of the Democratic Party) named Conni Harding leaped into the civic sphere like someone out of a Frank Capra film.

To say that Harding, a 45-year-old mother of six (four of her own and two stepchildren), had no immediate personal interest in preventing Target from desecrating the mostly lovely landscape of her hometown would be to tell an incomplete story. Conni and Luke Harding's two-story, Gambrell-style home, built in 1990, is situated on Union Street in tree-sheltered calm, up a slight slope, more or less on the opposite corner from the proposed building site. For the twelve years since they were married, the couple had been hoping against all capitalist logic that the 16-acre lot would remain empty. The site had been zoned for commercial use since the 1960s, and there was nothing in the owner's résumé to suggest that he had anything other than commercial exploitation in mind for the property. John "Jack" Egan, a wealthy Newport-based developer, was best known locally for his role in building Aquidneck Mall in aesthetically compromised Middletown, and he was not known to be a conservationist. Indeed, Conni had taken note when a few years earlier Egan had stripped the topsoil off the site to prevent trees from growing. That, Conni told me, might have given environmentalists ideas about preserving this particular site: the very visible red, white, and blue sign announcing "Retail For Lease—100,000 sq.ft." was a daily reminder that the land wasn't turning into a forest preserve anytime soon. But Conni and Luke were busy people—she works as an independent sales representative for a national jewelry company, and he owns a local heating, ventilation, and air-conditioning business. Because of her two youngest children, aged 10 and 4, Conni had managed to find time to involve herself in a public-school-funding controversy the year before, but she couldn't have told you the names of more than one or two town council members and certainly wasn't friends with any local politicians, including the most prominent resident of Portsmouth, U.S. Representative Patrick Kennedy, the son of Senator Edward Kennedy and nephew of the late president. What's more, in all her years living in Portsmouth, including her time at Portsmouth High School, Conni had given only passing thought to the sign that greets you on the way into town from the north: "Welcome Portsmouth—Birthplace of American Democracy Est. 1638."[2]

Then, one evening in early March, Conni got a call from a neighbor, Rich Cipriani. He'd seen an item in the *Providence Journal* about Target wanting to build in Portsmouth, and he thought Conni was the obvious person to call for two reasons: the first was that Target was going to ruin the Hardings' hard-earned tranquillity with a huge store and a 586-car parking lot across the street. The second, I suspect, was that there's a certain type of take-charge citizen in every town whom people tend to go to when there's trouble. I've met a few such natural leaders in my journalism career, and Conni Harding is one of them.

But this situation was more complicated politically, since Conni and Luke risked appearing excessively self-interested. "We were the most visible," she told me in August at Custom House Coffee, not far from the target of Target's development ambition. "Which put

---

2 Portsmouth bases this claim on its 1638 Portsmouth Compact, which purports to be America's first formal declaration of civic and religious freedom. The first white settlement on Aquidneck Island was established in part by Anne Hutchinson, a religious dissident who had been banished from the Massachusetts Bay Colony. Roger Williams, the co-founder of the Rhode Island colony, invited Hutchinson to resettle on Aquidneck.

us in a quandary: well, of course we're going to be crying 'poor me.' So for a few weeks I didn't know what type of role to take because obviously I'd be upset about it. And I didn't want it to become a 'not in my back yard' issue. But soon after all this happened it became an island-wide issue. There was just evidence of people all over the island who were calling us and didn't want it."

So Conni took the lead. She had once worked on a local Newport political campaign, as a high school student in 1977, and one of her cousins is a state representative from Winchester, Massachusetts. But Conni didn't consider herself a political person—she had been too busy over the years trying to make money to support two children after her first marriage ended, then helping to support four more children when she moved back to Portsmouth and remarried.

In her new political role, Conni, I think, was aided more by her long experience as a salesperson than by any direct experience in electoral politics. America is a sales and promotion culture as much as it is a democratic culture, and the idea of the self-reliant salesman—on his own with nothing to support him but his charm—is deeply embedded in the national psyche. The truth about sales is more complex, of course. The great modern American interpreters of the sales culture, the playwrights Arthur Miller and David Mamet, portray the salesman as a tragic figure enmeshed in a rigged game that he cannot really win. In fact, the salesman is often the victim of forces beyond his control (economic, political, and social), and no one would describe his job as easy or steady. But along with the rejection and occasional humiliation that comes with the territory, the American salesman develops a certain resiliency, a basic self-confidence that can pull him through difficult times and hostile environments. For every miserable Willy Loman I suspect there's at least one unflappable Conni Harding—willing to suppress fear and take the leap.

In sales, the hardest thing to do is make a cold call on an un-known customer in an unknown locale. Conni knew this from her two previous sales jobs, when she sold chemicals and spring wa-ter. That she could successfully sell these fundamentally antithetical products is the hallmark of a salesman's self-confidence—the feel-ing that one can sell anything to anyone. Of course, no one can sell anything to anyone, but a lot of Americans really believe they can. Whether this notion complements a democratic culture or not, I think it helped Conni, no fatalist, make the first crucial call.

First, Conni read all the local newspapers to "find out what was happening." She did not call the Portsmouth town administrator because instinctively she mistrusted the local political establish-ment, whose members include other landowners and real estate developers. Her first call was to her son's soccer coach, Ted Clem-ent (no relation to the supermarket owners), who also happened to be the executive director of the Aquidneck Land Trust, a nonprofit group that tries to preserve open land through combination pur-chases using both public and private money. Clement was somewhat pessimistic, Conni told me. "He said, 'Oh, Conni, it's a tough situa-tion . . . everything's legal that they could do.'" What made it tough was not only that the vacant land was already commercially zoned (as opposed to agricultural or residential) but that mostly middle-class Portsmouth badly needed more tax revenue to fund its public schools, and a big-box store would yield more money for the com-munity than an empty lot.

"So he said, 'You've got a tough road here,'" Conni recalled. "However, he also said, 'You've got to form a group immediately. You just have to, no matter what.'. . . So it's like coming to America [for the first time]. You've got to fight and get the best thing out of it."

Clement had cited the recent example of Middletown, where residents lost their fight to prevent construction of a Barnes & Noble, the chain bookstore, on the already overbuilt West Main Road (Route 114). But their opposition resulted in the preservation of 40 acres nearby, a compromise of sorts that benefited the Land Trust perhaps more than it did the neighbors of the new mega bookstore. "So," recalled Conni, "it was discouraging talking to him, yet we had to move forward."

Conni called a friend, Christine Jenkins, whose property abutted the building site on the other side of Union Street. Now she had the nucleus of an organization. Jack Egan was their opponent, but he was invisible to most residents and fortunately, according to Conni, not "an insider" with the local power structure. Target was the more visible enemy, since anyone who wanted to could visit one of its massive unsightly stores in nearby Dartmouth, Massachusetts, where big-box development was rampant. Nevertheless, she said, "the pro-development people are obviously going to say, 'Hey, there's a big rainbow and it's going to be good for the schools. We need the money. We don't have any choice.'" This was a "phony" choice, according to Conni, who in her previous fight against school budget cuts had learned that school funding was a question of social priorities as much as total tax revenue.

"So okay, I mean I'm calling people," Conni recalled. "Fifteen, twenty, thirty people now are aware of what's going on." By luck, "a girlfriend [Mil Kinsella], who lives way up the island," happened to stop by Town Hall on March 19 and noticed the posting of a meeting of Portsmouth's Design Review Board, scheduled for the next evening, to talk about Target's proposal. Conni, with her salesman's brio, called John Borden, chairman of the design board, to get acquainted. "He said, 'Oh, gee, you'll really be impacted.' But he just said [the proposal] goes to Design Review, then they come up with a nice design, like [Custom House Coffee], and then after that it will go to Planning and then to Zoning." Custom House Coffee's architecture was relatively traditional, with a peaked and gabled roof, but comparing a coffeehouse and a flat-roofed big-box Target was like comparing a tennis court and a football stadium. Conni gamely showed up the meeting with six allies, including Mil, Rich, and Christine, and they met the seven members of the Design Review Board as well as Target's local lawyer, Robert Silva of Middletown. To Conni's dismay, one member of the board was Allen Shers, who she knew owned a great deal of commercial property in town and would likely be friendly to Target.

As for Silva's presentation, "I felt like it was a joke," Conni told me. "They were looking at a three-and-a-half-acre building, and they're going to put 'character' on it. And they were talking about landscaping, and one guy said, 'Sir, I just have to be perfectly clear, I'm so against this . . .' Shers's face was red at one point or another. I don't think he was too happy." The date for Target's formal presentation was set two weeks hence, April 4. Outside, after the meeting, Conni spoke with Silva, who she says brazenly declared, "You know, this is going to happen."

Referred by Ted Clement, Conni contacted a Vermont foundation called the New England Grassroots Environment Fund, which encouraged her to create a formal, not-for-profit organization and apply for a grant. An activist resident of Middletown, Gail Greenman, offered tactical help in dealing with Silva—she'd fought him on other projects including the Barnes & Noble. But then Conni got a big break: a local weekly newspaper, the *Sakonnet Times*, showing considerable initiative, revealed that Target wasn't going to be the hoped-for cash cow for Portsmouth. Reporter Jill Rodrigues quoted Town Administrator Robert Driscoll as saying that the Target building, assuming an assessed value of $10 million, would contribute a paltry $100,000 a year in property taxes. The big gainer would be the state, which would get something like $1.4 million in sales tax revenue if Target generated $40 million in annual sales. "The state," Driscoll said dryly, "will get significant revenues in sales tax, while the town will get the droppings." With the town providing extra services—sewage, water, and more police to watch the influx of thousands of customers and their cars—Target was beginning to look less like manna from heaven and more like a pain in the neck from Minnesota, where the company is headquartered.

"So now we felt like, okay, now we have a fight. Now we have to educate the community," Conni said. Publicly, she kept insisting that "we don't mind smart growth . . . you know, nice little retail establishments with offices on top." Meanwhile, she got busy organizing. "We knew Target was coming back April 4, so I started calling people on April 1" to organize a meeting. Overnight, Conni had become a community organizer with a political base. "How do you motivate a volunteer army?" she wondered. "It was tough for me to say, 'You've got to be at this meeting, this meeting, and this meeting.' " In the end, 30 people crowded into her living room at 884 Union Street to found a new group, dubbed on the spot Preserve Portsmouth. "It just felt like the battle's on. It was wonderful."

For Conni, the most important thing was "just to have bodies" at the next Design Review Board meeting. With Christine functioning as database manager, they began to gather an email and phone list. On the evening of the meeting, 90 aroused citizens showed up at Town Hall, forcing the board members to convene in the Town Council chambers instead of in "the tiny little room the Design Review Board met in." When Bob Silva walked into the room with several representatives of Target, they were, to say the least, "taken aback."

"People were outraged," Conni recounted. "[The Target representatives] got up to show the preliminary design with the asphalt and just the big, huge signage. The Design Review Board was laughing at them: 'Have you read anything? Have you done your homework?' . . . I don't think they were used to it." It seemed unlikely that the board would approve a project so out of line with Portsmouth's general ambience.

And neither, most likely, were the Portsmouth business and political establishments. When I met with Council President Dennis Canario at the café in Clements', he didn't seem the type to court controversy or arguments, especially dressed, as he was that day, in black shorts, a sleeveless gray-and-black T-shirt, and white tennis shoes. A retired police detective who grew up in the quietest part of Portsmouth, Prudence Island, Canario was determined to show me he had not taken sides in the Target fight. A Democrat, Canario, 46, said he got into politics because "I deeply loved the town of Portsmouth." But he clammed up when I asked him which politicians he admired, although he did say he was inspired by his father, who volunteered to become the Portsmouth town game warden after he retired from his civilian Navy job. A Portsmouth councilman receives only $100 a month for serving, so Canario just might have been telling me the truth about why he ran for office.

Recently elevated, in December 2006, to council president, Canario said he had gotten word from the lawyer, Silva, that Target was interested in building on the Egan lot, and that he wanted to know "what we thought of it." Canario said he explained that Portsmouth's "Design Review Board is unique" because it required a "special use permit" for a building over a certain square footage, "and they look at the plans and they'll say either this building fits our community or it doesn't and you need to redesign it. Now if you look at where we are right now, Clements' Marketplace has that country-style look to it . . . [This is a] rural, country, bedroom community, versus city, heavy retail-type look."

Looking back, Canario insisted that "it wasn't a hostile type thing between Preserve Portsmouth and Target" and that Mr. Silva "indicated that Target was a community friendly business and that if there was going to be that much resistance then they weren't going to pursue it."

But pursue it they did, as community opposition mounted. On

May 23, the biggest paper on Aquidneck Island, the *Newport Daily News*, published an editorial criticizing the Target plan:

> While we're sure many shoppers would like to see a Target on the island, there are stores about a half-hour away in Dartmouth and Seekonk, Massachusetts. (Of course, as with most national retailers, that is not enough. Apparently, they will not be satisfied until there is one in practically every community.)
>
> And while the developers may tout a boost to the tax base, that promise has fallen short in Middletown, where a plethora of development has not kept taxes from increasing every year. Yet, as we have seen in Middletown, one commercial development begets another, multiplying like the proverbial rabbits. Once a community says "yes" to that kind of development, it becomes a lot harder to say "no" to subsequent proposals.

Preserve Portsmouth, meanwhile, hired an off-island lawyer, Jamestown Councilman Mark Liberati, because most of the competent local lawyers already represented developers and either couldn't or wouldn't have accepted an anti-development group as a client. All over town, Conni Harding's allies began planting lawn signs, 250 in all, with a diagonal line—the international safety symbol—drawn through the Target bull's-eye logo and a prominent "No" printed above. Some of the signs mysteriously disappeared after they were planted, and Conni suspected foul play by her opponents. With pressure building, Town Councilman Leonard Katzman—a lawyer, but not a developer—proposed an emergency, eight-week moratorium on retail developments over 55,000 square feet, a compromise to buy time. Apparently taken by surprise, Silva arranged a public meeting a few days later between Target, two council members,

Town Administrator Driscoll, and the town solicitor. Of the two council members present, Conni could count on the support of the Republican, Hubert "Huck" Little, a retired restaurant owner and substantial landowner on a still rural section of Union Street, but not William West, an African-American Democrat and retired trade union official, whom she counted as a probable foe.[3] Target told Little and West that the company would withdraw their plan if the Town Council didn't want them. "So we were excited for a day or two," Conni said.

But Silva was evidently buying time for his next move: just hours before the Town Council met on June 11 to consider the moratorium, Target rushed to file an application for a special-use permit from the Zoning Board of Review, obviously trying to circumvent the council if it passed the moratorium.

"They snuck in the special-use permit," Conni recalled with annoyance. "So I said, well, that was a bunch of hogwash. I mean, what were they trying to do? Hoping that the moratorium wouldn't go forward?" A call to the Department of Environmental Management convinced Conni and Mark Liberati that Target's application was incomplete and wouldn't win the board's approval.

The momentum seemed to have shifted to Preserve Portsmouth, and Conni was changing as well. Aware of the popular anger she had ignited, her first instinct had been to be polite to the local power structure. Ten days before the meeting, she had warned Town Administrator Driscoll that the council chambers weren't big enough to hold the expected crowd. Driscoll demurred, and then Conni's newfound political sense took over. Thinking a bit like the legendary radical organizer Saul Alinsky, she had a revelation: "I'm like, Hey, you know what? To me it sounds better to be bursting out of the seams; it's better for the effect." Sure enough, when the

---

3 West's race is notable because Portsmouth's population is overwhelmingly white (96 percent); barely more than 1 percent is African American.

council convened on June 11 at Town Hall, the room was packed to overflowing, with more than 140 people present inside and at least 50 more craning their heads through the windows from outside the building. By the time Conni took the microphone to testify in favor of the moratorium, she had emerged as a leading citizen—a veritable tribune—and she tried to muster the rhetoric to match her new role:

> We have a town that's still worth fighting for. There are towns all over this country that aren't worth fighting for anymore. There's sprawl, there's asphalt, there's big-box stores. I happened to live in the Bible Belt of big-box stores and worked in Rogers, Arkansas, where the first Wal-Mart went in. Those people wouldn't show up with 300 people at a meeting because the towns were not worth fighting for. We have a lot of issues in this town going on, but we're just pleading with you to give us an emergency moratorium so you can look at the bigger issues. We've got school safety, traffic, water quality, lots to look at. The emergency moratorium is in your control tonight to give to us. The other issues will be dealt with, if there were other things applied for. . . . But tonight you can do that for the people who elected you. God only knows what can happen. We don't want you to be the Town Council that let something like this in.

With Target very much on the defensive, Silva had evidently chosen tactical discretion over confrontation and did not attend the meeting. Thus, it was left initially to Director of Business Development Bill Clark to question the restriction of development rights on behalf of Jack Egan and Target. Clark himself remained cautious: "It's not my intention to become the most unpopular person in town," he said, but he wanted to remind people that other local owners had "been paying taxes on [their] property based on the idea that maybe they could develop about 25 percent of it" and that now "you're telling the person that now suddenly you can do about 9 percent or 10 percent."

Throughout the hour-and-a-half meeting, the citizens and elected officials of Portsmouth had maintained a worthy decorum. But finally, when council member William West boldly spoke up for commercial property owners, emotions spilled over. "I don't know what effect the moratorium will have on anyone planning on bringing their business. . . . We're trying to balance out the tax rate. Part of that helps having commercial business in town. If you're against the big box, go down the street to Raytheon; there's a bunch of big boxes on Raytheon; go to Hodge's Badges [a badge and award-ribbon manufacturer]. . . ." The crowd erupted angrily and West turned testy: "Quiet please, if you don't mind! I have the floor! We have a big box at Hodge's Badges. . . . If you're only upset or concerned about not having commercial, then that's a different animal. . . . You also have the owner of the property. . . . He has a right to develop the property. There are other people here who are real estate agents, and that's what their jobs are supposed to be. That person has . . . paid taxes on it and has a right to develop it."

Then, West challenged the audience, asking if Preserve Portsmouth had "decided on purchasing the property and donating the development rights" to the Aquidneck Land Trust. "You know, that's something you could do." West's impromptu suggestion that a grassroots organization of middle-class homeowners purchase a 16-acre parcel of prime commercial real estate was as preposterous as his comparison of high-tech, high-paying Raytheon to low-tech, low-paying Target. The crowd again turned audibly restless, to the point where Canario had to twice pound his gavel to restore order. West refused to show his hand: "This is going to be a difficult decision for us to make on this moratorium. I mean, there are a lot of implications."

There it was, the line drawn between the interests of the many and the interests of the few, between popular sovereignty and the power of money and property. Middletown couldn't beat the big money, and neither even could Newport, symbol of the old big money. In the end, though, the council couldn't ignore the people. When Canario called for a vote, the moratorium passed unanimously, though Conni said she detected some ambivalence. "I knew we had four votes," she recalled. "But some of the hands went up when they looked around and saw everyone else's." Ironically, only Karen Gleason, the council's lone radical, initially dissented—she had wanted a more stringent moratorium and contradicted Conni's plea that development opponents needed first to "take baby steps." When the measure passed, a full-throated cheer burst forth from the crowd.

Target must have been rattled, for in the aftermath of the vote, Silva lost his composure and committed a grave tactical error. Two days later, he was quoted in the *Providence Journal* claiming that the moratorium would never hold up in court if it were challenged because the Town Charter didn't specify "a clear process for a moratorium"—a fair, if somewhat belligerent legal point. But then he took another, perhaps fatal, step: "I don't fault the council for what they did," he said. "It was mob rule last night." In two sentences, Silva had summed up the profound dilemma, and the contradictions, of American democracy. Clearly used to getting his way with politicians, Silva bore no ill will toward the elected officials of Portsmouth, whom he regarded essentially as allies of his client. The council, he implied, would have acted more responsibly were if not for the intimidation of the "mob"—that is, Conni Harding and the partisans of Preserve Portsmouth. For Silva, it was the people, not their elected representatives, who were the enemy.

This was too much, even for some of the more development-friendly council members. Council Vice President James Seveney, a Portsmouth native who works at Raytheon, struck back, calling Silva's description of the meeting "wrong."

"It was not a mob scene," he told Gina Macris of the *Providence Journal*. "It was not anything close to that. It was an orderly meeting with a lot of people. Everyone behaved very well." Furthermore, "everyone has a right to meet with the Town Council and speak their piece . . . They can meet any time they want, and in as large a group as they want."

Under the headline "Republic of Portsmouth," the *Providence Journal* had felt compelled to editorialize in defense of self-government:

> Citizens gather at their places of public assembly and try to persuade their elected officials to do what citizens want. Sometimes they are noisy, even angry. That's okay, as long as they obey the rules. . . . Portsmouth's comprehensive plan describes its character as "semi-rural," and by law the Town Council must protect that character. But citizens who think that Portsmouth needs more jobs and tax revenue have a right to push the council to water down its protection of that character, and maybe change it someday. And if it does, citizens who like peace and quiet more than jobs and tax revenue have a right to boot the incumbents out of office. (We'd be sympathetic if Portsmouth decided to keep out more ugly big-box stores, with their wind-swept parking lots).

When I asked Dennis Canario whether he thought mob rule had swung the vote, the excruciatingly cautious council president hemmed and hawed before finally responding, "No, I think it was democracy."

But the fight wasn't over. Silva's comment had further galvanized the opposition. "I loved it," Conni recalled, since Silva had succeeded only in flushing out more opponents to Target. Up to that point, "I didn't know where certain people stand, and then they were getting agitated by this attorney. I was like, yeah, this is gravy."

On July 16, Town Building Inspector George Medeiros concluded that Target's last-minute special-use application was not "substantially complete" because it failed to include drainage plans and a study of how the influx of customers and cars would affect the already heavy traffic on West Main Street. The following Saturday, Conni organized a Preserve Portsmouth picnic at Glen Park that raised $6,000. For good measure, she wrote a letter to the chief executive officer of Target and his board of directors in Minneapolis "informing them that we don't want them here." The next big hurdle was to be on August 1, when the moratorium was set to expire. The only issue on the council docket would be a motion to extend the moratorium, and Conni busied herself readying the troops. This time the meeting would be held in the much larger Portsmouth Middle School auditorium.

Then, on July 25, Target announced that it was giving up. Trent Luger, the company's real estate development manager, presented the news directly to Robert Driscoll. In a press release the company stated: "Target is committed to serving the people of Aquidneck Island. We have decided to rescind our application in the town of Portsmouth due to project costs. We will continue to serve our guests in the community at our existing stores."[4] Conni celebrated, but not for long. Now she had to fear complacency, lest Egan line

---

4 Actually, the type of "guests" Target would have attracted to Portsmouth were one of the main reasons locals opposed the store. As Conni put it, "I'm sorry, but if an extra 100,000 people are coming to this thing, you're going to get a creepy element coming in . . . right next to our middle school. Why do you think Target has the most unbelievable forensics unit? The government taps into their forensics department; how did they find the killer of that Overland Park, Kansas, girl who was abducted? Target has fabulous cameras and everything for a reason. Creepy people go there."

up another big-box tenant. Indeed, by the time I got to town on the afternoon of August 1, the anti-Target signs were already disappearing, and Conni had to drive me a good distance in her big SUV, a Chevy Suburban, before we found one. All things considered, though, she had kept her group disciplined and together for the meeting that night.

When I entered the auditorium, the first thing I noticed was a reproduction of Henri Rousseau's famous painting *The Sleeping Gypsy* overlooking the 85 or so people seated in the hall. A pretty good political metaphor, I thought, since the vigilant members of Preserve Portsmouth could not afford to rest with the lions of real estate and their lawyers prowling about. Indeed, the Target controversy had roused the biggest lion in the Aquidneck pride, Jack Egan, who sat attentively with his lawyer, Charles Allott, and with Robert Silva's law partner, David Martland, throughout the proceedings. Egan was an alert, fit, and handsome man of 75, with a trim white mustache and quick eyes that seemed to take in everything. As one speaker after another pronounced him or herself in favor of property rights, I began to sense that a counterattack might be in play.

To be sure, Preserve Portsmouth stalwarts like Werner Loell, a German immigrant, returned to the microphone to support a proposed six-month moratorium—"we don't want to look like Middletown do we? . . . Do we?"—but the defeated forces of the real estate lobby now were insistently raising their voices. What's more, one of Conni's allies on the council, Huck Little, was absent. Without Little, Allen Shers, the landowner whose commercial property on West Main would be restricted under the moratorium, could declare with greater impunity: "Please note: we are not a rural community, we are a suburban community. . . . Property owners have rights too."

Other commercial-property advocates repeated the mantra "Development Is Inevitable," and Bill Clark reiterated William West's specious equivalency between Raytheon's "big boxes" and retail "big boxes." I began to wonder whether Preserve Portsmouth's power had peaked. Clark even mocked the anti-development forces: "We're seeing what we call the BANANA—Build Absolutely Nothing Anywhere Near Anything." Allott, Egan's lawyer, also spoke, asserting his clients' "rights." Finally Conni, who had not planned to testify, was compelled to rise, if for no other reason than to remind the council that Preserve Portsmouth wasn't going away. She announced that the group would host a speaker on "smart growth" at a local country club the next month. Meanwhile, the radical Karen Gleason wanted to know why Assistant Town Planner Gary Crosby had recommended a 55,000-square-foot minimum size for the moratorium since in theory "with no limit on the number of structures, we could have 200 55,000-foot buildings under the plan." This doomsday scenario, while exaggerated, served to shift momentum back to the fear of big boxes rather than the fear of offending developers. "I don't want to wake up and find we're in Dartmouth or Middletown," she said. "We have to be careful not to make exceptions for certain special interest groups, for developers." She was seconded by Preserve Portsmouth's lawyer, Mark Liberati, who warned about the "vested rights of developers" if no moratorium were passed.

In the end, Crosby's bland proposal for a "planning charrette"—a sort of community workshop in land use and zoning—seemed to steady everyone's nerves. On August 23, all of Portsmouth would be invited to attend the meeting, at which groups of 10 or so people would sit around tables for intensive planning discussions. Somehow, it was hoped, talking it out in small groups would allow the public, the developers, and the town planners to agree on how Portsmouth should look in 20 years.

Meanwhile, Council President Dennis Canario, dressed for the meeting in an impeccable, buttoned-up dark suit, demonstrated real talent for reducing political tension. Earlier, Canario had told me that nearly everyone on Aquidneck Island was up in arms about plans to ship liquefied natural gas up Narragansett Bay to Providence and Fall River. Residents fear terrorist sabotage, since, as Canario himself had warned, one ship explosion could have a devastating impact on the island. So with a politician's instinct, he turned his constituents' fears to his advantage. When someone mentioned the gas plan in passing, Canario deftly replied, "My extensive experience in law enforcement tells me that terrorists don't follow Target." The auditorium erupted in the laughter of relief.

There was no doubt now that a six-month moratorium extension would pass. But all the talk of property rights had taken its toll on the council. West, Seveney, and Peter McIntyre, a Republican council member, wanted it known that they too respected developers' privileges, and West was visibly unhappy with any moratorium at all. As the council's discussion wound down, Councilman Len Katzman offered an amendment to Section 2 of the ordinance, the "Duration" clause. In its original wording, the clause ended with the sentence, "The council reserves the right to extend the moratorium for one (1) five-month period." Katzman proposed that it be stricken, and the council agreed. In this form, the measure passed unanimously.

Katzman, I suspected, was making a conciliatory gesture to the commercial real estate men in the room. He surely knew that the council could declare a new moratorium on January 31, 2008. For the time being, the "system" had worked. A compromise forged from democratic debate had prevented the immediate ruination of the corner of West Main and Union and its residential surroundings.

When the meeting adjourned I rushed up to Jack Egan to get some comment. He didn't want to talk, gesturing me toward his lawyer. I prefer interviewing principals, so I waited 15 minutes and approached Egan again as the crowd thinned. When he looked at the name on my business card, a light of recognition appeared in his eyes. Egan was old enough, and evidently rich enough, to have known my real estate developer and insurance magnate grandfather, who had built his share of undistinguished housing and commercial buildings on the east coast of Florida, including Palm Beach Gardens, where I lived for two years as child. We gossiped about this coincidence until Conni and Luke walked by on their way out of the building. On impulse, I introduced Egan to his principal antagonist, the woman who almost single-handedly had cost him the Target deal and presumably a lot of money.

Ever the promoter, Egan was all smiles when he greeted Conni and Luke, I assumed for the first time. But it turned out that Egan had met Luke before, in a construction context.

"Yeah," Egan offered with forced cheerfulness. "I used to use this guy on a lot of jobs, until he screwed one up and I fired him." Whether this was a calculated warning shot aimed at Conni or just a nasty outburst born of pent-up anger, Egan's remark abruptly ended the conversation. Obviously, Luke's heating and air-conditioning business depended very much on developers like Egan, and the Hardings needed income to pay the tuitions and expenses of their combined family of eight. It occurred to me that Egan might have been making a preemptive threat in anticipation of objections to his next potential big-box tenant.

Earlier that day, Dennis Canario had tried to persuade me, with contradictory reasoning, that the Target fight had left no ill will in town: "I don't think that Target backed down under pressure. . . . They didn't want to be where people didn't want them. . . . I think the end result is that everyone's a winner here."

But everyone wasn't a winner in Portsmouth, any more than everyone is a winner in American democracy. Effective democracy requires the acceptance of defeat, and it wasn't yet clear whether Jack Egan was the loser or Conni Harding the victor.

P

ortsmouth, Rhode Island, may be a model of fair and functioning local democracy; Chicago may be its polar opposite. I pretend to no objectivity about the politics of my home county and state. Having grown up in a suburb outside Chicago, in Cook County, Illinois, I had had most of my illusions about representative democracy shattered in August 1968, when Mayor Richard J. Daley's police force violently suppressed antiwar demonstrators, many of them supporters of Eugene McCarthy, in Grant Park during the Democratic National Convention.[1] Since 1931, the city and the county it dominates have been—with only brief respites—the fief

---

1 A federal-government-appointed investigation of the convention violence, known as the Walker Report, dubbed the actions of Chicago's forces of law and order "a police riot." The behavior of Daley's officers led Senator Abraham Ribicoff to denounce their "Gestapo tactics" during his nomination speech for George McGovern. The cameras then focused on the furiously animated mayor on the convention floor, shouting what some lipreaders interpreted as "Fuck you, you Jew son of a bitch! You lousy mother-fucker! Go home!" Daley's spokesman, however, said he had merely called Ribicoff a "faker."

of a Democratic Party machine that tolerates very little opposition from the Conni Hardings of the world.[2] Today, at the head of that machine stands Richard M. Daley, the six-term mayor of Chicago and the son of Richard J., the founder of the current machine and himself a six-term mayor. When Richard J. died in 1976, there was hope for a time that Chicago was ready for real democracy, but the son fought his way back into power, and his autocratic grip on the city, the county, and to some extent the state of Illinois makes him the most powerful local political boss in all of America. Chicago endures as the epitome of the one-party town; 49 of 50 seats on the city council, all citywide offices of any importance, and most elected county posts and judgeships are held by Democrats.

Moreover, Daley's influence in the national Democratic Party is proportionally immense. In 1993, when President Bill Clinton needed extra help to push NAFTA through a Democrat-controlled Congress, he turned to Daley and Daley's younger brother, William, an ambitious lawyer, for help. William Daley essentially became Clinton's NAFTA "campaign manager," charged with coordinating lobbying between corporate America (represented by the Business Roundtable), Republican House Minority Leader Newt Gingrich (who strongly supported NAFTA), and the New Democrats (pro-business Democrats) led by Clinton and his colleagues on the Democratic Leadership Council. For his stellar work in defeating organized labor and the followers of Ross Perot, the younger Daley was, fittingly, appointed to the cabinet position of Secretary of Commerce in 1997. In 2000, Clinton once again called on the Daleys to help ram through Permanent Normal Trade Relations (PNTR) with China, another trade-lib-

2   The most noteworthy interruption of the machine's control of City Hall was the brief (1983-1987) tenure of Mayor Harold Washington, an African-American Democrat and former U.S. representative turned reformer, who profited from a split among white candidates seeking to assume the mantle of Richard J. Daley.

eralization measure that was bitterly opposed by labor unions and a majority of Democratic House members.

The Daley/Clinton alliance in the 1990s is crucial to understanding the power structure of today's Democratic Party.[3] Franklin D. Roosevelt was the first national Democratic "boss" to martial systematically the nearly universal support of American trade unions, and since 1932, organized labor has functioned more or less as a subsidiary of the Democratic Party. In exchange for their political support, labor leaders were rewarded by Democratic administrations (and in periods of Republican presidencies by the usually Democrat-controlled Congress) with laws that facilitated union organizing, patronage appointments for union officials, and straight-out grants of public money to labor's various education and political-action arms. Thus, the AFL-CIO leadership in the 1950s and '60s barely objected to either America's anti-Communist Cold War agenda or the Vietnam War, policies that in a European country would likely have brought union militants into the streets. In their heyday, in 1953, when 27 percent of workers belonged to one, American labor unions were famously conservative because they were so rich—in part thanks to the patronage of the Democrats.

Meanwhile, a free-trade consensus had taken hold of the country's leaders as part of their overall Cold War strategy to check the Soviet Union. Lowering import tariffs to encourage nations like Japan and Italy to manufacture electronics, cars, shoes, and textiles for export—in order to blunt Communist influence on those countries' labor unions and to isolate the Russians economically—directly reduced the power of American unions and gradually

---

3 By 2007, the power relationship had changed within the party. Barack Obama had become the favored presidential candidate of the Daley family, to the great chagrin of the Clintons. With Mayor Daley's sponsorship, Obama enjoyed access not only to wealthy Illinois contributors but also to the sage counsel of Daley's political adviser and former City Hall bureau chief of the *Chicago Tribune*, David Axelrod, and Daley's former chief of staff, John Schmidt.

eliminated millions of unionized manufacturing jobs. Paradoxically, and self-destructively, the unions tolerated "free trade" in the name of fighting Communism. But in truth they were demonstrating fealty to the leadership of the Democratic Party.

Not since before Roosevelt, however, had a Democratic administration proposed anything so brazenly anti-union as NAFTA and PNTR, and the Daleys' abandonment of their traditional support for organized labor shocked many Democrats who truly believed that theirs was the party of the working class. Unlike Cold War tariff reductions to strengthen the anti-Communist cause in Europe and Asia, NAFTA and PNTR were solely intended to protect American investments in Mexico and China, and to efficiently exploit cheap labor in those countries. These "free trade" measures were guaranteed to wipe out large numbers of American factory jobs, yet the Democratic leadership—now ambitious to raise campaign money from corporate political action committees—shamelessly promoted them as beneficial to unions and the lower middle class.

By 2004, Chicago faced an employment and wage crisis not so different from that of the much smaller Utica. The manufacture of steel, electronics, televisions, and cars had virtually disappeared, along with the slaughterhouses and meatpacking industry that once defined the city. The "city of broad shoulders" now in fact had very little good-paying work left for its large population of broad-shouldered workers. For many members of the former industrial working class, the only available employment was low-wage jobs in non-union, big-box retail stores like Wal-Mart or Target—the very companies that lobbied so hard for NAFTA and PNTR so they could buy their goods cheaper abroad than in the United States. But whereas an old-style factory job with health and pension benefits paid $10 to $20 an hour, the big-box stores and fast-food franchises paid as little as minimum wage ($5.15 nationwide at the time, but $6.50 in Illinois) to around $10 an hour, with minimal benefits.

Unions had taken note of America's industrial decline and Wal-Mart's commensurate rise but done little to confront the Democratic Party leadership about its new anti-union policies.[4] With each factory shutdown, poor Chicago neighborhoods, particularly black and Latino ones, simply got poorer. And fiercely anti-union Wal-Mart seemed utterly impervious to labor-organizing attempts; today, not a single Wal-Mart in North America is unionized. In April 2005, in Jonquière, Quebec, when a union successfully organized the local Wal-Mart, Wal-Mart simply closed the store.

When in 2004 Wal-Mart sought permission from the Chicago City Council to build its first stores in the city, there was predictable and angry opposition. But no Conni Harding emerged to lead the fight, perhaps because in boss-ruled Chicago, the Democratic Party machine tends to overwhelm all opposition. Which is not to say that such women have never tried to fight Chicago City Hall over the years. In 1961, a local woman named Florence Scala led the fight against the Daley machine's plan to build a huge new branch of the University of Illinois in the middle of her old Italian neighborhood on the city's near West Side. Scala knew that the campus would dismember and effectively destroy the area she called home; her group, the Harrison-Halsted Community Group, argued correctly that the university branch could be built elsewhere on vacant or decrepit industrial land. They took their fight all the way to the U.S. Supreme Court, where they lost. The patriarch Daley would not be moved—he wanted the campus near the downtown section known as the "Loop," so he built it using the city's power of eminent domain. Today, very little of this once thriving neighbor-

---

4 During the administrations of Ronald Reagan and the first George Bush, Chicago's most powerful congressman, Democrat Daniel Rostenkowski, helped ease the passage of White House-initiated free-trade policies and lowered tariffs that contributed to killing off the substantial television-making industry in his own Northwest Side district.

hood remains, except for a small and largely nostalgic smattering of restaurants along Taylor Street. And, perhaps more important, the courageous and talented Florence Scala faded from public life; like Cindy Sheehan, she was exhausted and beaten by political party power, in this case the Daley machine.

Still, there were objections to the Wal-Mart proposal. In 2001 Wal-Mart surpassed General Motors as the nation's second largest corporation in revenue (in 2002, it passed ExxonMobil as the country's largest, where it remains today), and its arrogance is legendary. Used to placing its stores in depressed areas desperate for any employment, the Arkansas-based company (which once boasted Hillary Clinton, then-Governor Clinton's wife, as a board member) had learned to be tough in situations where it was received with less than open arms. In Chicago's poorest black neighborhoods, located on the city's South and West sides, residents needed the work Wal-Mart would bring, but some local leaders understood the accompanying costs. No small merchant could compete with Wal-Mart's discounts, so neighborhood retailers would inevitably be driven out of business. At the same time, Wal-Mart's reputation for low wages, minimal benefits, and ferocious anti-unionism preceded it everywhere it sought to build.

So while Alderman Howard Brookins Jr. welcomed Wal-Mart's proposal to build a store—and the 330 jobs it would bring—on the site of a former steel plant in his South Side 21st Ward, Alderman William Banks, the chairman of the City Council Zoning Committee, balked. "We have serious questions about the labor practices of Wal-Mart and [company] practices in general," Banks declared. Banks was seconded by Dennis Gannon, president of the Chicago Federation of Labor, who noted that the company was the largest in America, "yet they can't give a worker dignity and justice in the workplace." Brookins objected to what he and 41st Ward Alderman Brian Doherty viewed as interference with the tradition of aldermen controlling development and zoning within their wards. So did Alderman Emma Mitts of the West Side 37th Ward, where Wal-Mart proposed to build a second store, on the site of an old shampoo factory. Brookins and Mitts threatened political retaliation, and Dwight Gunn of the 37th Ward Pastors Alliance added that "we believe it is our duty to fight for the economic development of our community."

As the controversy boiled, Mayor Daley declared his support for Wal-Mart. Like his father, Richard M. is famous for his convoluted language, and he has always had difficulty articulating a clear point of view. When in an interview with the *Chicago Tribune* he posed the seemingly rhetorical question—"Who decides you are a good corporate citizen? How much money you give to politicians? How much money you give to charities?"—he unwittingly raised the issue of Wal-Mart's political donations to the two major parties. At the same time, he astutely dodged the central question of megarich Wal-Mart's miserly pay scale.

The local Democratic Party was now split as it had never been before during the tenure of either Mayor Daley. On April 19, Rev. Jesse Jackson, still a potent local and national political figure (whose son Jesse Jr. represents Illinois's Second Congressional District, including a large piece of the city's South Side), stepped into the fray. In reference to the mass cult suicide of Rev. Jim Jones and his followers, he called Wal-Mart the purveyors of "Kool-Aid and cyanide. The Kool-Aid is the cheap prices. The cyanide is the cheap wages. The cyanide is the cheap health benefits." Jackson had been emboldened by his involvement in a successful campaign to reject a proposed Wal-Mart in mostly black Inglewood, California, and he attempted a repeat performance in his adopted hometown. Jackson said that Wal-Mart and the other big-box chains provided cheap prices, but that their long-term impact was depressing wages and destroying small businesses. "The Wal-Martization of the country is like a Trojan horse," he declared. "It's exciting on the outside, but on the inside is a machinery that destroys competition."

Meanwhile, Daley posed another public question, though not necessarily a coherent one. "We have Wal-Marts all over the suburban area," he said. "That's something I can't understand. If they are all over the suburban area, why is someone objecting when they build one in the city?" Daley's position was in direct contradiction to his family's ferocious chauvinism about their native city, which they have always run as though no other governments existed. Hardly anybody, other than a federal judge, ever dares to tell the Daleys what to do in their fiefdom. If the Daley machine has an ideology, it is the paramount importance of local control. But, as we shall see, Daley's logic is the logic of party loyalty, above and beyond any other system of thought.

The battle lines had been drawn, but this was Chicago, not Portsmouth, or Inglewood, and the mayor would have his way. Wal-Mart pitched in with push polling and a heavy-handed telephone lobbying campaign that offended even its supporters on the City Council, but nothing could stop the company's incursion into Daley's Chicago except Daley himself.[5] On May 26, the City Council approved by 32 to 15 the smaller, 150,000-square-foot Wal-Mart in the poorer of the two proposed locales, the city's Austin neighborhood, on the far West Side. On the proposal to build in the more "racially diverse" neighborhood of Chatham on the far South Side—an area with more whites than Austin—the council voted 25 to 21 in favor, one vote short of the required 26 majority. Thus was the desperation of poor black Chicagoans exploited and the political interests of Mayor Daley served.

But the friends of labor weren't quite finished. Two months after

---

5 The public-relations firm Wal-Mart hired used a phone bank to call Chicago residents and ask them whether they wanted new jobs to come to their community. Those who answered yes were then transferred to the offices of City Council members.

the council vote, as if to compensate for giving in to Wal-Mart, two groups of aldermen proposed a minimum-wage and baseline-benefits ordinance worth about $13 an hour for employees of big-box stores. The sponsors of one ordinance included aldermen who had voted to let Wal-Mart build, so it seemed destined to pass. But to pass, a bill must first come to the floor of a legislative body, and there are many ways to delay or altogether prevent inconvenient laws from ever coming to a vote. Despite the best efforts of Joe Moore, sponsor of the second big-box minimum-wage bill, Wal-Mart, Daley, and the retail-store lobby prevented the ordinance from coming to the floor of the council for two years. In the mean time, after its partial victory in the Chicago City Council, Wal-Mart, normally a faithful contributor to the Republican Party, discovered the advantages of backing local Democrats. Up to February 2004, Wal-Mart made 85 percent of its donations to federal candidates to Republicans.[6] But Wal-Mart was happy to contribute a check for $1,000 to Democratic Alderman Emma Mitts, Wal-Mart's fervent backer and host to the new Wal-Mart store at the corner of Grand and Kilpatrick Avenues. During the debate, Mitts had declared, "This a free country, and we look for low prices," so perhaps she had offered her services too cheaply. (Since their first contribution, Wal-Mart has given Mitts another $6,500.) When Wal-Mart broke ground on its first store, on the grounds of a vacant Unilever plant, in February 2005, the *Chicago Tribune* described the ceremony, with Alderman Mitts presiding, as something that resembled "a corporate pep rally."

But the minimum-wage initiative wouldn't die. On July 26, 2006, the Chicago City Council, in what seemed an open rebellion against the mayor's rule, voted overwhelmingly, 35 to 14, to require stores of at least 90,000 square feet to pay their employees

---

6 By January 2008, Wal-Mart had acknowledged the shift in control of Congress to the Democrats by increasing the Democratic share of its donations for federal candidates to 43 percent.

a minimum of $9.25 an hour plus $1.50 in fringe benefits, with an automatic raise to $10 and $3 respectively by 2010. Supporters of the ordinance cheered in the packed council gallery when the roll was called. "This is a great day for the working men and women of Chicago," Alderman Moore exulted.

Hardly radical or confiscatory, the big-box minimum wage was still too much for Wal-Mart and Daley. Because he is somewhat more polished than his frequently crude father, Richard M. Daley sometimes fools liberals into thinking he is a softer touch than his forebear. That he is conscious of his image manifests itself in appearances at fashionable events and fund-raisers, such as the Chicago premiere of the film *Ocean's Thirteen*, which benefited the International Rescue Committee. If you looked at the photograph of Daley, his wife, Eleanor, and Bruce Willis, published in the September 2007 issue of *Vanity Fair*, you might think the mayor was something of a sophisticated fashion plate, like the star of the movie, George Clooney.

The *Vanity Fair* photo-op, however, did not hint at Daley's autocratic side, which was perhaps best illustrated by the boss's surprise, dark-of-night shutdown of Meigs Field, a small, city-operated lakefront airport near downtown Chicago that Daley wanted replaced by a public park. Just before midnight on March 30, 2003, with no warning to the Federal Aviation Administration, Daley ordered bulldozers under police escort to rip into sections of the nearly 4,000-foot runway and thus render it unusable for takeoffs and landings. With the airport closed at 10 p.m., there was no one on hand to object to the destruction, but even if there had been, who could they have called, since the Chicago police were accomplices in the covert action?

Daley justified his sneak attack by claiming concern over possible airborne terrorist attacks on nearby downtown. But no one believed the threat of terrorism was anything other than a pretext.

"This is a pure and simple land grab," Steve Whitney, founder of the group Friends of Meigs Field, told the *Chicago Sun-Times*. "If it was fear of terrorists, he could have just told us," an air traffic controller told the newspaper. "By doing this it makes it too expensive for the state or federal government to say, 'We'll buy it from you.' This guarantees him his park." As *Sun-Times* columnist Mark Brown put it, Daley's fait accompli grew out of "the rule of clout" as opposed to the rule of law.

Daley, having recently been reelected with 80 percent of the vote, defended himself in his habitually rhetorical fashion: "Why did we act so quickly? Because the fear exists right now. To do this any other way would have been needlessly contentious and jeopardized public safety—and prolonged anxiety among Chicagoans—for months and maybe even years." But Secretary of Homeland Security Tom Ridge said his agency was never consulted about Meigs and potential terrorism and that he was "disappointed" by the closure.

So if the Meigs Field shutdown was, as the air traffic controllers union termed it, "the epitome of arrogance," then Daley's response to the passage of the big-box minimum-wage initiative was unsurprising. In September 2006, the "Supreme High Commander," as *Sun-Times* columnist Brown describes the mayor, vetoed the ordinance—Daley's first veto after 17 years in office. "I understand and share a desire to ensure that everyone who works in the city of Chicago earns a decent wage," Daley wrote to the City Council, explaining his decision. "But I do not believe that this ordinance, well intentioned as it may be, would achieve that end. Rather, I believe it would drive jobs and business from our city, penalizing neighborhoods that need additional economic activity the most." Alderman Moore, a previously loyal Democrat, replied "I'm angry, but not surprised." As the pro-minimum-wage forces reorganized, it might have appeared that the 34 votes necessary to override the veto could be secured. But Daley had already converted enough aldermen to halt the rebellion. "I think just by virtue of the fact that the message was, 'this was important to the mayor,' [it] was enough to convince a couple of my colleagues to switch their votes," Moore said in an interview. "These are aldermen who have traditionally been almost 100 percent in lockstep with the mayor." In the end, Daley flipped three aldermen who had voted for the minimum wage, and on September 13 the override vote fell three votes short, 31 to 18, with one alderman absent.

Why did Aldermen Shirley Coleman, Danny Solis, and George Cardenas switch sides? Loyalty to the mayor and fear of his wrath counted heavily, to be sure. But there were other factors: namely, political survival and money. Bitterness over the treachery of the pro-Wal-Mart aldermen ran so high in the following election year that the three turncoats, and nine other incumbent aldermen who had opposed the big-box minimum-wage initiative, found themselves challenged by union-backed candidates in the February 2007 primary election. Organized labor poured $2.6 million into the campaign coffers of the 13 insurgents.

Mayor Daley, putative friend of the common man, still self-consciously residing in the working class South-Side neighborhood of Bridgeport where he grew up, countered by organizing the First C.D. Victory Political Action Committee to raise money for his council loyalists. First C.D. collected $662,450 for the first half of 2007, including $100,000 from Wal-Mart and $10,000 from the non-union Target Corporation, which already had nine stores in Chicago and typically pays its employees $7 to $10 an hour. The Daley/Wal-Mart PAC then contributed $217,705 to alderman candidates. Coleman received $72,000 but still lost. Cardenas survived, along with Solis. Freedom-loving Emma Mitts won renomination, as did her pro-Wal-Mart colleague Brookins, who still hoped for a big shopping center in his ward—for Wal-Mart hadn't given up on placing a store on the South Side. In all, six labor-backed candidates

defeated Daley-backed incumbents, and one beat a Daley-support-
ed candidate for an open seat. In Chicago, as in many one-party
cities and states, nomination is tantamount to victory in the general
election.

Was this at long last the flowering of direct democracy in
Chicago? When the council failed to override Daley's veto of the
minimum-wage ordinance in September 2006, Moore had defiantly
declared: "We will be back. I can assure you this will not go away."
But it wasn't long before Moore felt the consequences of his ren-
egade campaign. In the ensuing primary, while labor ran its slate
against the pro-Wal-Mart aldermen, Moore himself was obliged to
fight off an unusual primary challenge from Don Gordon, a political
neophyte claiming to be "non-partisan." Despite a $200,000 contri-
bution from organized labor, Moore barely won a run-off against
Gordon, who opposed the big-box minimum-wage bill and received
$60,000 (about half of his total contribution) from David Herro of
Harris Associates, a Chicago firm with large investments in Wal-
Mart. Moore's margin of victory was only 247 votes. Perhaps it was
no coincidence that, as of this writing a year later, the big-box minimum-wage ordinance had still not been reintroduced in the City
Council. Despite the net gain of seven labor-backed seats—more
than enough to override a Daley veto, it would seem—Moore appeared to be hesitating, saying in August 2007 "Well, we are con-
sidering it."

Robert Penn Warren's classic political novel, *All the King's Men*,
chronicles the career of a reformer turned machine politician, Willie Stark, who is known simply as "The Boss." Warren describes
the brutality of boss rule. In one scene, when the state's auditor has
been caught stealing public money, the state legislature, hostile to
Stark, moves to impeach the auditor, principally to embarrass Stark.
Against apparent political logic, Stark uses his power to block the
impeachment from going forward. Stark's calculation concerns the

arithmetic of loyalty rather than the calculus of public perception and political honesty. Instead of giving in to his rivals and letting his puppet drown, he upbraids the auditor, Byram White, for his indiscretion and greed and then lectures him on duty:

> Now you know what you're supposed to do. You're
> supposed to stay pore and take orders. I don't care
> about your chastity, which from the looks of you you
> don't have any trouble keeping plenty of, but I mean
> it's poverty and obedience and don't you forget it.
> Especially the last. . . . There just aren't going to be any
> one-man bonanzas. You got that? . . .
> I'm going to stop this impeachment business for
> you. But don't go and get the notion it's because I love
> you. It's just because those fellows [in the legislature]
> can't get the idea they can just up and knock off
> somebody. Are my motives clear?

White meekly assents, then signs a letter of resignation that Stark can date whenever he pleases. It's not hard to imagine such a scene occurring in Chicago, in a meeting between Richard Daley and a recalcitrant alderman—say, Coleman, Cardenas, Solis, or, for that matter, Joe Moore—who needs a lesson on political loyalty and independence. In the language of boss rule, the alderman from the 49th Ward was getting a little too rich on union money and way too independent from his party's leader. Without suggesting any corruption on the part of Moore, I wonder how long it might be before such an encounter takes place between the boss of Chicago and the new hero of the Chicago working class. As Moore no doubt understands, boss logic has a political logic all its own.

One day in the spring of 1984, during the economic boom of the Reagan years, I visited Thornton Bradshaw, then chairman of RCA, high above Manhattan in his 53rd floor office at 30 Rockefeller Center. Bradshaw was by then a senior corporate statesman, the very model of a distinguished chief executive officer at a time when corporations, after almost a two-decade period of unpopularity, were back in fashion. Bradshaw was much sought-after in those days—indeed, he was on everybody's party and board of directors A-list—because, although he was a Republican, he maintained friendships with liberal Democrats as well as with rich, conservative businessmen. His association with the intellectual Aspen Institute, his three degrees from Harvard, and his bail-out and hands-off stewardship of the distressed, liberal (London) *Observer* when he was president of Atlantic Richfield, one of the seven large oil companies, had endeared him to the foundation establishment, which is how we met.

"Brad," as he was known, was going to take me to lunch at the Century club, itself a symbol of democratic, intellectual merit, since the Century has always prided itself on accepting members (in those days only men) for their accomplishments in the world of arts, letters, and science rather than because of their wealth. But instead of meeting me at the club on West 43rd Street, he asked me to "30 Rock," from which we would walk the seven or so blocks to the club.

When I was ushered into Brad's very large office, complete with fireplace, television, and paintings of old-fashioned sailing ships, I found him in the company of an Italian shoeshine man in his 80s named Joe, who was seated on a short stool behind the desk, busily snapping a cloth over the chairman's shoes. Bradshaw seemed a bit embarrassed to be seen in this posture, but the shine continued while we made small talk, and the tradesman finally was dismissed. A rather handsome man of medium stature with neatly combed gray hair, Bradshaw was an elegant dresser (he favored hand-made suits from Savile Row and shoes from John Lobb of London), and placing what I recall was a brown fedora on top of his head, we descended on an express elevator to the ground floor and walked out into a brilliantly sunny and crowded Manhattan lunch hour. But the mob of people on Fifth Avenue was difficult to navigate and as we bumped and maneuvered our way through the crush of shoppers, tourists, and businessmen, Bradshaw turned to me and commented, "It's a bit like walking through the kitchen on the way to the dining room."

I relate this anecdote because it contrasts so sharply with an assumption about democracy that is dearer to Americans than the right to vote—that we live in a classless society free of hereditary aristocracy. Along with this belief is the profound and related conviction than any poor person in America can become rich through hard work and education and intelligence. Imbedded in the popular imagination through pulp literature, such as the nineteenth-century series by Horatio Alger Jr., upward social and economic mobility is a central tenet of American life—a balm that excuses all other injustices and inequality. In a country that fears class conflict—and does its utmost to pretend there is no such thing—the ability to change classes for the better remains a powerful element underlying the American social contract. If Americans suddenly lost faith in their chances of significant financial advancement, it would likely cause greater social upheaval than any number of Vietnam wars or racial conflicts.

To fully subscribe to the American faith in upward mobility, one must believe that Thornton Bradshaw's shoeshine man could have become Thornton Bradshaw.[1] Indeed, in Alger's most famous novel, *Ragged Dick* (1868), the protagonist is an impoverished bootblack. Early in the story, when Dick buys breakfast for his friend Johnny, Alger, as narrator, takes the occasion to summarize his philosophy of self-improvement:

> Now, in the boot-blacking business, as well as in higher avocations, the same rule prevails, that energy and industry are rewarded and indolence suffers. Dick was energetic and on the alert for business, but Johnny the reverse. The consequence was that Dick earned probably three times as much as the other.

Later on, through pluck and trustworthiness, Dick attracts assorted mentors and benefactors, like Mr. Whitney, who emphasizes the benefits of hard study and hard labor. Himself a wealthy, self-made man, Whitney informs Dick that "all labor is respectable, my lad,

---

1 According to Thornton Bradshaw's daughter, Priscilla Page, he grew up in a "very poor, working-class family" in Bogota, New Jersey. However, he also had a rich uncle: Bradshaw's paternal aunt was married to William T. Grant, the retail-store magnate. Grant helped pay Bradshaw's way through Phillips Exeter Academy, an elite boarding school in New Hampshire.

and you have no cause to be ashamed of any honest business; yet when you can get something to do that promises better for your future prospects, I advise you to do so." Another benefactor, Mrs. Greyson, even insists to her young daughter that Dick is not really poor: "Dick cannot be called poor, my child, since he earns his living by his own exertions." As Alger optimistically puts it, "[Dick] knew that it would take him a long time to reach the goal which he had had set before him, and he had patience to keep on trying. He knew that he had only himself to depend upon, and he determined to make the most of himself—a resolution which is the secret of success in nine cases out of ten."

In fact, however, it is not Dick's persistence, determination, and "street education" that eventually make him a success. Self-reliance is a great virtue in Alger's world, but luck, not work, is the deciding factor in success. In the end, Dick gets ahead by saving the drowning son of a well-to-do businessman, who rewards the hero by giving him a job. Suddenly, he is "a young gentleman on the way to fame and fortune." Dick is not rewarded for any intrinsic value in his work but rather for the virtue of his character—for waiting patiently for his big chance and never complaining about being poor.

Even African Americans, the most victimized of any class except possibly Native Americans, have at times subscribed to the ethos and possibility of self-improvement, against every dismal reality of American social life. At the turn of the century, following the failure of Reconstruction to equalize the races, when segregation was institutionalized throughout the South and blacks were largely stricken of their right to vote, the most powerful and influential black leader in America was Booker T. Washington, who devoted his life to creating, as professor Louis Harlan wrote, "the Horatio Alger myth in black." In his largely ghostwritten (by Max Bennett Thrasher, a white man) autobiography, *Up From Slavery*, Washington preached the virtues of hard work and practical education (as opposed to "mere book education") and offered himself as the exemplar of the self-made black man. "From slavery," wrote Harlan, "the most degraded condition imaginable, there could be no other direction than up. And Washington described the hardships of his early life as a challenge to be up and doing, not as a deterrent." In Washington's recollection of the early days of the Tuskegee Normal and Industrial Institute, the all-black school he founded in 1881, adversity was the essential prerequisite to success.

> Gradually, by patience and hard work, we brought order out of chaos, just as will be true of any problem if we stick to it with patience and wisdom and earnest effort. As I look back now over that part of our struggle, I am glad that we had it. I am glad that we endured all those discomforts and inconveniences. I am glad that our students had to dig out the place for their kitchen and dining room. I am glad that our first boarding-place was in that dismal, ill-lighted, and damp basement. Had we started in a fine, attractive, convenient room, I fear we would have "lost out heads" and become "stuck up." It means a great deal, I think, to start off on a foundation which one has made for one's self.

Nowhere did Washington blame white people, or the American ruling class, or politicians for the low status of his racial brethren. Throughout his life, as Harlan wrote, "his manner toward powerful whites was deferential to a fault," while at the same time he "ruled over the black community with the iron hand of a machine boss."

The reality of the rags-to-riches narrative in post-Civil War America was, of course, quite different from that described by Alger and Washington. As the historian William Miller pointed out in a groundbreaking 1949 study of the backgrounds and status of 190 top businessmen in the late nineteenth and early twentieth centuries, "Poor immigrant boys and poor farm boys together actually make up no more than 3 per cent of the business leaders," and the lower-class boys "who become business leaders have always been more conspicuous in American history books than in American history." Two of Miller's collaborators, Frances W. Gregory and Irene D. Neu, followed up his work by examining the industrial elite of the earlier Gilded Age:

> Was the typical industrial leader of the 1870s . . .
> an escapee from the slums of Europe or from the
> paternal farm? Did he rise by his own efforts from a
> boyhood of poverty? Was he as innocent of education
> and of formal training as has often been alleged? He
> seems to have been none of these things. American by
> birth, of a New England father, English in national
> origin, Congregational, Presbyterian, or Episcopal in
> religion, urban in early environment, he was rather
> born and bred in an atmosphere in which business
> and a relatively high social standing were intimately
> associated with his family life.

For those who did arrive from "the slums of Europe" during the great wave of immigration from 1890 to 1921, it wasn't so easy to get ahead. Sentimental success stories about newly minted Americans have tended to obscure the facts of economic life for those new arrivals. The American historian John Bodnar wrote that "Occasional success existed for some but generally continual toil in the strata they entered upon arrival in industrial America was the fate of most newcomers if they remained. . . . While instances of immigrant children attaining occupational ranks above those held by their parents existed, however, progress was neither inevitable nor simply a function of time." Bodnar cites a study of Boston by Stephan Thernstrom, which found that 13 percent of immigrant workers born in the 1850s "were able to climb out of blue-collar positions in which they started." In 1900-1909, the study found that only 14 percent moved up the economic ladder. "From a sample of Italians, Romanians, and Slovaks in Cleveland who were born between 1870 and 1890 only 14 of every 100 starting their careers in blue-collar jobs were able to move to a higher standing during their careers," Thernstrom discovered. Meanwhile, in New York, "only 14 percent of unskilled Italians were able to enter white-collar positions and an additional 10 percent acquired the designation skilled worker." As Bodnar summarized, "Generally immigrants were likely to find mobility horizontal rather than vertical or no mobility at all." Immigrants in general, including their children, did better in less socially stratified cities like Milwaukee, where Germans dominated the immigrant pool. In more class-ridden cities like Boston, the barriers to upward mobility were greater. There, Bodnar writes, "in the 1880's, 77 percent of the sons of unskilled immigrants remained unskilled themselves."[2]

Even during the more egalitarian era of the Jackson Administration—the period so famously studied and celebrated by Tocqueville—there is little evidence of dramatic upward mobility. The unfortunately unsung historian Edward Pessen acknowledged *Democracy in America* as "frighteningly prescient" and "the most penetrating single book yet written on American civilization." But

---

2 According to George Borjas, an economist at Harvard University, the prospects for upward mobility among contemporary immigrants haven't improved much. His study, published in a 2006 issue of *The Future of Children,* found that "the second-generation workers in the 2000 cross-section (whose parents made up the immigrant workforce in 1970) have a lower economic status than the second-generation workers in the 1970 cross-section (whose parents made up the immigrant workforce in 1940). If these historical trends continue for the next few decades, the forecast for the economic performance of the children of today's wave of immigrants could be bleak."

on the matter of rags to riches, Pessen wrote in a seminal 1971 essay, the great French sociologist got it wrong, as have many other historians inspired by Tocqueville. As Pessen paraphrased Tocqueville's view:

> According to the egalitarian thesis the United States was a society dominated by the great mass of the people, who composed the middling orders. Unfortunate minorities aside, few men here were either very poor or very rich. . . . Flux ruled this dynamic society; riches and poverty were ephemeral states in this kaleidoscopic milieu. . . . Deference gave way to strident rule of the masses, as the beleaguered rich turned their backs on a politics permeated by vulgarity, opportunism, and other loveless expressions of popular power. Social and economic democracy followed on the heels of, as they were in part caused by, political democracy. In a society that exalted work over status, class barriers loosened and diminished in significance. And a near if not a perfect equality of condition resulted from the unparalleled equality of opportunity that in Tocqueville's time complemented the abundant natural resources, the technological advances, and the human energy that had been present in America since its settlement.

Tocqueville was explicit in his support of this idea. "In a democratic society like that of the United States . . . fortunes are scanty," he wrote, since "the equality of conditions [that] gives some resources to all the members of the community . . . also prevents any of them from having resources of great extent." Furthermore, Tocqueville said, with his penchant for vast generalizations, "In America most of the rich men were formerly poor." Elsewhere, he elaborates, "In no country in the world are private fortunes more precarious than in the United States. It is not uncommon for the same man, in the course of his life, to rise and sink again through all the grades which lead from opulence to poverty."

Pessen demolished these assertions by studying the tax records of the wealthy elites of New York, Boston, Philadelphia, and Brooklyn, where he found precious little rags-to-riches movement. For example, he discovered, "about ninety-five per cent of New York City's one hundred wealthiest persons were born into families of wealth or high status and occupation; three per cent came of 'middling' background; only two per cent were born poor. As small a portion of Boston's one hundred wealthiest citizens started humble, with perhaps six per cent originating from middling families."

Pessen limited his critique to the second quarter of the nineteenth century, but he could just as well have been commenting on contemporary myths about American equality. "Popular ideology notwithstanding, the era of the common man was remarkable above all for how few rich men were in fact descended of common folk. When it is compared with earlier periods in American history, the age of egalitarianism appears to have been an age of increasing social rigidity."

After the stock market crash of 1929, as the nation plunged into the Great Depression and mass unemployment, studies by sociologists like Robert and Helen Lynd revealed that the economic victims of the calamity—mostly people of humble or middle class means—tended to blame themselves, not the rich or the social elites, for their plight. Similar to Ragged Dick, millions of downwardly mobile Americans in the 1930s apparently felt that financial misfortune was as much a bolt from the blue as was financial success. This anti-Marxist, anti-class consciousness helps explain the failure of the U.S. Socialist Party or Progressive Party (apart from the exceptional Bull Moose candidacy of President Theodore Roosevelt in 1912) ever to obtain more than 17 percent of the popular vote in a presidential election. It also speaks to a psychology of both optimism and fatalism that is ingrained in the American character.

Yet if Americans of inferior classes tend not to resent the upper class, the American upper class, in my experience, most certainly tends to disdain the lower classes and is determined to maintain its superior status. Class-consciousness is very much alive among the rich, which may be why the political elite that draws its financial support from wealthy contributors works so hard to suppress any notion of class division in America. (The best example of this aversion to public discussion of class was when the well-born George W. Bush accused his well-born opponent, Al Gore, of engaging in "class warfare" by employing mildly populist rhetoric during the 2000 election campaign.)

If poor and middle-class Americans really knew how the rich viewed them, they might well be troubled. But if they faced up to the stark statistics of what is, in fact, the prevailing *social immobility* in their country, they might be very disillusioned about the American dream.

Nowadays, the rags-to-riches story is embodied in ultra-successful entrepreneurs like Stephen Jay Ross, the late chairman of Time Warner, and the aforementioned S. Daniel Abraham, the billionaire founder of Slim-Fast, the diet-drink giant, and a quiet power within the Democratic Party. That these men were born into modest families does nothing, however, to contradict the basic facts of American economic life. These facts get little publicity, even though the extremes of American wealth and poverty are fairly well known and often sensationally publicized. It's hard to ignore the vast wealth of private-equity magnates like Stephen Schwarzman, the billionaire CEO of Blackstone Group, who hired the rock star Rod Stewart to perform at his 60th birthday party—a service for which Stewart generally charged $1 million at the time. If you live in New York, the opulent lifestyles of Schwarzman and his ilk contrast starkly with the thousands of homeless people who populate the sidewalks and parks of the city.

But these comparisons are obvious ones, and they obscure the less dramatic story of class immobility. The media will happily report on the excesses of the rich because it's easy, titillating, and fun. In the same vein, they will revel in spectacular financial collapses by high-profile millionaires like the profligate supermarket heir Huntington Hartford. It is left to less sexy reports like *Women's Labor Market Involvement and Family Income Mobility When Marriages End*, a 2002 study by two economists at the Federal Reserve Bank in Boston, to present the real facts about social mobility in America. In their research, Katharine Bradbury and Jane Katz found that of the poorest fifth of American families surveyed in 1988, 53.3 percent were still in the bottom fifth of the economic ladder in 1998. Another 23.6 percent made it up one rung to the second-lowest quintile of income earners, 12.4 percent made it to the third, 6.4 percent reached the second, and only 4.3 percent settled in the top fifth.

Looking down from the top, the story was almost identical in the rarity of significant proportions of people making big class shifts. Bradbury and Katz found that 53.2 percent of people in the top fifth of income earners in 1988 remained in the top bracket a decade later, 23.2 percent fell to the second-highest bracket, 14.9 percent dropped to the third quintile, 5.7 percent fell to the fourth quintile, and 3.0 to the fifth quintile.

In their 1995 book, *America Unequal,* and an updated piece published in *Dynamics of Child Poverty in Industrialised Countries* (2001), economists Sheldon H. Danziger and Peter Gottschalk examined the economic fate of two different, racially diverse groups of children, each for ten years. In the first group studied, from 1970 to 1980, the children, ranging in age from just born to five, found themselves pretty much locked into the economic class of their birth. Dividing the kids by their family's income into five separate segments, the researchers found that of the children constituting the poorest 20 percent of the sample, six in 10 stayed in the bottom economic bracket after 10 years, and eight in 10 remained in the two lowest income brackets at the end of the same period. The children studied from 1980 to 1990 (again ranging from just born to five) fared slightly worse: for the children in the lowest quintile, six in 10 remained where they were, and nine in 10 stayed put in the lowest two quintiles. The Reagan-driven "supply side" boom of the 1980s had helped not at all. The lesson is unmistakable: if you're born poor, you're likely to stay poor.

On the other hand, if you're born wealthy, you're likely to stay the same. Danziger and Gottschalk found that of the children belonging to the wealthiest 20 percent of families surveyed in 1970, only 2.4 percent had fallen to the lowest income bracket, and 6.5 percent to the bottom two quintiles, a decade later. There was even less downward mobility in the 1980 group. Only .5 percent of children belonging to the richest quintile fell to the poorest quintile 10 years later, and only 1.7 percent dropped into the lowest two brackets.

As the wealth gap has increased in America, so has nostalgia for a supposed golden era when income inequality was far less pronounced. At the end of 2005, according to the economist Emmanuel Saez, the richest 1 percent of Americans possessed 21.8 percent of the nation's wealth, while the top 10 percent owned fully 48.5 percent. These numbers surpass even the highs seen at the end of the Clinton presidency, in 2000, when the top 10 percent owned 47.61 percent of the nation's wealth and the top 1 percent controlled 21.52 percent. This grotesque concentration of wealth was second only to the pre-Depression boom year of 1928, when the class imbalance was at its height and the top 10 percent and top 1 percent of rich Americans controlled 49.3 percent and 23.9 percent, respectively, of the nation's wealth.[3] It was this wealth stratification that led *The Economist* magazine, tribune of free market and capitalist orthodoxy, to conclude in December 2004 that "the United States risks calcifying into a European-style class-based society."[4]

If there was never quite a golden age of American economic equality, there have been periods of national effort to pull ordinary people up the economic ladder, particularly during the New Deal and the immediate post-World War II era. The bipartisan Servicemen's Readjustment Act of 1944, popularly known as the G.I. Bill, guaranteed money for higher education, low-interest housing loans, unemployment compensation, and low-cost medical care to millions of returning veterans of the military. Its social and economic impact was enormous. Under the auspices of the Veterans Administration, out of a total of 16 million veterans, 2.4 million people received home loans from 1944 to 1952, and 7.8 million were able to attend colleges and universities, with the government's support, until 1956. As writer Pete Hamill described it, the G.I. Bill was revolutionary in its leveling effect:

> Millions of Americans, of all races, had their lives
> changed forever by the G.I. Bill, which guaranteed an
> education for those who had fought and survived a
> great war. For the first time in our history, the gates of

---

3 The first decade of the twenty-first century is often compared with the pre-income-tax Gilded Age of the 1870s, '80s and '90s. But such analogies are difficult to make accurately, since without systematic reporting of taxable income, the pre-1913 wich were frequently able to hide their assets from tax assessors.

4 In the same editorial, *The Economist* noted that "thirty years ago the average real annual compensation of the top 100 chief executives was $1.3 million: 39 times the pay of the average worker. Today it is $37.5 million: over 1,000 times the pay of the average worker."

academia were opened to men and women from every conceivable background. The rigidities of class crumbled. Children of longshoremen, mechanics and factory workers walked into the classrooms of the Ivy League. The children of policemen became lawyers. Infantrymen became professors of literature. Men and women who spoke Italian or Yiddish at home with their immigrant parents absorbed the elegant theories of quantum theory or semiotics or symbolic logic. When I was going to college on the Korean War version of the G.I. Bill, there were still a few students using their benefits from World War Two. They were intense, serious (but not solemn) men. I remember asking one of them if he felt intimidated by a philosophy course he was taking. "Intimidated?" he said, with a thin smile. "Hell, no. I was in the Battle of the Bulge."

In 1953, at the same time as the G.I. Bill was in full swing, union membership in America, as a percentage of the total workforce, peaked at 27 percent. Such a high percentage of organized laborers, combined with a top marginal income-tax rate that peaked at 94 percent in 1944-45 and remained above 90 percent until 1964, and an inheritance tax which reached a high of 77 percent in 1942, also reduced some of the more extreme advantages of the upper class. Indeed, most everyone was getting richer throughout the 1950s and '60s. The peak of statistical economic equality occurred from 1966 to 1974, when the wealth gap was its narrowest. According to the U.S. Census Bureau, during those eight years, the bottom fifth of American families owned about 5.5 percent of the nation's wealth and the top fifth controlled about 41 percent. It's probably no co-incidence that total union membership peaked at 20.3 million in 1978 and has been falling rapidly every since. Today's 1920s-style wealth gap parallels the decline of the American working class, the loss of union power, and the dramatic reduction of the top income tax rate, which in 1964 fell to 77 percent, in 1982 to 50 percent, and in 2003 to 35 percent, where it remains today. The inheritance tax, meanwhile, has also fallen from its New Deal high to 45 percent in 2007, with the first $2 million of an estate exempt from the tax altogether (up from $675,000 in 2001 and $60,000 in 1942). In 2006, union membership had fallen to a total of 15.4 million, which was 12 percent of the total workforce. More telling was that as a result of "free trade" agreements, de-industrialization, and "outsourcing" of factory work to cheap-labor locales such as China and Mexico, only 7.4 percent of private-sector workers belonged to unions.

Horatio Alger completes his iconic novel with the assurance that all will be well: "Here ends the story of Ragged Dick. As Fosdick said, he is Ragged Dick no longer. He has taken a step upward, and is determined to mount still higher." As for Thornton Bradshaw's bootblack, Joe, he ended his career where he started—on a stool, a good foot below the desk.

Most contemporary American pundits and politicians will say that they consider equal access to primary and secondary education to be a fundamental pillar of American democracy. The idea of universal education not only as a tool for upward mobility but also as the cure to any number of social ills is virtually universal in America. Thanks in part to the examples set by the brilliant, classically educated patrician Jefferson and the brilliant, self-educated poor boy Lincoln, most Americans would probably say that widespread, readily available education goes hand in hand with a healthy democracy—that formal schooling is a fundamental right nearly as important as the right to vote.

But beyond this assumed link between an educated citizenry and an effective democracy, there is little that Americans agree on when it comes to schools: who gets to use them and for what purpose. Like Booker T. Washington, George W. Bush and much of the American right believe that education is essentially just a means to a better economic life, not an end in itself and certainly not a prerequisite to popular sovereignty. But "liberals" don't necessarily disagree. Growing up in the supposedly revolutionary 1960s, I was inundated, along with millions of other Americans, by Advertising Council television commercials that endlessly repeated the slogan "to get a good job, get a good education." We were adjured not to be a good citizen or a happier, more insightful person, but just to get a decently paying position, preferably in an office. Such a prosaic and frankly practical approach to education argues against "fancy" teaching, the "mere book learning" (including the mastery of dead languages and classical cultures such as ancient and democratic Athens) that Booker T. Washington considered pretty much useless.

But if the American educational system was nothing more than a giant vocational school, then we wouldn't demand so much of it and criticize it so severely when it fails. As Peter Schrag wrote in the September 2007 *Harper's Magazine*, Americans have historically asked far too much of their public schools:

> Win the Cold War; beat the Germans and the Japanese
> in the battle for economic supremacy; outduel the
> Chinese and Indians in the training of scientists and
> engineers; Americanize millions of children not just
> from Southern and Eastern Europe . . . but from a
> hundred Third World cultures . . . make every child
> "proficient" in English and math; educate the blind, the
> mentally handicapped, and the emotionally disturbed to
> the same levels as all others; teach the evils of alcohol,
> tobacco, marijuana, cocaine, heroin, and premarital
> sex; prepare all for college; teach immigrants in their
> native languages; teach driver's ed; feed lunch to poor
> children; entertain the community with Friday-night
> football and midwinter basketball; sponsor dances and
> fairs for the kids; . . . serve as the prime (and often the

only) social-welfare agency for both children and parents
... [and bridge] the rapidly growing gaps in earnings
between the very rich and almost everyone else.

Nevertheless, Americans remain resolutely optimistic about the potential of education to create both a more democratic society and a better American. Even George Horace Lorimer, the somewhat cynical dean of how-to-succeed writers at the turn of the nineteenth century, could not entirely reject the notion of education as an intrinsically democratic benefit for all. Lorimer was the longtime editor of the widely circulated *Saturday Evening Post* magazine, and his best-selling *Letters from a Self-Made Merchant to His Son*, first serialized in 1901-02, constituted a template for popularized "practical wisdom" as opposed to largely intellectual education. In this, Lorimer became a kind of Booker T. Washington for the WASP middle class. His own secret to success, as Lawrence Grauman Jr. and Robert S. Fogarty wrote, was to "soothe a public grown weary of radicalism, war, social discord, and weary even of the rhetoric of uplift." Lorimer's mass-market magazine formula promoted "the themes of business success, 'public affairs' and romantic fiction—themes which could be overlapped and co-mingled so as to reveal the romance and adventure of commercial enterprise, or the politics of professional ambition." No sentimentalist of the Horatio Alger variety, Lorimer created a fictional Chicago meatpacking magnate, John Graham, whose signal character trait is a seeming absence of illusion and his contempt for serious academic training.

I recognize Graham's personality as authentic because I grew up in a similarly self-promoting business milieu, the Republican Chicago suburbs of Wilmette and Winnetka. Graham's language is to some extent the language of my highly successful businessman grandfather, who never graduated high school, and cared not at all whether my father went to college.[1] But immensely practical and self-reliant though he purports to be, Graham could not deny the value of at least *some* formal education. In his letters to Pierrepont, a Harvard undergraduate, Graham warns his son "not to understudy."

> What we're really sending you to Harvard for is to get a little of the education that's so good and plenty there. When it's passed around you don't want to be bashful, but reach right out and take a big helping every time, for I want you to get your share. You'll find that education's about the only thing lying around loose in this world, and that it's about the only thing a fellow can have as much of as he's willing to haul away. Everything else is screwed down tight and the screwdriver lost.

"Everything else" presumably was wealth, property, and social and political power. Education was still there for the taking, for a rich boy as well as a poor one.

But Graham (and Lorimer) remain cynical about the fundamental purpose of education: "Does a College education pay?" he writes to his son.

> Does it pay to feed in pork trimmings at five cents a pound at the hopper and draw out nice, cunning, little "country" sausages at twenty cents a pound at the other

---

1 Lorimer was, like my grandfather, the son of a Chicago preacher, though my great-grandfather was an evangelical Christian and Lorimer's father was a mainstream Baptist minister. Lorimer dropped out of Yale to work for a time for the Chicago meatpacking mogul Philip D. Armour, while my father dropped out of Rollins College to find adventure in Mexico and, eventually, success in business.

end? . . . You bet it pays. Anything that trains a boy to think and to think quick pays; anything that teaches a boy to get the answer before the other fellow gets through biting his pencil, pays.

College doesn't make fools; it develops them. It doesn't make bright men; it develops them. A fool will turn out a fool, whether he goes to college or not. . . . And a good, strong boy will turn out a bright, strong man whether he's worn smooth in the grab-what-you-want-and-eat-standing-with-one-eye-skinned-for-the-dog school of the streets and stores, or polished up and slicked down in the give-your-order-to-the-waiter-and-get-a-sixteen-course-dinner school of the professors. But while the lack of a college education can't keep No. 1 down, having it boosts No. 2 up.

In the end, it's the school of life that counts most ("the man who hasn't licked stamps isn't fit to write letters"), though it helps if the curriculum is organized by a rich father. Dismissing Pierrepont's notion of going on to graduate school, Graham affirms:

> You're not going to be a poet or a professor, but a packer, and the place to take a post-graduate course for that calling is the packing-house. . . . There's a chance for everything you have learned, from Latin to poetry, in the packing business, though we don't use much poetry here except in our street-car ads., and about the only time our products are given Latin names is when the State Board of Health condemns them. So I think you'll find it safe to go short a little on the frills of education; if you want them bad enough you'll find a way to pick them up later, after business hours.

Besides, "some men are like pigs, the more you educate them, the more amusing little cusses they become, and the funnier capers they cut when they show off their tricks. Naturally, the place to send a boy of that breed is to the circus, not to college."[2]

It would be easy to laugh at Lorimer's anti-intellectualism—indeed his anti-idealism—if it weren't so pervasive in American society. So many of the "frills of education" are central to what makes an educated citizen: music, art, literature, and foreign languages tend to be the first things that are cut when a public-school system runs low on money. President Bush's pet education project, the under-funded "No Child Left Behind" legislation, seeks to impose minimum achievement standards for math and reading, but not much more. The shallow rigidity of this federal mandate led Howard Dean to dub the program "no child left untested."[3]

But the fundamental fraud contained in Lorimer's bromides is the implication that all Americans (other than what he called "niggers") enjoy equality of access to good schools and good teachers ("the only thing lying around loose in this world"), not to mention the frills. After four leisurely years at Harvard, pampered, spendthrift Pierrepont can always find the time to read poetry, because no matter how harsh a taskmaster, his father has guaranteed him permanent employment (even if it starts at the bottom of the company) and, most probably, a tidy inheritance. Meanwhile, even the most virtuous Ragged Dick of today must make do with the no-frills education of overcrowded classrooms, lack of books and science equipment, and undisciplined students who, whether because of poverty

---

2 This sort of folk-business metaphor is a second cousin to my grandfather's warning against excessive greed: "Pigs get fed, hogs get slaughtered."

3 The parents who send their children to my local public grammar school, P.S. 87 in Manhattan, set an annual fund-raising goal of $300,000 from private sources to pay for art teachers and other "frills."

or broken homes, distract the already harassed teachers from the task of teaching.[4]

Today's American system of education, both primary and secondary, is probably more distinguished by its inequality and social stratification than by its universality. At the extremes of the divide between haves and have-nots, we still find persistent racial discrimination. Minority blacks and Hispanics in American public schools almost inevitably fare worse than their white counterparts. This is principally because public schools continue to be funded locally, primarily from property tax revenues, a system which guarantees that wealthy cities, towns, and counties will have more money to spend on public education than poor ones. Since minorities remain a disadvantaged economic class, impoverished big-city schools with high minority enrollments produce more failures than better-off suburban schools.

Jonathan Kozol has chronicled the separate and unequal saga of public education and recently found that big-city schools were just as segregated as they were when the U.S. Supreme Court declared, in its 1954 *Brown* v. *Board of Education* decision, that racially segregated schools were unconstitutional because separate education necessarily meant unequal, inferior education for blacks. As of 2003, Kozol wrote in *The Shame of the Nation: The Restoration of Apartheid Schooling in America*, the percentage of black and Hispanic students in the Chicago public-school system was 87 percent; Washington, D.C., 94 percent; St. Louis, 82 percent; Philadelphia and Cleveland, 79 percent; Los Angeles, 84 percent; Detroit, 96 percent; and Baltimore, 89 percent. Kozol asserts, however, that "even these statistics, as stark as they are, cannot begin to convey how deeply isolated children in the poorest and most segregated sections of these cities

---

4 In Horatio Alger's fairy-tale world, Ragged Dick is able to hire another street urchin, who had briefly attended public school before his father's death, to be his tutor.

have become." The physical distance between the races has created an "achievement gap between black and white children, which narrowed for three decades up until the late years of the 1980s—the period in which school segregation steadily decreased—[but] started to widen once more in the early 1990s when the federal courts began the process of re-segregation by dismantling the mandates of the *Brown* decision."[5]

Notwithstanding the simplemindedness of the slogan "To get a good job, get a good education," the correlation between education and economic success in America is undeniable. So, too, is the correlation between prosperity and voting. As for income, according to the most recent U.S. Census, Americans with advanced degrees (master's, professional, or Ph.D.) earn an average of $79,946 annually; those with a B.A. (the standard degree of a college graduate) make an average of $54,689 (median of $40,166); high school graduates earn an average of $29,448 (median of $21,079); and those who do not graduate high school make an average of $19,915 (median of $13,085). As for voting, in the 2004 national elections the U.S. Census Bureau found an exact correlation between income and electoral participation. In its survey, the bureau discovered that

---

5 In the summer of 2007, the Supreme Court in a 5-4 vote struck down desegregation plans in the Louisville and Seattle school districts. In his majority opinion, Chief Justice John Roberts wrote, "Classifying and assigning schoolchildren according to a binary conception of race is an extreme approach in light of our precedents and our nation's history of using race in public schools.... The way to stop discrimination on the basis of race is to stop discrimination on the basis of race." In a dissenting opinion, Justice Stephen Breyer argued that "the plurality's approach risks serious harm to the law and for the Nation. Its view of the law rests either upon a denial of the distinction between exclusionary and inclusive use of race-conscious criteria ... or upon such a rigid application of its 'test' that the distinction loses practical significance. Consequently, the Court's decision today slows down and sets back the work of local school boards to bring about racially diverse schools.... The last half-century has witnessed great strides toward racial equality, but we have not yet realized the promise of *Brown*. To invalidate the plans under review is to threaten the promise of *Brown*. The plurality's position, I fear, would break that promise."

in households with incomes of $150,000 and above, 78 percent of eligible family members voted. For families with household incomes of $30,000 to $40,000, the rate of participation fell to 54 percent; for those with incomes between $10,000 and $15,000, the rate was 39 percent. According to the congressionally chartered National Conference on Citizenship, 62 percent of college graduates voted in the 2004 elections, while only 31 percent of high school dropouts went to the polls. In short, the better the education one receives in America, the more likely one is to take part in the democratic system.

Race exacerbates the income gap between the educated and the less educated, but class matters too: poor white children also suffer disproportionately from under-funding of schools. Even when the federal government intervenes to redress the inequality of school funding that results from the heavy reliance on property taxes, poor school districts are regularly shortchanged, regardless of their racial makeup. In a September 2007 editorial, the *New York Times* noted that federal Title I money, intended to give extra help to poor school districts, was simply being used by states to excuse them from their own obligation to provide equal funding to poor districts: "In practice, many states have continued to shortchange those high poverty schools, while using Title I money to make up the difference."

According to the U.S. Department of Education, local contributions to public schools amount to 44 percent of the total funding, compared with 47 percent that comes from state governments and only 9 percent from Washington. As America's great leveler, the federal government has an implied responsibility to maintain broadly democratic access to primary education, which is compulsory to the age of 16. But it is falling far short of the country's stated mission of offering every child, rich or poor, a more or less comparable opportunity for a decent education. In effect, the class bias of property-tax funding is fundamental in judging whether American public schools are "democratic" in spirit as well as in practice.

But what about the Horatio Alger versions of post-primary-school success? Everyone knows the story of a poor kid who made it to Harvard via the public-school system. But the odds remain solidly against such rags-to-the-honor-roll narratives. As a percentage of the total student population, 88 percent of American school children (PK-12) attend public school; the remaining 12 percent, or 6.5 million, are enrolled in a variety of religious and secular private schools. Because they cost money, private schools still attract the sons and daughters of the socially prominent and wealthy elite (George W. Bush attended Phillips Academy Andover in Massachusetts, and Al Gore attended the St. Albans School in Washington). But in most towns and cities, there is really only one option, the local public school. Contrary to the egalitarian premise of American education, a higher percentage of the favored few who graduate from private school go on to college than do graduates of public high schools. For the high school senior class of 2002-03, the National Center for Education Statistics found that 44 percent of public-school graduates went on to four-year colleges, compared with 80 percent of private-school graduates. Seventy-two percent of public-school graduates did enter some post-high school program, including two-year junior colleges; the comparable number for private-school graduates was 93 percent.

Getting into college is hard enough for a person of modest means. But assuming the best—that someone like Ragged Dick's urchin tutor succeeds in prepping his pupil for collegiate life—how hard is it for an ordinary American to gain entry to the best colleges and universities? To be sure, it's not easy for anyone to get into an Ivy League school. But it certainly helps if your father or mother was a graduate of the institution and has some money. Tocqueville was right in noting the anti-aristocratic convictions abroad in nineteenth-century America, but a hereditary aristocracy of sorts survives in higher education. So-called legacy admissions make up an estimated 10 to 15 percent of each class in the eight Ivy League colleges, according to the universities themselves. At Harvard, the children of alumni are nearly four times as likely to be admitted as other applicants. At a less elite private institution, the University of Notre Dame, the legacy ratio is even higher: 22 to 24 percent of each entering class consists of the children of alumni. In all, *The Economist* noted in 2005, "three-quarters of the students at the country's top 146 colleges come from the richest socio-economic fourth, compared with just 3 percent who come from the poorest fourth."

However, this "inherited" advantage for some applicants to high-profile colleges is not necessarily what is keeping the poor and minorities down in American society. (Indeed, the wealthy Ivy League schools compensate heavily for this class skew with generous scholarship money for minorities and students who can't afford to pay tuition and living expenses upwards of $40,000 a year.) The typical high school graduate from a modest background looks closer to home when he or she applies to college: this is principally because state universities offer substantially lower tuition—about half the price in most instances—to in-state residents. But public secondary education is becoming more expensive, beyond the reach of the poor but also of the lower-middle-class students who do not qualify for sufficient financial aid to go to college. Tuition inflation has risen dramatically over the past 20 years: according to the College Board, in 1986, the average annual tuition and fees at a public university was $2,628. The same education today costs, on average, $5,836. Among private institutions, the increase has been similarly steep: in 1986, it cost $12,375 to go to a private college for one year; today it costs $22,218.

Along with rising costs, poor blacks and Latinos face new barriers to higher education because of rollbacks in "affirmative action," the doctrine under which college admissions officers could establish quotas using race as a criterion. Under the latest Supreme Court ruling, colleges can consider an applicant's racial origins but cannot fix a minimum number for each incoming class. No doubt, affirmative action has allowed statistically less-qualified blacks into colleges ahead of whites, but given the built-in disadvantage of being black in American society, affirmative action has seemed a fair method of compensation.

As a result of the federal government's help with direct financial aid and subsidized loans, the percentage of blacks 18 to 24 enrolled in college rose from 13 percent in 1967 to 33 percent in 2005, a 151 percent increase. Among the white and Hispanic population in the same age bracket, the percentage rose from 27 percent to 39 percent over the same four decades, a 45 percent increase. When separated out, Hispanics, for whom English is often their second language, still fared the worst, with an increase in college enrollment from 13 percent in 1972 to 25 percent in 2005.[6]

However, the increased cost of going to college combined with the political backlash against affirmative action threaten to reverse this 40-year trend of educational mobility. At the public University of California, Los Angeles, for example, only 96 of the entering freshman class of nearly 5,000 in 2006 were black, the lowest number since 1973. Studies predict that if current legal trends opposed to affirmative action (whether they are hard quotas or less stringent considerations of race) continue, there will be a decline in the number of blacks and other minorities going to college. Two Princeton professors, Thomas Espenshade and Chang Chung, analyzed data from 1997 from three highly selective private research universities to project what impact eliminating all affirmative-action programs would do to their student bodies. They determined that college ac-

---

6 In 1972, the U.S. Census Bureau offered for the first time the choice of identifying yourself as Hispanic as a separate category from white.

ceptance rates for blacks would fall from 33.7 percent to 12.2 percent; for Hispanics, from 26.8 percent to 12.9 percent.

Right-wingers often argue that affirmative action is "un-American" because it steals places from white children who deserve the same chance for success as blacks. However, Espenshade and Chung found that the acceptance rate for whites under a no affirmative action policy would rise by only .5 percent at the three schools. Asians, they found, would be the greatest beneficiaries of a race-blind policy; their acceptance rate would jump from 17.6 percent to 23.4 percent.

As of this writing, darker skin color—and the legacy of slavery—still mattered as much as democratic principle in the American school system. The larger question is this: how far will the country's legal and political establishments go in re-segregation—with its inevitable de-democratization—of education?

Whenever possible, promoters of the free market try to equate the blessings of American democracy with the thrill of unfettered capitalist consumption. Though no proof exists that the freedom to buy guarantees democracy, propagandists for the American system of capitalism want everyone to make the connection anyway: that freedom of choice in politics is nearly the same thing as freedom of choice in a store.[1]

I suspect that the merging of the right to shop with the right to vote is why Americans—and foreign visitors—are so obsessed with the retail side of life in the United States. Indeed, journalists often refer to political primary campaigning as "retail politics," as if politicians were simple commodities and voters were buying stock in candidates in the hope of receiving a return on their investment. In the same vein, politicians often exhort voters to shop before Christmas as a kind of democratic-patriotic duty. Meanwhile, advocates

---

1 Totalitarian China, one-party Singapore, and autocratic Russia are three states that harmonize some version of a "free" consumer economy with the absence of democracy.

of legal abortion resort to a consumer metaphor to justify their position, as in "pro-choice" or "a woman's right to choose"; whereas opponents of legal abortion are labeled "anti-choice," which sounds practically un-American.

So closely linked are democracy, freedom, and capitalism in the minds of many Americans that they are sometimes moved to say very odd things. Nearly a decade after he was taken hostage at the U.S. Embassy in Tehran, the diplomat Morehead Kennedy was asked by WOR, a New York City radio station, to comment on the occasion of the bicentennial of the U.S. Constitution. Speaking on WOR's topic, "A More Perfect Union: Prominent Americans Reflect on Our Constitution," Morehead sounded as if he had been bottle-fed as a baby inside the University of Chicago economics department by a nanny named Milton Friedman:

> In 1979, I was the acting head of the economic section
> at our embassy in Tehran, and I was held hostage for 444
> days. You don't appreciate what freedom is until you've
> been deprived of it. When I came home my first instinctive
> reaction was to go shopping. I sort of sashayed around:
> maybe I was going to buy this and maybe I was going
> to buy that, but what I was exercising was purchasing
> power. The Constitution, we often forget, was designed to
> ensure that consumers could get a wide variety of things
> by breaking tariff barriers between the states. These are
> critical things we often take for granted. Until you've been
> deprived of them, you don't know what they are.

Whatever the flaws in Kennedy's interpretation of the founding of America, he was clearly expressing something deeply imbedded in the American psyche—the belief that consumer choice and freedom are inextricably linked. Tocqueville identified the country's materialistic cravings, noting that the "passion of the Americans for physical gratifications is vehement" (though "not indiscriminating"), and he made the connection between unfettered buying and democracy in terms not very different from Morehead Kennedy's:

> Americans believe their freedom to be the best instrument and surest safeguard of their welfare: they are attached to the one by the other. They by no means think that they are not called upon to take a part in the public weal; they believe, on the contrary, that their chief business is to secure for themselves a government which will allow them to acquire the things they covet, and which will not debar them from the peaceful enjoyment of those possessions which they have acquired.

While many American cynics believe the political and legal systems to be rigged in favor of the rich (or, in the case of the resentful followers of Ronald Reagan, rigged in favor of the poor and the blacks), most Americans assume that the market is fair and that a hardworking, ordinary citizen can buy whatever he or she wants, or needs, at a reasonable price. American politics might be corrupt, remote from the public, and sometimes ridiculous, but shopping was more or less pure, accessible to all and no laughing matter. Conni Harding of Portsmouth, Rhode Island, and millions of other mothers were genuinely outraged when it was revealed in the summer of 2007 that Chinese manufacturers were using lead paint in the production of toys. Similarly, when I interviewed Dennis Canario at Clements' Market, the ultra-prudent president of the Portsmouth Town Council became livid when the subject turned to rising gasoline prices and the likelihood that oil was being manipulated for political purposes:

Let's talk about the price of oil. Every time something
even looks to be a storm, prices shoot up. This never
happened years ago.... When gas was a buck a gallon,
we would have hurricanes and [prices wouldn't change]
... but now they're getting the people to believe that
anything in the $2 range is a deal! Which is absurd! It
is absurd! They've actually brainwashed society to think
that we'll never see $2.50 a gallon again. But boy, you
know, you can get it for $2.60, $2.70, you're in a deal.
Come on!

No political issue, Iraq included, came close to inciting Canario in
our two hours of conversation the way the price of oil did. Indeed,
this determinedly conservative man sounded almost like a left-wing
populist once he warmed to the subject:

Now think about the big picture. If they were taking
this money to build more refineries, for energy research,
that's okay.... But we're making the rich richer. They're
getting millions and billions and millions of dollars in
bonuses. That's where our working money is going. So
it saddens me to think that a Republican administration
is using this, whatever you want to call it—maybe
propaganda—to make people think it's okay. And we're
feeding the rich.

Little wonder that businessmen, bankers, politicos, and sociologists
follow The Conference Board's monthly consumer confidence index
with such keen interest. If Dennis Canario and others like him lost
faith in America's free-market consumer culture, the whole democratic premise of the country might collapse.

To be sure, propagandists work tirelessly to shore up belief in the American economy and the importance of spending money on goods and services. Total advertising spending in America, for the most part entirely unregulated, amounted to $149.6 billion in 2006, or just over 1 percent of the gross domestic product. Advertising, according to the historian Daniel Boorstin, is "the characteristic rhetoric of American democracy." An hour of watching network or cable television or listening to American commercial radio confirms his thesis. The aforementioned free-market theorist Joseph Schumpeter, writing in the early 1940s, acknowledged the immense power of American advertising:

> Economists . . . have begun to discover that . . .
> consumers do not quite live up to the idea that the
> economic textbooks used to convey. On the one hand
> their wants are nothing like as definite and their
> actions upon those wants nothing like as rational and
> prompt. On the other hand they are so amenable to
> the influence of advertising and other methods of
> persuasion that producers often seem to dictate to them
> instead of being directed by them. The technique of
> successful advertising is particularly instructive. There is
> indeed nearly always some appeal to reason. But mere
> assertion, often repeated, counts more than rational
> argument and so does the direct attack upon the
> subconscious which takes the form of attempts to evoke
> and crystallize pleasant associations of an entirely extra-
> rational, very frequently of a sexual nature.

With so much advertising in support of the ideal of free choice, I sometimes wonder whether this, too, is a manipulation—indeed, that the actual variety of choices might not measure up to the fervent wish for free choice in the market. As in politics, where the parties strictly limit the choice of candidates on the ballot, Americans who go shopping might have fewer choices than they are led to believe. U.S. Census Bureau data on retail stores reveals that the sales of chain stores are growing significantly faster than those of single retail outlets. The Census said that between 1992 and 2002, sales for companies with more than 100 "establishments" grew by 102 percent, from $648 billion to $1.3 trillion. In 1992, these big-chain enterprises accounted for 34 percent of all retail sales in the country; by 2002 they had 43 percent of the market. For the single-unit stores, the trend was in the other direction: in 1992, they had 40 percent of all retail sales, and by 2002 their share had fallen to 35 percent. Although the total sales of the individual stores also increased during the decade studied—from $758 billion to a little over $1 trillion—they were declining relative to the whole market, which had grown by 61 percent in the same period. Americans en masse were shopping more and more, but they were buying increasingly from mass-market outlets like Wal-Mart and Target, which offer lower prices than traditional Main Street stores.[2]

Clearly, many American consumers have fewer choices of stores today than they had fifteen years ago. When Wal-Mart comes to town, smaller, local retailers disappear, unable to compete with the big-box economies of scale. Anyone who lives in a small or medium-size American town can attest to the Wal-Mart effect: very simply, Main Street can't compete and dies. Certainly the products at Wal-Mart are cheaper than at the old hardware store, but another question arises: Does Wal-Mart offer as many products to choose

---

2 In 2002, the nation's 685,000 single-unit stores still outnumbered the 259,000 big-chain outlets belonging to 457 companies with 100 or more stores. But the lead is rapidly shrinking, even as the chains consolidate. In 1992, single-unit stores totaled 998,000 compared with 264,000 outlets belonging to 540 chains with more than 100 establishments.

from as the combined inventories of the five or six stores it drives out of business?[3] Journalist Barry C. Lynn has noted the increasing worldwide consolidation of manufacturing since the laissez-faire Reagan Administration relaxed enforcement of antitrust laws: firms ranging from the glass-container giant Owens Illinois to the Italian sunglass maker Luxottica dominate their markets while "consolidation reigns in banking, meatpacking, oil refining, and grains." But however powerful some manufacturers may be, Wal-Mart is in some ways even more powerful, with about 10 percent of all retail sales in the United States (upwards of 30 percent for some goods) and revenues close to the combined totals of the next six largest retailers. Lynn calls Wal-Mart a "monopsony" due to the company's "ability to dictate price to its suppliers, because the suppliers have no real choice other than to deal with [Wal-Mart]." He argues that the "ultimate danger of monopsony is that it deprives the firms that actually manufacture products from obtaining an adequate return on their investment" and thus "tends to destroy the machines and skills on which we all rely."

But for the purposes of determining whether Americans have a truly "democratic" consumer culture, we need to know Wal-Mart's effect on choice and range of products. Mass merchandisers obviously want to focus their efforts on promoting and stocking their best-selling items, so the incentive for manufacturers would seem to be to please the retailer first and the consumer second. Ideas for experimental or speculative products, no matter how interesting or innovative, would tend to be shelved in the drive to satisfy Wal-Mart with products that are sure to sell. Specialty items that sit too long on the shelf would also tend to disappear. The ruthlessly efficient Barnes & Noble chain, for example, carries many more books and

---

3 Conni Harding said she was delayed sending me a video I needed transferred to a DVD because the Wal-Mart in Newport had put her local photo/video store out of business.

titles than the typical independent bookstore, but its store managers are much quicker to pull slow sellers from the shelves than a small independent owner who knows his or her customers. The question becomes whether companies like Barnes & Noble, with its 15 percent share of the book market, and Wal-Mart force their suppliers to limit the variety and number of products they offer consumers in the name of greater efficiency and higher profits. Economics and common sense suggest that this is an inevitable result of monopsony. According to John B. Kirkwood, professor of law at the University of Seattle and a former antitrust official in the Federal Trade Commission, manufacturing firms under relentless pressure from giant retail firms may "curtail their investment in the industry" and "consumers may eventually pay higher prices or have fewer choices."

Anecdotal evidence suggests that suppliers are responding to retail-chain demands for ever higher profits and efficiencies by simply producing fewer items or, as they're known in the trade, SKUs—Stock Keeping Units. According to the *Wall Street Journal*'s Deborah Ball, the Swiss-based food giant Nestlé reduced its SKUs by 20 percent in 2006 and by another 10 percent in 2007. But she didn't attribute the reduction in the variety of products to the power of chain stores. According to Ball, Nestlé "faces a predicament that is increasingly common in the corporate world, as a wave of consolidation creates megaliths that are bigger than ever, and now need to be rationalized."

"It is surprisingly easy for a food maker to come out with too many new products," wrote Ball. "When sales are slow, brand managers often think they can win back consumers with something new." Isn't that the very point of free-market consumer choice—more innovation and more choices? Evidently not at Nestlé. In addition to cutting SKUs, Paul Grimwood, the head of Nestlé's British candy business, had "cut the number of future innovations by more than half." In this new culture of anti-variety,

U.K. customers could no longer buy "low-carb versions of Kit Kat and Rolo" or "Double Cream chocolate bars, a premium candy make with extra cream and high quality cocoa from Ecuador."

For my part, shopping in a non-chain store has become a luxury, which fortunately I can afford. I find big boxes difficult to navigate and am often frustrated by their poorly designed displays, the lack of expertise and attention by the salesclerks, and the generally alienating atmosphere, which seems designed to accommodate forklifts instead of humans. In the huge Duane Reade drugstore chain in my work neighborhood of Noho in New York City, the basic products I want are usually only offered in the largest-size quantities (which I don't want), the checkout lines are invariably long, there never seem to be enough cashiers, and the ones there are look they'll have to work Sundays for the rest of their lives. Some Duane Reades stay open 24 hours, which can be a great convenience if your child falls ill in the middle of the night. But in my experience, they take longer to fill prescriptions—up to an hour and longer—than individually owned pharmacies.

Small family-owned pharmacies are increasingly hard to find in New York and its environs, however. When I came down with a very painful "swimmer's ear" infection on the East End of Long Island in the summer of 2007, I went to see an eye, ear, and throat specialist in Southampton named Anthony Caruso. He prescribed antibiotic drops, which I was anxious to take as soon as possible, so I asked his nurse where the nearest drugstore was located. She and the front- desk clerk simultaneously suggested two chain drugstores, Rite Aid and CVS, so I pressed them further for the name of a "regular" drug store. Overhearing me, Dr. Caruso mentioned a place called Southrifty. As it turned out, the good doctor knew of it because his parents had once owned it! The two assistants seemed entirely unaware of Southrifty's existence.

With some difficulty (when I passed the big CVS I almost gave in) I found Southrifty, located off the main drag on a narrow commercial street. The place was full of customers, but a sympathetic-looking female clerk quickly handed my prescription to the pharmacist. Meanwhile, I was free to relax on the store's cushioned banquettes, which is something you would never find in a chain store. When I got my medicine fifteen minutes later, the clerk invited me to begin my treatment on the banquette. I used to get similarly personal treatment at University Pharmacy near my office on West 4th Street in New York, but it's now a Duane Reade.

Obviously, there's more to a healthy democracy—and to life—than the freedom to buy the commodities of your choice. Though media and culture are increasingly commodified in the United States, many people still make the distinction between the life of the stomach and the life of the mind. In this realm, Americans rightly have prided themselves on having the freest media in the world with the fewest legal restrictions placed on them by the government. But once again, a similar question arises about democratic choice: does the freedom to publish or broadcast virtually anything in fact guarantee a wide variety of information and viewpoints? I think not. Just as the marketplace of goods tends to be narrowed by the dominance of chain stores, so, too, is the marketplace of ideas and information threatened by the increasing concentration of ownership.

When I drive down the main thoroughfares of just about any American town or city, I'm struck by the numbing sameness of the national chain stores and fast-food franchises I pass. I feel the same way about newspapers and television news programs. There is a stultifying uniformity in American journalism that limits choice for the consumer who is also a citizen. The conglomerate media not only discourages competition; it breeds uniformity of opinion. Tocqueville noted this suffocating lack of intellectual diversity, although rather than blaming the media he attributed it to the "unlimited power of the majority" to suppress minority views. Long before there was Rupert Murdoch or a Gannett newspaper chain, he wrote: "I know of no country in which there is so little true independence of mind and freedom of discussion as in America . . ."

> In America, the majority raises very formidable barriers to the liberty of opinion: within these barriers an author may write whatever he pleases, but he will repent it if he ever steps beyond them. Not that he is exposed to the terrors of an auto-da-fé, but he is tormented by the slights and persecutions of daily obloquy. His political career is closed forever, since he has offended the only authority which is able to promote his success. . . . Works have been published in the proudest nations of the Old World, expressly intended to censure the vices and deride the follies of the times. . . . But the ruling power in the United States is not to be made game of; the smallest reproach irritates its sensibility, and the slightest joke which has any foundation in truth renders it indignant; from the style of its language to the more solid virtues of its character, everything must be made the subject of encomium. No writer, whatever be his eminence, can escape from this tribute of adulation to his fellow-citizens. The majority lives in the perpetual practice of self-applause; and there are certain truths which the Americans can only learn from strangers or from experience.

I am often reminded of Tocqueville's words when I pick up the *New York Times* or the *Washington Post*, knowing how much genuine news they have suppressed and distorted since President George W. Bush began his campaign to invade Iraq. Over the past five years, the great metropolitan dailies have been distinguished less by what they have revealed in their pages than by what they have left out. During the hysterical run-up to war in March 2003 the *Times* and *Post*, along with most of the American media, published largely false information about Saddam Hussein's weapons programs, much of it originating with scare propaganda leaked to *Times* reporters Judith Miller and Michael Gordon of the *Times* by Bush Administration officials. These immensely destructive stories helped pave the way to war. But it is the self-censorship of the *Times* and the *Post*—America's two most influential newspapers—that may be most indicative of the lack of diversity and choice in America's "marketplace of ideas." One example is perfectly illustrative: the *Times'* refusal to publish, for more than a year, James Risen's crucial revelation about the Bush Administration's illegal, warrantless wiretapping program conducted by the National Security Agency. Had the paper of record published Risen's scoop before the 2004 election, public outrage might well have swung the contest to John Kerry. Instead, the *Times* waited until December 2005 to tell the world, and then only because Risen was about to publish his revelation in a book. As *New York* magazine's Joe Hagan described it,

> In the fall of 2004, Risen had brought a massive scoop to his editors: Beginning in the days after September 11 [2001], he discovered, the Bush Administration had authorized the National Security Agency to eavesdrop on foreign calls into the United States without court-approved warrants.
>
> When the *Times* first approached the White House with the story that fall, [Washington Bureau Chief Philip] Taubman took the lead editorial role, beginning a series of meetings with Bush officials. General [Michael] Hayden, the NSA director, took him on a

personal tour of the agency's headquarters and tried
to impress upon him the importance of its secret
programs. Taubman also met personally with then-
national-security adviser Condoleezza Rice, a close
friend of his for more than twenty years. Six months
before the 2004 election, Taubman had thrown a lavish
dinner party for Rice at his house in Washington.

Shortly after Taubman was briefed by the Bush
administration, [*Times* Executive Editor Bill] Keller
himself met with Rice, Hayden, and others. "I think
they were shocked they were having to share this with
journalists," Keller recalls. But, sitting on a potentially
explosive piece of news that could tip the presidential
election to John Kerry, Keller was persuaded by the
administration's counterarguments and decided against
publishing Risen's revelations.

I quote this article at length in order to illustrate the routine intimacy
that exists in America between powerful politicians and powerful
media and the self-censorship that results. None of this is news to
Washington insiders, but it might be news to the general public if
they knew just how far outside the system they are. Keller says the
administration was "shocked" to be sharing a secret with journalists,
but they needn't have been alarmed. Sympathetic by instinct and
training to political power, the executive editor of the nation's
preeminent establishment newspaper, abetted by his publisher
Arthur Ochs Sulzberger Jr., wasn't about to "share" the big secret
with the sovereign people of America, at least not in time for them
to make an informed judgment at the polls. Neither, for that matter,
was Risen, who evidently felt his duty to himself came before his
patriotic duty to inform his fellow citizens. Hagen described Risen
as "beyond furious" that his bosses refused to publish his scoop. Yet

there was nothing preventing Risen from quitting the paper and taking the story elsewhere.

For the ordinary "consumer" of news, robbed by the *Times* of the information they most need to govern (and protect) themselves, the question becomes: Where can they shop for alternative news? Like the consumer offered the choice of several big-box retail outlets, the American news consumer can buy a different daily newspaper or watch a different television station. As with the choice between Wal-Mart and Target, though, the actual selection of items on the shelf is more limited than customers may realize. They could, for example, read the *Washington Post* instead of the *New York Times*, but the paper that broke the Watergate scandal exhibited extraordinary self-censorship of its own during the Bush regime. In November 2005, the *Post* revealed the existence of CIA secret "black site" prisons—in Thailand, Afghanistan, and "several democracies in Eastern Europe." These hidden dungeons had been established for the legally questionable purpose of interrogating "terrorist" suspects away from the meddling fingers of U.S. courts and human rights lawyers. But despite the outrage generated by its scoop, the *Post* declined to say where in Europe the prisons were located, citing the U.S. government's alleged concerns about "possible terrorist retaliation." The *Post*, assuming for itself the mantle of government censor, said that it wasn't "publishing the names of the eastern European countries involved in the covert program, at the request of senior U.S. officials" who "argued that the disclosure might disrupt counterterrorism efforts in those countries and elsewhere and could make them targets." The *Post* did not seem concerned that countries hosting these secret detention/torture centers would thus escape public scorn and criticism, as well as possible sanctions by the European Union.

As with the chain stores, consumer choice in media is limited by the concentration of ownership. The great press critic and journalist A. J. Liebling remarked that "freedom of the press is guaranteed only to those who own one," and this observation remains a fact of life, even in the age of bloggers. According to the most recent figures from Free Press, a nonprofit media watchdog, 91.8 percent of all U.S. television stations are group owned; and of commercial radio stations, 74.5 percent belong to conglomerates and chains. Newspapers, still the principal generators of what passes for "news," are 81 percent chain-owned, according to Free Press. One-third of newspaper owners control four-fifths of all newspapers. Only 11 cities have two or more independently owned competing newspapers, and 12 cities have two newspapers operating under so-called joint operating agreements, in which a single entity runs the business operations for both papers. With the nearly complete demise of United Press International, America has only one major general wire service, the Associated Press. This press cooperative, owned by 1,500 member newspapers nationwide, must compete with Reuters on national and international news, and with Bloomberg on business news, but in many state capitals, and in large segments of the federal bureaucracy, the AP is the only serious journalistic presence.

Certainly, conglomerate ownership and only one major wire service account for much of the numbing sameness of newspapers, TV news, and non-fiction book publishing from coast to coast. But it doesn't explain everything. The Internet, only about fifteen years old and with its tens of thousands of news bloggers, myriad websites, and powerful search engines, is supposed to combat conventional self-censorship by newspapers like the *Times* and the *Post*. Promoters of this new medium cite scoops by websites such as The Memory Hole—which posted the first photographs of coffins bearing U.S. soldiers killed in Iraq—as an example of the declining pre-eminence of conventional media. So, too, is Amazon.com cited as the last word in democratic accessibility to any book on any subject. With all this access to information, how can any government secret be kept? But availability doesn't always equal access. If you need a specialty electric plug right away and Wal-Mart doesn't stock it, in theory you can order it off your computer—but only if you know where to look.

With news about the government, however, you can't always know what you're looking for or what you need. If the information isn't in the pages of your local newspaper, paper or electronic, you probably won't stumble across it on the Internet either. In any event, websites don't have staffs of experienced reporters, like the *Times* and the *Post*, and they can't muster the resources to hire them. Indeed, a great deal of blogging involves the rehashing of news from the same old sources: newspapers, television, and radio. If "everything gets out eventually on the Internet," as its partisans suggest, then how were Risen and the *Times* able to keep the Bush Administration's secret about NSA's warrantless wiretapping program for so long?

The monolithic nature—indeed, the anti-diversity—of the American media extends beyond its news content. Politically, the major media tends to express conventional editorial opinions in line with the political power structure in Washington. Syndicated columnists rarely stray beyond the strict parameters of what is considered appropriate discussion, and newspaper editorials are remarkably uniform on the great issues of the day, such as "free trade" and war. According to journalist John Nichols, the top 20 most widely circulated newspapers supported the very controversial North American Free Trade Agreement in 1993. The only large paper Nichols could find that opposed NAFTA was the family-owned *Toledo Blade*, the 81st biggest daily in the country. In 2000, when Congress was debating another hotly contested trade deal, Permanent Normal Trade Relations with China, the media was similarly pro-"free trade." In the fall of 2002, when the Bush Administration was driving the country into war, the American press, apart from the consistently skeptical Knight Ridder Washington bureau (now part of the Mc-

Clatchy chain), was asleep at the wheel if not actively enabling the President's lies about Saddam's capacity for making nuclear, chemical, and biological weapons. On the editorial pages of the major papers, the position on invasion was for the most part either favorable or equivocal.

In a *Columbia Journalism Review* article published in the aftermath of the Iraq debacle, Chris Mooney analyzed editorial-page opinion about the then-imminent Iraq invasion in the *Washington Post, New York Times, Chicago Tribune, Los Angeles Times, USA Today,* and *Wall Street Journal.* "Many foreign papers," wrote Mooney, "viewed [Secretary of State Colin] Powell's [February 2003 United Nations] presentation more skeptically, but the endorsements from these six leading domestic editorial boards—four of which would ultimately support the war—strengthened Bush's hand considerably." Mooney chronicled some of the worst editorial-page judgment in the history of American journalism: "Irrefutable" was how the *Washington Post* described Powell's fraudulent testimony about the Iraqi dictator's weapons program. The *New York Times* said Powell "may not have produced a 'smoking gun,'" but his speech left "little question that Mr. Hussein had tried hard to conceal one." In fact, Saddam was concealing nothing of importance, but that didn't prevent the *Wall Street Journal* from insisting that Powell's statement was "persuasive to anyone who is still persuadable."

On the alleged alliance between Saddam and Osama bin Laden, also false, the *Wall Street Journal* was similarly sure of itself and its friends in the Executive Branch: "Saddam Hussein is probably too clever to get caught openly canoodling with Osama bin Laden, but the evidence . . . shows that they share the same evil purposes." The *Chicago Tribune* added that Powell's linking of Iraq and Al Qaeda "fleshed out evidence that Iraq harbors an active terrorist network linked to Al Qaeda." The right-wing *Journal* and conservative, pro-

Republican *Tribune* were not ideologically isolated in their views: the liberal *New Yorker* magazine and its correspondent Jeffrey Goldberg had already done as much as any other major publication to establish a connection between Saddam and bin Laden. And as of this writing, editorial-page diversity was shrinking more and more. In July 2007, the conservative press baron Rupert Murdoch's News Corporation purchased the *Journal*, but this was unlikely to make its right-wing editorial page any more balanced. Before the invasion of Iraq in March 2003, all 175 of Murdoch's News Corporation newspapers worldwide endorsed Bush's war plan.[4]

Even the Knight Ridder chain, which had benefited from exceptional reporting by three of its own journalists, John Walcott, Warren Strobel, and Jonathan Landay, that contradicted the administration propaganda on Saddam's "weapons of mass destruction," opted for equivocal language in its leading papers. On March 19, the day before the invasion began, the *San Jose Mercury News* editorialized with caution verging on optimism: "If the dice roll just right—if all of these things happen just as the White House is betting they will—then America may be able to emerge from this conflict with credibility intact and with a good base for rebuilding alliances." The *Miami Herald* was worse in its avoidance of drawing critical conclusions based on information from its own reporters. On the eve of the invasion, while insisting that the President's "case never fully convinced us," the *Herald* editorial page nevertheless encouraged its readers to accept Bush's claims: "This, admittedly, is a leap of faith. But we must take it because war is upon us now. We need to leave for later the sober, thoughtful evaluation of what led the world to this pass." Evidently inspired by deep loyalty to

---

4 *The New Yorker*, once a beacon of independent good sense and liberal opinion, has been owned since 1985 by the Newhouse family, which controls the largest privately held magazine and newspaper company in the United States, Advance Publications.

the commander-in-chief, the editorial writer went on: "We now must face what lies ahead—and on that count, we stand with the president and with our troops."

Meanwhile, the two most skeptical major editorial pages hedged their bets with the most equivocal sort of prose: "So the United States," wrote the *Los Angeles Times*, "apparently will go to war with few allies and in the face of great international opposition. This is an uncharted path . . . to an uncertain destination. We desperately hope to be wrong in our trepidation about the consequences here and abroad." The *New York Times*, claiming firmness of purpose, outdid itself in disingenuousness: "This page has never wavered in the belief that Mr. Hussein must be disarmed. Our problem is with the wrongheaded way this administration has gone about it."

But this is always the way American administrations have "gone about" marshaling popular and media support for war. In America, the customer isn't always right; nor is the advertiser always telling the truth.

S hort of outright insurrection, nothing tests a democracy's integrity—or that of an ambitious politician—more than war. Mass mobilization of soldiers and of public opinion conducts its own war against individual choice and self-government. Wartime hysteria, usually generated by government propaganda about foreign threats, discourages citizens from functioning as actors in their own political fates. In wartime political leaders and generals surge to the fore, cults of personality flourish, and public pressure for "patriotism" encourages people to follow rather than to think for themselves. In such an atmosphere, opposition to war by elected officials can invite harsh criticism and even ridicule from the war party, usually led by the president of the United States himself. An antiwar politician, especially one with his sights on the White House, risks ruining his political career if he doesn't give in to the prevailing national sentiment.

If we include the Cold War, it's fair to say that the United States has been almost continually at war—or at least on a war footing—since December 7, 1941, when the Japanese bombed Pearl Harbor. In those 66 years, the American republican system has been severely tested. During the Truman Administration and the communist witch-hunts of Senators Joseph McCarthy and Richard Nixon, the constitutional rights of free speech and the freedom of association, as well as the right not to have to be a witness against oneself, were curtailed in many ways, legally (through the imposition of loyalty oaths and the issuing of subpoenas to testify before hostile committees of Congress) as well as psychologically and economically (though blacklisting and public denunciation). Certainly, the 1950-53 Korean War, fought largely by the United States with United Nations approval against the "worldwide communist threat," contributed to the suppression of civil liberties in America and encouraged a climate of fear that harmed the nation's traditions of tolerance and freedom.

These well-documented affronts to constitutional liberty, however, are just one part of the politics of war in America. Not nearly enough has been written by historians and journalists about the uses of war in domestic politics, and the ways in which these politics distort and manipulate the democratic process itself. [1] For example,

---

1 One commentator who did understand the domestic political power of war was the newspaper publisher Joseph Pulitzer, who in the aftermath of the Spanish-American War criticized President William McKinley's military occupation of the Philippines. Writing in 1899 in the *North American Review*, Pulitzer noted that "We saw in the recent [1898] elections how 'loyalty to the flag' was made synonymous with loyalty to the President. No man in Congress, no ambitious politician anywhere, can oppose the President's policy without 'going against the party.' And to go against the party, whenever the President chooses to enter upon a war of 'criminal aggression' is, in the view of the party organs and orators, to commit treason."

Pulitzer advocated a constitutional amendment limiting the president to one six-year term to discourage the chief executive from making war with an eye toward re-election. "If this were done we should no longer see the President beginning on the very first day of his term to plan and work for a second term. We should not see our Presidents indulging in the menace of a foreign war to make capital for reelection, as President Harrison did in the Chili affair and President Cleveland did in the Venezuelan incident, or actually leading the country into a war of conquest and 'empire,' as Mr. McKinley has done in the Philippines."

President Harry Truman's hard-line anti-Soviet "Truman Doctrine" speech of March 12, 1947, can be said to have marked the formal launch of the Cold War in America, but it also directly affected the following year's election.[2] Besides facing a strong Republican opponent in Thomas E. Dewey, Truman had to fend off two challengers inside his own party, the segregationist Senator Strom Thurmond and the left-wing breakaway candidate, former Vice President Henry Wallace, who ran under the Soviet-friendly Progressive Party banner. Wallace was the greater threat to Truman, for he was a national figure who would have succeeded to the presidency in 1945 upon Roosevelt's death had FDR not replaced him with Truman on the ticket. Thus, Truman likely had more than just Soviet containment on his mind when he and his advisers crafted his bellicose foreign policy. Containment of a prominent Soviet-sympathizing political rival in a close race could not have been far from their thinking. As Edward Pessen recounted in his critical study of the Cold War, *Losing Our Souls*,

> In 1948 Progressive party members in Illinois were refused police protection despite being shot at, beaten, and victimized by stonings and kidnappings. In South Carolina, the murderer of what he called a "nigger-lover" from Henry Wallace's Progressive party was sentenced to all of three years in jail. The governor of Ohio, in refusing to act against a mob that ransacked the home of a Communist party leader, said that "no pattern had been established" and urged the victim to "go back to Russia."

Attacks on communists proved useful against Republicans and

---

2 Winston Churchill's "iron curtain" speech on March 5, 1946, in Fulton, Missouri, can be said to have marked the informal launch of the Cold War.

the staunchly anti-communist Thomas Dewey as well. Campaigning in Indiana, Truman claimed that "the Communists are doing everything in their power to beat me. They have taken over [Wallace's] Third Party and are using it in a vain attempt to split the Democratic Party. The Republicans have joined up with this Communist-inspired Third Party to beat the Democrats. . . . The Republicans financed the Third Party to get on the ballot right here in Indiana."

Intimidation of Wallace and his supporters had significant implications in states like boss-ruled Illinois, where, as the historian Zachary Karabell explains, Wallace was kept off the ballot "in a clever court maneuver" (Thurmond also did not appear on the Illinois ballot). Truman defeated Dewey in Illinois by a slim margin of 33,612 votes, and it's probable that Wallace, with his strong labor following, would have taken enough votes away from Truman to swing this crucial industrial state to Dewey. Whatever ultimately persuaded Truman to promote an aggressive anti-Soviet foreign policy, it is clear that Cold War rhetoric and anti-communist hysteria served him well in domestic electoral politics. As the historian Melvyn Leffler wrote: "Truman's anti-Communist rhetoric was marvelously effective. His political advisors were convinced that strong leadership and bold talk against the specter of Communism would redound to the president's political advantage and revive his chances for victory in the 1948 elections."

The red scare tactics of the Truman-McCarthy period have been thoroughly examined—and harshly criticized—by historians across a broad range of opinion, and by innumerable public figures, many of them staunch anti-communists. With the exception of right-wing apologists like William F. Buckley and Norman Podhoretz, most Americans realize that McCarthyism was a gross overreaction not only to the perceived Soviet threat but also to a very minor American political movement. McCarthyism, not Trumanism, is nowadays employed as an epithet to intimidate would-be intimidators. In retrospect, McCarthy seems more a symptom of a much larger political phenomenon than its cause. As bad as McCarthyism was for American democracy, its principal actor was only one United States Republican senator. Under pressure from the mainstream media, particularly CBS's Edward R. Murrow, and from his own party, which had begun investigating charges of corruption against him, McCarthy's influence declined rapidly and the junior senator from Wisconsin died in 1957, a broken man and a drunk.[3]

To understand what war—hot or cold—does to American democracy, an even more useful period to examine is the last three years of the administration of President Woodrow Wilson, from 1917 to 1920. Wilson's reputation today remains essentially positive, even glorious. This professor-turned-politician is remembered for the most part as a visionary who was martyred in the cause of world democracy and peace. A self-styled idealist who called World War I "a war to end all wars," Wilson claimed that America was fighting to make the world "safe for democracy," not for any crass political motives. For these reasons, millions of high school students have been taught more about Wilson's Fourteen Points and his failed crusade for American entry into the League of Nations than about George Washington's or Dwight Eisenhower's prescient, regrettably unheeded farewell addresses, which argued for restraint in foreign policy and against the dangers of a large, permanent military establishment.

---

3 McCarthy's downfall began when he accused the U.S. Army itself, in 1953, of covering up internal communist infiltration. The Army responded with its own charges: that McCarthy had sought preferential treatment for a former aide, an Army private. Even though President Dwight Eisenhower was a Republican, he ultimately refused to cooperate with McCarthy's investigation of the Army (the president invoked "executive privilege") and the subsequent "Army-McCarthy" hearings, broadcast on national television by ABC, exposed McCarthy to intense scrutiny and criticism. Although the Senate subcommittee cleared McCarthy of the corruption charges, his reputation took a beating from which it never recovered.

But the Woodrow Wilson of dramatic oration and lofty principles was also an intolerant demagogue whose repressive policies and personal ambition sullied his stated aspiration to save the world from war and corruption. Long before there was McCarthyism, there was Wilsonianism, with its own "red scare" tactics and assaults on civil liberties that may have made Joe McCarthy envious. Although he had always insisted he was trying to avoid war, as early as his December 7, 1915, State of the Union Address to Congress, Wilson was hinting at the war-fevered crackdown to come:

> The gravest threats against our national peace and safety have been uttered within our own borders. There are citizens of the United States, I blush to admit, born under other flags but welcomed under our generous naturalization laws to the full freedom and opportunity of America, who have poured the poison of disloyalty into the very arteries of our national life; who have sought to bring the authority and good name of our Government into contempt, to destroy our industries wherever they thought it effective for their vindictive purposes to strike at them, and to debase our politics to the uses of foreign intrigue. . . . A little while ago such a thing would have seemed incredible. Because it was incredible we made no preparation for it. We would have been almost ashamed to prepare for it, as if we were suspicious of ourselves, our own comrades and neighbors! But the ugly and incredible thing has actually come about and we are without adequate federal laws to deal with it. I urge you to enact such laws at the earliest possible moment and feel that in doing so I am urging you to do nothing less than save the honor and self-respect of the nation. Such creatures of passion, disloyalty, and anarchy must be crushed out.

What was incredible, and ugly, was the ferocity of Wilson's anti-democratic impulse. As Senator Daniel Patrick Moynihan wrote in his book *Secrecy*, Wilson's "plea . . . astonishes still, as much for its passion as for what it proposes. . . . No president had ever spoken like that before; none has since."

Wilson disingenuously campaigned for reelection in 1916 as a peace candidate; his slogan, "He kept us out of war," was a critical tactic in his very narrow victory over the Republican Charles Evans Hughes. But getting into World War I was uppermost in Wilson's mind. As historian Walter Karp wrote in *The Politics of War*, "As he [Wilson] once confided to his wife, he himself ached for the opportunity 'to impel [the people] to great political achievements,' achievements that, in Wilson's view, the ignoble masses were incapable even of desiring without strong leaders and strong governments to drive them."

Wilson got his way, and from his speech before a joint session of Congress on April 2, 1917, calling for a declaration of war against Germany, until October 2, 1919, the day he suffered a massive stroke while campaigning frantically for Senate ratification of the Treaty of Versailles, the great proponent of democracy engaged in the most anti-democratic domestic crusade in American history. Wilson's self-righteousness encouraged coercion, rather than persuasion, and he resorted to moral blackmail and brute force when faced with domestic political opposition, whether to his war plans or to his vision for postwar peace. For example, if the treaty and the League of Nations were not approved, there would result "in the vengeful Providence of God, another struggle in which, not a few hundred thousand fine men from America will have to die, but as many millions as are necessary to accomplish the final freedom of the peoples of the world." As the historian Anders Stephanson wrote, Wilson's messianic obsession with making the League into what Wilson called a "wholesale moral clearinghouse" meant that opponents of his vision were heretics:

An order or organization supposed to embody the absolute principles of Right, the universal interests of humankind, tends to render any opposition to it inhuman or criminal. Wars to eradicate deviance from Right dehumanize the enemy. It is partly against this background that one must see the extraordinary fury of domestic repression, public and private, legal and extralegal, that took place in the United States once the country had entered the war: loyalty programs, savagery against "hyphenated" Americans and perceived dissenters from the American way of life, even lynchings. Radical movements were destroyed. Criticism of the war became illegal, and numerous people were imprisoned. Neither the experience of the Second World War nor even of the McCarthyist 1950s compares to the repression of domestic dissent during World War I. Wilson himself sensed no contradiction here in his odes to democracy and the popular voice, just as he saw no contradiction in arguing for public diplomacy while conducting it completely by himself, and just as he saw no contradiction in denouncing "imperialism" and intervention in the affairs of other nations while sending armies into Mexico and revolutionary Russia.

Wilson did not just suppress free speech with the passage of the Espionage Act in 1917, and its more drastic amended version, the Espionage Act of 1918, sometimes known as the Sedition Act. To be sure, these draconian laws were intended to stifle dissent over the war—in its amended 1918 version, the Espionage Act made it illegal to do just about anything that was perceived as interfering with the war effort, and its language is astonishing in its blatant disregard for the Bill of Rights. Among other things, a person could be prosecuted if he or she were to "willfully utter, print, write, or publish any disloyal,

profane, scurrilous, or abusive language about the form of government of the United States, or the Constitution of the United States,
or the military or naval forces of the United States, or the flag . . .
or the uniform of the Army or Navy of the United States, or any
language intended to bring the form of government . . . or the Constitution . . . or the military or naval forces . . . or the flag . . . of the
United States into contempt, scorn, contumely, or disrepute." A socialist pamphleteer, Charles Schenck, fell victim to the new law for
advocating peaceful resistance to the military draft in the summer
of 1917 and was sentenced to 15 years in jail (though he served only
six months).[4]

---

4 Schenck's conviction was upheld unanimously by the Supreme Court in 1919 in
one of the worst blows to the First Amendment in U.S. history. Justice Oliver Wendell
Holmes Jr. wrote the opinion, employing the kind of specious logic that is so preva-
lent in wartime, and thereby illustrating a lack of political independence in what is
supposedly the nation's most disinterested and unpoliticized court: "The character of
every act depends upon the circumstances in which it is done. The most stringent
protection of free speech would not protect a man in falsely shouting fire in a theater
and causing a panic. . . . The question in every case is whether the words used are
used in such circumstances and are of such a nature as to create a clear and present
danger that they will bring about the substantive evils that Congress has a right to
prevent. It is a question of proximity and degree. When a nation is at war many things
that might be said in time of peace are such a hindrance to its effort that their utterance will not be endured so long as men fight and that no Court could regard them
as protected by any constitutional right." Schenck was merely general secretary of
the Philadelphia branch of the Socialist Party and hardly a danger to anyone but himself. As the constitutional lawyer Alan Dershowitz wrote, "The example of shouting
'Fire!' obviously bore little relationship to the facts of the Schenck case. The Schenck
pamphlet contained a substantive political message. It urged its draftee readers to
think about the message and then—if they so chose—to act on it in a lawful and
nonviolent way. The man who shouts 'Fire!' in a crowded theater is neither sending a
political message nor inviting his listener to think about what he has said and decide
what to do in a rational, calculated manner. On the contrary, the message is designed
to force action without contemplation. . . . The analogy is thus not only inapt but also
insulting. Most Americans do not respond to political rhetoric with the same kind of
automatic acceptance expected of schoolchildren responding to a fire drill."

But Wilson, the would-be messiah, also targeted political rivals, most prominently Eugene Debs, the leader of the Socialist Party of America, who had done remarkably well in his run for president against Wilson and four other candidates in 1912. The 900,000 votes won by Debs that year amounted to 6 percent of the popular vote, the highest percentage ever for a socialist in an era when socialist and other left-wing mayors were being elected in cities such as Milwaukee and Schenectady. Debs's subsequent opposition to Wilson's push for war placed him in political jeopardy, and it was only a matter of time before the weight of the law came down on him. After making an antiwar speech in Canton, Ohio, in June 1918, Debs was arrested and convicted under the 1917 Espionage Act. He served more than two years in the Atlanta Federal Penitentiary until President Warren Harding commuted his sentence on Christmas Day 1921.

Less well known today is the prosecution of Robert Goldstein, a film producer who at one time had been connected with D. W. Griffith. In 1917, Goldstein released a movie innocuously titled *The Spirit of '76*, though the response of the war-fevered government was anything but innocuous. As described by Zechariah Chafee Jr. the great legal scholar of the period, Goldstein's silent film was little more than a patriotic montage that celebrated the American Revolution. Goldstein made the movie before the war, and so he couldn't have anticipated that Wilson's violent attachment to his new British war ally would result in a jail sentence. Writing when the Espionage Act was still in force and the stroke-incapacitated Wilson still occupying the White House, Chafee himself was risking his career and possible prosecution when he published *Freedom of Speech* in 1920. This may account for the terseness of the following passage:

> [*The Spirit of '76*] contained such scenes as Patrick Henry's Speech, the Signing of the Declaration of Independence, and Valley Forge. After a year and

a half of work the picture was finished, just before
the outbreak of our war with Germany. The film was
displayed in Los Angeles to the usual audience, which
was not shown to contain either soldiers or sailors.
The government thereupon indicted Goldstein for
presenting a play designed and intended to arouse
antagonism, hatred, and enmity between the American
people, particularly the armed forces, and the people
of Great Britain, particularly their armed forces,
when Great Britain was "an ally" of the United States,
because one scene, the Wyoming [Valley, Pennsylvania]
Massacre, portrayed British soldiers bayoneting women
and children and carrying away girls. The film was
seized, the business was thrown from prosperity into
bankruptcy with a loss of over $100,000, and Goldstein
was convicted of attempting to cause insubordination,
etc., in the armed forces and sentenced to ten years in
the federal penitentiary at Steilacoom, Washington.

Chafee allowed himself a small joke when he remarked on the
"unfortunate" case name of *United States* v. *The Sprit of '76*, but this
was not a time for irony or joking, since political satire could very
well land you in jail during the Wilson Administration. The point
of Wilson's spear in his crusade against sedition was his Attorney
General, A. Mitchell Palmer, who often acted to halt subversion before it even occurred.[5] Using the Espionage Act and the Alien Act
of 1918 (which targeted foreign-born anarchists and revolutionaries
for deportation), Palmer's notorious campaign targeted thousands
of suspected communists and anarchists, who were supposedly slip-
ping into the United States from Europe and Russia intending to

---

5 Wilson had wanted to name Palmer his secretary of war, but Palmer declined
because of his Quaker pacifism.

foment revolution. The Palmer Raids, conducted by employees of the U.S. Department of Justice, began in earnest on November 7, 1919, the anniversary of the Bolshevik Revolution, and culminated in January 1920 with the arrest of more than 3,000 members of the Communist and Communist Labor parties. From the start, the government also grabbed innocent bystanders who happened not to speak English. In his history of American crackdowns on civil liberties, First-Amendment advocate Christopher Finan described one raid, on November 7, which targeted the Russian People's House in New York City's Union Square. Government agents arrested about 200 people, mostly students: "Approximately 75 percent of those arrested were guilty of nothing more than being in the wrong place at the wrong time, and many were quickly released." Outside New York, "others were not so lucky. Nearly 100 men were locked up in Hartford, Connecticut for almost five months" on suspicion of being communists. In all, the raids netted over 4,000 alleged communists, of whom 800 were deported, including the prominent radical Emma Goldman.

In the atmosphere of Wilsonian hysteria, not only were left-wing militants with foreign names arrested and deported; so, too, were legally elected representatives to Congress and state legislatures denied their seats. Victor L. Berger, a socialist elected to the Fifth District of Wisconsin in 1918, was excluded from Congress at the beginning of its new session in April 1919. Running a second time in a December 1919 Wisconsin special election against a fusion Democrat-Republican candidate, Berger won again. By now convicted under the Espionage Act for vocally opposing the war, Berger presented his credentials to the House once more, in January 1920, and was once again excluded, by a vote of 330-6. Three days before Berger was refused his seat, five socialists elected to the New York State Assembly were denied theirs as well, by a resounding 140-6 vote.

Although Wilson has been celebrated as a tragic visionary, it's not hard to find, even among his admirers, voices critical of his heavy-handed promotion of American entry into the League of Nations and his self-destructive refusal to accept Senator Henry Cabot Lodge's "reservations," which doomed the League. Godfrey Hodgson, a sympathetic biographer of Wilson's close friend and adviser, Col. Edward House, says, implausibly, that Wilson "hated war," but he is clear on what he views as Wilson's failings as a politician, in contrast with the wily tactician House: "Faced with opposition, Wilson's instinct was that anyone wicked enough to disagree with him must endorse his noble vision or face his messianic wrath." However, the portrait favored by admirers of the twenty-eighth president as an idealistic amateur among cynical professionals—particularly Clemenceau, Lloyd George, and Lodge—understates Wilson's ability to marshal popular support and his genuine tactical skills in day-to-day politics. Wilson may have been headstrong and "vainglorious," in Walter Karp's description, but he was no fool about building a political career and getting elected.

It is an enormous irony that Wilson came to prominence during the high-water mark of the Progressive Era, since this Virginia-born, Georgia-reared conservative was an out-and-out racist of the most conventional sort. The southerner Wilson presided over the segregation of the civil service and once said to a group of black protesters that "segregation is not a humiliation but a benefit, and ought to be so regarded by you gentlemen." Moreover, Wilson's stated adherence to the cause of Progressivism was at best opportunistic and at worst specious. Yet his anti-progressive, anti-populist instincts did not prevent him from succeeding in politics. As Karp wrote,

> As long as domestic affairs remained predominant,
> Wilson was on a collision course with the entire reform
> movement. . . . The solution to his problem Wilson had

arrived at long before he ever faced it, when he praised the domestic political advantages of the Republican "plunge into international politics [by way of the Spanish-American war]." If he could make another such plunge and "impel" the nation to "great national triumphs" abroad, he could not only avert failure but reap glory as well. As soon as he took office, therefore, Wilson began trying to persuade the American people that the true spirit of reform was to be expressed not at home, but in a new altruistic foreign policy, a policy, in Wilson's words, of "service to mankind."

Of course Wilson and Truman were not the only presidents to use war—or war-like belligerence—to advance their political ambitions. To be sure, there have been other presidents and politicians who have exploited war—or at least their war records—to personal advantage. Theodore Roosevelt, with his charge up San Juan Hill in Cuba during the Spanish-American War, and Lyndon Johnson, with his volunteer flight on a single combat mission in World War II, inflated their war service to great and exaggerated heights in order to increase their appeal as candidates.

Other politicians with even less distinguished war records, such as Richard Nixon, also understood the power of war, or the threat of war, in moving the electorate. The ambitious Nixon, running for the Senate in 1950 against Democratic Congresswoman Helen Gahagan Douglas (he called her the "pink lady"), needed to match the belligerence of President Truman's Democratic Party, which was already using the Cold War to great political advantage. Melvyn Leffler wrote,

In fact, many of [Truman's enemies] cared little about foreign policy, but they were eager to capitalize on anti-Communist impulses to achieve domestic goals or serve selfish interests, the most immediate of which was winning elections. Politicians like Richard M. Nixon initially found anti-Communism an irresistible tool to clobber political foes, win votes, discredit the New Deal, and attack the executive branch.

The persecutor of Alger Hiss would ultimately ride anti-Communism to the vice-presidency and then the Oval Office.

Even the great internationalist Wilson displayed scant interest in world-shaping foreign policy or war-making until he gained high national office. "Before his presidency," wrote Anders Stephanson, "Wilson had showed no signs of reforming zeal in foreign affairs.... A single memorandum, some scattered remarks, revealing nothing so much as a strong desire to be safely in the middle, an inkling that the experience of war had opened up possibilities for better national government at home: rather a meager sum total for a well-known scholar of political systems."

Besides James Polk, architect of the expansionist war against Mexico in 1846, perhaps no president has entered the White House with a less altruistic vision of foreign affairs or of war-making than George W. Bush. Having already avoided military service in Vietnam by using his father's influence to enter the Texas Air National Guard, Bush had no political interest in 2000 in promoting an ambitious foreign policy. To make matters worse, this candidly provincial son of a worldly father found himself frequently embarrassed by his lack of basic knowledge about foreign countries, famously failing in a 1999 television interview to name the leaders of India and Pakistan, countries that were just then facing off in a potential nuclear confrontation over Kashmir. Bush initially made a point of presenting himself as cautious and unlearned in foreign affairs, apart from his relations with Mexico as governor of Texas. In an April 2000 interview with PBS's Jim Lehrer, the then presidential candidate said, "I'm a fast learner, and listen, [but] I am not going to play like I've been a person who's spent hours involved with foreign policy. I am who I am." In his October 3, 2000, campaign debate with Vice President Al Gore, Bush portrayed himself as an anti-Wilsonian:

> I don't think we can be all things to all people in the world. I think we've got to be very careful when we commit our troops. The vice president and I have a disagreement about the use of troops. He believes in nation building. I would be very careful about using our troops as national builders. I believe the role of the military is to fight and win war and therefore prevent war from happening in the first place.

But, like Wilson, Bush quickly learned the uses of war for political gain. According to his fired campaign ghostwriter, Mickey Herskowitz, Bush was already thinking about the potential political benefits of war before he was elected. In an interview with the journalist Russ Baker published in October 2004, Herskowitz said:

> It [Iraq] was on his mind. He said to me: "One of the keys to being seen as a great leader is to be seen as a commander-in-chief." And he said, "My father had all this political capital built up when he drove the Iraqis out of Kuwait and he wasted it." He said, "If I have a chance to invade . . . if I had that much capital, I'm not going to waste it. I'm going to get everything passed that I want to get passed and I'm going to have a successful presidency."

Whatever his learning curve, after the terrorist attacks of September 11, 2001, Bush largely reinvented himself as the direct heir to Woodrow Wilson, minus some of the rhetoric about international cooperation. Like Wilson, Bush leaned heavily on the concept of "self-determination" to justify his "liberation" of the oppressed Iraqi people. Like Wilson, he seemed to be ignorant of the contradiction in his "vision." As Joseph Schumpeter observed: "To try to force the people to embrace something that is believed to be good and glorious but which they do not actually want—even though they may be expected to like it when they experience its results—is the very hall mark of anti-democratic belief." So complete has been the transformation of Bush from the parochial parody of a Texas "good ol' boy" to "nation builder" and crusader for democracy that by 2007, historians like Godfrey Hodgson could assert that the current Bush Administration "is unmistakably Wilsonian," that is, "the idea that it is the destiny of the United States to use its great power to spread American ideas of democracy and the American version of capitalism to the world." Bush himself invoked Wilson in a November 2003 speech in London eight months after the invasion of Iraq. With Queen Elizabeth II and all of British officialdom in attendance, the new slayer of dragons and dictators made pointed reference to his newfound Wilsonian heritage when he declared,

> The last President to stay at Buckingham Palace was an idealist, without question. At a dinner hosted by King George V, in 1918, Woodrow Wilson made a pledge; with typical American understatement, he vowed that right and justice would become the predominant and controlling force in the world. . . . At Wilson's high point of idealism, however, Europe was one short generation from Munich and Auschwitz and the Blitz. Looking back, we see the reasons why. The League of Nations, lacking both credibility and will, collapsed at

the first challenge of the dictators. Free nations failed to recognize, much less confront, the aggressive evil in plain sight. And so dictators went about their business.

Following Wilson, Bush has used his rhetoric of freedom to launch an aggressive assault on freedom in the United States—including the most important amendments in the Bill of Rights—in order to dampen dissent against the Iraq War as much as to fight terrorism. Bush may not be systematically arresting opposition leftists and deporting them, or silencing filmmakers, but police in New York during the Republican Convention of 2004 did make mass arrests of antiwar demonstrators on largely fraudulent, and utterly unconstitutional, grounds. Instead of the Espionage Act and mass deportation under the Alien Act, we have the USA PATRIOT Act (Uniting and Strengthening America by Providing Appropriate Tools Required to Intercept and Obstruct Terrorism Act of 2001), Homeland Security Act, secret prisons, and "rendition" of terrorist suspects to "third party" countries where they are interrogated without lawyers present and tortured. The "Bush Doctrine" justifying preemptive war evidently also justifies preemption of the Constitution.[6]

---

6 Perhaps President Bush's most spectacular flouting of the Constitution is his profligate use of so-called signing statements. Charlie Savage of the *Boston Globe* has chronicled the worst of these abuses, in which the President, according to Savage, asserts the "power to set aside any statute passed by Congress when it conflicts with his interpretation of the Constitution." Thus, when Congress, for example, sent Bush a bill banning torture in the interrogation of criminal suspects, Bush signed the law but declared, in a separate statement, that "the executive branch shall construe [the law] in a manner consistent with the constitutional authority of the President ... as Commander in Chief." He argued that the freedom to "construe" the law as he sees fit "will assist in achieving the shared objective of the Congress and the President ... of protecting the American people from further terrorist attacks." In all, notes Christopher Kelley, a political scientist at Miami University of Ohio, Bush has claimed the right to disobey at least 1,149 laws since taking office. According to the Constitution, the President is obliged to "take care that the laws be faithfully executed," so the unprecedented number of signing statements represents a systematic assault on the very concept of the separation of powers.

Like Truman with his loyalty oaths, Bush's war on civil liberties is only one piece of his politics of war. Along with his chief political strategist, Karl Rove, Bush immediately seized on the imagery of war—and of external threats—in his 2004 reelection campaign. On the crudest level, this involved repeated use of the "terrorist threat"—reminiscent of Wilson's bogeyman of foreign-born radicals—to frighten people into agreement with his war policy. On the more sophisticated level of media imagery, Bush and Rove frequently melded pictures of freedom and democracy with images of victory in war. The most famous of these staged photo events was Bush's landing on the deck of the aircraft carrier *USS Abraham Lincoln*, which was festooned with a banner that read "Mission Accomplished." The pictures said, in effect, "trust your courageous war leader," while the ship's name associated Bush with the great emancipator who had freed an enslaved people. No more would Saddam Hussein "go about his business" unchecked, tyrannizing a subject people.

Again and again in the 2004 campaign against the Democratic challenger John Kerry (an actual combat veteran of Vietnam), Bush emphasized his commitment to freedom and democracy, at the same time invoking the alleged dangers of changing presidents during a war. Vice President Dick Cheney made this threat explicit when he told an audience in Des Moines, Iowa, on September 7, 2004, "It's absolutely essential that eight weeks from today, on November 2nd, we make the right choice, because if we make the wrong choice then the danger is that we'll get hit again—that we'll be hit in a way that will be devastating from the standpoint of the United States, and that we'll fall back into the pre-9/11 mind-set, if you will, that in fact these terrorist attacks are just criminal acts and that we are not really at war." Bush repeatedly referred to himself as a "war president" and during the campaign often spoke on the campaign trail with uniformed soldiers as a background. In keeping with the theme of war leadership, *USA Today* made the Bush-Lincoln comparison without prompting, in an article datelined Gettysburg and head-lined "It's clearly a campaign for commander in chief":

> The issue [of whether it was wise to elect Kerry and change the commander in chief] reverberates in Gettysburg, site of the bloodiest battle of the Civil War. One wartime president, Abraham Lincoln, delivered a classic address here on the sacrifices and valor of soldiers.

The newspaper went so far as to quote Lincoln's plea to voters during his 1864 reelection campaign that "it is not best to swap horses while crossing the river." However preposterous was the analogy between the U.S. Civil War and the invasion of Iraq, or between Lincoln and Bush, the strategy worked. Whatever fraud may have occurred in Ohio, the state that decided the election, there is little doubt that Bush legitimately won the popular vote (by 3 million or so votes), and his slightly more than 62 million votes were the most cast for a presidential candidate in history.

The ironies of Bush's successful use of Lincoln for political gain are manifold and disturbing. As the historian Eric Foner wrote in *The Nation* magazine, "Like Bush, Lincoln spoke of the United States as a beacon of liberty, an example to the world of the virtues of democracy. But he rejected the idea of American aggression in the name of freedom." Moreover, Lincoln, rather than exploit war to his political advantage, nearly destroyed his political career by opposing President James Polk's war against Mexico.

Polk was a Democratic Party functionary whom John Quincy Adams considered "just qualified for an eminent County Court lawyer." But this unimaginative technician, much like Bush, nonetheless understood how to put war to work in the cause of his political ambition. "He was not a man of nuance," wrote Anders Stephanson.

"But he knew what he wanted and accomplished it completely. One of the things he wanted most was territorial expansion, at which he was an astonishing success." But Polk had to get elected first. "Following his party's platform, [Polk] made Texas 'reannexation' an issue in his [1844] presidential election campaign, claiming with little justification that Texas had been a part of the Louisiana Purchase and had been shamefully given up in 1819 by Adams (then Secretary of State) in the treaty with Spain." Once in the White House, and with Texas joining the union in 1845, "Polk was to use this commanding [executive] power to push the country into war with Mexico and nearly with Britain as well." Ultimately, Polk provoked the war with Mexico by marching U.S. troops through Texas to Point Isabel at the mouth of the Rio Grande, not far from Matamoros, Mexico, allegedly to help settle the location of the new, and disputed, international border between the two countries. In doing so, the U.S. army, under the command of General Zachary Taylor, had entered territory claimed by Mexico; as Colonel Ethan Allan Hitchcock wrote in his diary, "It looks as if the government sent a small force on purpose to bring on a war, so as to have a pretext for taking California and as much of this country as it chooses." Eventually, the Mexicans, claiming U.S. aggression, sent troops across the river, and on April 25, 1846, they clashed with American soldiers.

On May 3, the Mexican army shelled Fort Taylor (near what is now Brownsville, Texas), Polk claimed that the United States had been invaded, and Congress declared war on May 13. By the time a peace treaty was signed in February 1848, U.S. territory had vastly increased and Polk had acquired an enduring reputation of boldness and vision (though he did not seek reelection and died three months after his term in office ended). Like Bush, Polk dressed up his land grab in grandiose slogans such as "manifest destiny," but this Tennessee slave-owner sought land and political gain above all else. Lincoln, by contrast, for the most part responded to the Mexican war by doing precisely what was not politically expedient. His Whig Party, a minority in both houses at the start of the war, had initially opposed Polk because they feared the potential extension of slavery into land taken from Mexico. But, like many of the Democrats who voted for the Iraq War resolution in October 2002, the Whigs lost their nerve when faced with the popular war fever stoked by Polk. In all, only 14 Whig members of the House, and two in the Senate, voted against the declaration of war.

Lincoln's party became more aggressive toward Polk when it gained the majority in the House in the August 1846 elections, but it never tried to stop the war. That year, Lincoln was elected to Congress from the Seventh District of Illinois, and during the campaign he spoke pragmatically—his "only utterance on the subject," according to the historian David Herbert Donald—at a pro-war rally in his district. As Lincoln biographer Stephen Oates wrote, "In private . . . Lincoln may have had misgivings about the war and Polk's defense of it. But caught in the middle of a campaign in superpatriotic Illinois, with the war spirit flaming across the Seventh Congressional District, he held his tongue about whatever doubts he had and drifted with the winds of popular opinion."

So it was all the more remarkable, and principled, for Lincoln, as a freshman congressman, to denounce a popular and victorious war nearing its end, as he did on December 22, 1847, and again on January 12, 1848. At the beginning of the 30th Congress (the session convened in December 1847, more than a year after the 1846 election), Polk had requested more money to finish the war, and brazenly (very much in the manner of Bush's insistent connecting of Saddam Hussein with Al Qaeda) reiterated his spurious claim that Mexico had provoked the conflict by invading Texas and "shedding the blood of our citizens on our own soil." The Whigs struck back with Lincoln as one of their principal spokesmen. His first salvo was to introduce eight resolutions demanding that Polk present to the House "all the facts which go to establish whether the particular spot of soil on which the blood of our *citizens* was so shed, was, or was not, *our own soil.*" As the historian Bernard DeVoto wrote, Lincoln's second oration, three weeks later, gave

> the President what-for. It was quite a speech, and—with the rest of his war record—it retired Lincoln to private life. . . . He was gratuitously offending the Seventh District [of Illinois], which by then had lost some sons in war, and he might have been content to stand on his party's record. For nine days before, on January 3, 1848, by a strict party vote and a majority of one, the House of Representatives had adopted another resolution, by George Ashmun of Massachusetts, which formally decided that war had been "unnecessarily and unconstitutionally begun by the President of the United States."

Historians differ on exactly why Lincoln came out against the Mexican war so vociferously at so late a stage. Writes the Oxford historian Richard Carwardine,

> No doubt part of Lincoln's purpose here was to impress his congressional colleagues. No doubt it was also, with the presidential election of 1848 on the horizon, to secure an advantage for his party (with the bloodiest fighting now over, Whigs would be less vulnerable to accusations of disloyalty). But Lincoln's earnestness, even biblical fervor, in pressing the charges sprang, too, from a determination to expose what he privately described as "a foul, villainous, and bloody falsehood." It sprang from his conscientious objection to unprovoked aggression against a feeble neighbor for territorial gain.

Though he pragmatically accepted the Mexican cession, he continued to stress that Whigs, the champions of intensive cultivation of the social order, "did not believe in enlarging our field, but in keeping our fences where they are and cultivating our present possession, making it a garden, improving the morals and education of the people, devoting the administration to this purpose."

As Lincoln later wrote to his law partner, "Allow the President to invade a neighboring nation, whenever *he* shall deem it necessary to repel an invasion, . . . and you allow him to make war at pleasure," which would place "our President where kings have always stood."

Lincoln's January 12 speech rings out with eloquence and outrage of a sort that has nearly disappeared from public life in America. President Polk, he charged, was

> deeply conscious of being in the wrong; that he feels the blood of this war, like the blood of Abel, is crying to Heaven against him; . . . that originally having some strong motive . . . to involve the two countries in a war, and trusting to escape scrutiny by fixing the public gaze upon the exceeding brightness of military glory—that attractive rainbow that rises in showers of blood—that serpent's eye that charms to destroy—he plunged into it, and has swept *on* and *on* till, disappointed in his calculation of the ease with which Mexico might be subdued, he now finds himself he knows not where. How like the half insane mumbling of a fever dream, is the whole war part of his late message!

Proud of his powerful speech, Lincoln found himself not only ignored by Polk but also largely abandoned by his party, which, content with the Ashmun resolution, did nothing to press for adoption of Lincoln's resolutions. "For some reason," Oates wrote, "not a single Whig rose to defend him" after "prowar Democrats from the South . . ." replied "in condescending verbal salvos." By prior agreement with home-state Whig rivals, Lincoln was not supposed to stand for reelection from his district, but he very much wanted to be asked. In this hope he was disappointed. "Condemnation from Democrats was to be expected," wrote Donald, "but Lincoln was troubled by the faintness of praise he received from fellow Whigs." Privately, the criticism from prominent Illinois Whigs was considerable—they, too, recognized the vote-getting power of war—and no reelect-Lincoln movement materialized.

Eschewing bitterness, Lincoln nevertheless campaigned hard for the presidential nomination and eventual election in 1848 of General Zachary Taylor, hero of the Mexican war. But his efforts on behalf of his party again went unrewarded. After President Taylor took office in 1849, Lincoln tried hard to get appointed to the powerful and well-paid post of commissioner of the General Land Office, but his attacks on the war came back to hurt him. Lincoln's Whig rival for the job, Justin Butterfield, had not supported Taylor's candidacy, but he hadn't publicly opposed the war against Mexico. Taylor's Secretary of the Interior Thomas Ewing already favored Butterfield, but anti-Lincoln lobbying from important Illinois Whigs made up the secretary's mind. This campaign, according to Donald, included "a letter declaring that Lincoln's stand on the Mexican war had rendered him 'very unpopular, and inflicted a deep and mischievous wound upon the Whole Whig party of the State.'" Lincoln did not return to electoral politics until his unsuccessful campaign for Senate in 1858 against Stephen A. Douglas.

The parallels with today's politics of war are unmistakable. In his January 12 speech, Lincoln criticized Polk's war policy as "wandering and indefinite."

First, it is to be done by a more vigorous prosecution of the war in the vital parts of the enemy's country; and, after apparently talking himself tired on this point ... then he suggests the propriety of wheedling the Mexican people to desert the counsels of their own leaders, and, trusting in our protection, to set up a Government from which we can secure a satisfactory peace, telling us that *"this may become the only mode of obtaining such a peace."* But soon he falls into doubt of this too, and then drops back on to the already half-abandoned ground of "more vigorous prosecution." All this shows that the President is in no wise satisfied with his own positions. First, he takes up one, and, in attempting to argue us *into* it, he argues himself *out* of it; then seizes another, and goes through the same process; and then, confused at being able to think of nothing new, he snatches up the old one again, which he has some time before cast off. His mind, tasked beyond its power, is running hither and thither, like some tortured creature on a burning surface, finding no position on which it can settle down and be at ease.

Besides its uncannily apt description of George W. Bush and his Iraq policy, Lincoln's language gives the lie to any favorable comparison between himself and the current president. As this most unpopular and falsely predicated war drags on to its indefinite conclusion, Bush wanders "hither and thither" while the "opposition" Democrats dither and the blood continues to flow. The great difference is that there is no Lincoln on the horizon to save us—and no new political party with the power to restore democratic sovereignty to the people.

After Hillary Clinton surprised pollsters and analysts by narrowly beating Barack Obama to win the 2008 New Hampshire Democratic primary, *Time* magazine proclaimed on its cover, "It's the Voters, Stupid." *Time*'s thesis, elucidated in the article's subtitle, appeared to be that ordinary American citizens remained the masters of their own political fate: "Forget the experts. Forget the polls. Forget the TV ads. How the American people defied the odds, upended expectations and gave us a real race."

There was considerable irony in *Time*'s citing of a Clinton primary victory as evidence of democratic vitality. To date, Hillary Clinton's political career has been conspicuous less for its popular appeal than for its intimate connection to the Democratic Party leadership (in particular, her husband, Bill, the former president and the party's one-time champion fund-raiser) and powerful business interests (Wal-Mart and Wall Street). Rather than representing "the voters' revenge," as *Time* asserted, Hillary Clinton's victory in New Hampshire was revenge by the Clintons against an ambitious young troublemaker of half-African parentage who had shocked his party's leadership by daring to challenge her and then win in Iowa two weeks earlier.

What *Time* (and so many of the pollsters) seemed to ignore was the enduring power of the party system in America—that intricate network of elected officials, civil servants, patronage workers, and donors with business ties to the government who work in concert at election time to maintain their jobs and their power. It also glossed over the enduring power of money in American political campaigns. For more than fifteen years as leaders of the Democratic Party, the Clintons not only had raised a great deal of money but had done a great many favors for a great many people. In turn, such grateful clients of political patrons are usually more than willing to solicit campaign contributions on behalf of their benefactors; on Election Day they're eager to turn out the vote for their sponsors' friends and allies. As a freshman senator from Illinois (where he hadn't lived until adulthood), even with the support of the powerful Daley family machine, Obama could not expect, at least in the early stages of the campaign, to call in political debts in the quantities necessary to match the debts owed the Clintons.[1]

But Obama was was no amateur when it came to competing with the Clintons for organized financial support in the upper reaches of American society; his most audacious maneuver was to tap deeply

1 In New Hampshire, Hillary could rely on the former governor and current Democratic Senate candidate Jeanne Shaheen, and her husband, Bill, a veteran party powerbroker who had chaired Al Gore's presidential campaign in the state and co-chaired the 2008 Clinton campaign there and nationally. (Bill Shaheen was forced to resign his campaign post a month before the primary after he made comments to the press playing up Obama's youthful drug use as a potential liability during a general election.) On primary day, the Shaheens, "the closest thing to [New Hampshire] political royalty," according to the *Boston Globe*, went all out for Hillary. Somehow, 300 drivers were recruited to transport elderly voters to their polling places around the state, part of an effort that helped put Clinton over the top. Obama, despite all the money he had already raised, was still, at this point, largely reliant on television advertising and the goodwill of his supporters.

into Hillary Clinton's base of banks, corporations, and Washington lobbying firms. By the end of January 2008, Obama had actually raised more money than his rival—who was, at the outset, favored by most party officials and the Wall Street establishment—by $137 million to $117 million (at the end of April, he had increased his total primary receipts to $257 million compared with Clinton's $191 million).[2] To compete with the Clintons, Obama needed to create his own fund-raising machine, and he went right to work upon entering the Senate in 2005. As journalist Ken Silverstein wrote in *Harper's Magazine* in November 2006, before Obama declared his candidacy for president, the freshman senator from Illinois

> quickly established a political machine funded and
> run by a standard Beltway group of lobbyists, P.R.
> consultants, and hangers-on. For the staff post of
> policy director he hired Karen Kornbluh, a senior aide
> to Robert Rubin [now director and chairman of the
> Executive Committee of Citigroup, America's largest
> commercial bank], when the latter, as head of the
> Treasury Department under Bill Clinton, was a chief
> advocate for NAFTA and other free-trade policies
> that decimated the nation's manufacturing sector (and
> the organized labor wing of the Democratic Party).
> Obama's top contributors are corporate law and
> lobbying firms (Kirkland & Ellis and Skadden, Arps,
> where four attorneys are fund-raisers for Obama as
> well as donors), Wall Street financial houses (Goldman
> Sachs and JPMorgan Chase), and big Chicago
> interests (Henry Crown and Company, an investment

---

2 The huge sums raised by Clinton and Obama in their primary duel guaranteed that the 2008 presidential campaign would be the most expensive in history.

firm that has stakes in industries ranging from telecommunications to defense [including General Dynamics]).

As a result of his early courting of the U.S. financial and corporate establishment, Obama could boast of a growing campaign war chest with the potential to match Clinton's when he officially announced his candidacy in February 2007. His early victory in Iowa stunned the Clinton campaign, but it shouldn't have, given the money and effort he expended to win. To be sure, Obama's stated opposition to the Iraq invasion, his superior campaigning skills, and his attractive smile and incessant calls for "change" elicited genuine popular support. But the money didn't hurt.

By February 5, 2008, so-called Super Tuesday, the Clintons were back in the running, but they were clearly losing altitude. A big loss on January 26 in South Carolina, where Obama enjoyed overwhelming black support, proved a significant setback for the former first lady and her consort, as well as for the neo-populist former senator and vice-presidential candidate, John Edwards, who left the race after finishing third in his home state. Next, Hillary prevailed in symbolically important Florida on January 29 by a wide margin, though she won no delegates there.[3] One on one with Obama on Super Tuesday, Mrs. Clinton prevailed in most of the biggest states with the most delegates—California, New York, New Jersey, Massachusetts, and Tennessee—while Obama won his home state of

---

3 Florida and Michigan were stripped of their delegates by the Democratic National Committee for moving their primaries ahead of Super Tuesday against the wishes of the national party leadership. The major candidates agreed not to campaign in the two states, but that didn't stop Clinton from keeping her name on the ballot in Michigan—where Edwards and Obama stayed off—and celebrating her popular-vote victory in person in Florida, where all three major candidates' names appeared on the ballot. Clinton argued that the Michigan and Florida delegates should be seated at the convention.

Illinois, Georgia, Minnesota, and barely carried a popular majority in Missouri, where the two candidates split 72 delegates. Other less populated states went for Obama, in party caucuses and popular votes, giving Obama an estimated 842 delegates to Clinton's 828. But the built-in, party-sponsored advantages of the Clintons were still significant.

Along with the perquisites garnered from eight years in the White House—big lecture fees and lucrative book contracts for Bill and a safe Senate seat for Hillary—came the grave responsibility of maintaining the flow of campaign cash to the national Democratic Party. While Bill officiated at countless party fund-raisers, Hillary established her own leadership political action committee, "Hill PAC"—a collection basket for redistribution to fellow Democrats and for promotion of party interests—when she entered the Senate in 2001. During her first six-year term as senator, Hill PAC collected nearly $9 million, of which $1.5 million went to Democratic candidates for federal office, including the "independent" Connecticut Senator Joe Lieberman. These contributions took on greater significance in light of the competition between Clinton and Obama for the votes of 849 so-called superdelegates (794 if Michigan and Florida were not permitted to have their delegates seated at the convention)—delegates to the national convention who were neither elected in primaries nor chosen by party caucuses open to the public.[4]

---

4 According to the political scientist Rhodes Cook, superdelegates were created by the Democratic Party after the 1980 campaign as a "firewall to blunt any party outsider [who] built up a head of steam in the primaries"—largely in response to Jimmy Carter's successful insurgency in 1976. As such, this was a partial return to the pre-1972 McGovern era, when far fewer delegates were selected by popular vote and state party bosses chose a majority of the total delegates who went to the convention. The figure of 849 superdelegates could change at any time; New York, for example, suffered a net loss of one superdelegate when Governor Eliot Spitzer resigned over a sex scandal in March 2008.

The Democratic superdelegates consist mostly of elected officials—governors, U.S. senators (including Hillary Clinton and Barack Obama themselves), and U.S. representatives—but also such party grandees as Bill Clinton and veteran campaign strategist Donna Brazile, and moneymen such as Terry McAuliffe, Bill Clinton's ace fund-raiser and the former chairman of the Democratic National Committee. Two critically important superdelegates enjoyed dual roles as elected officials *and* moneymen—the long-time Clinton loyalists Senator Charles Schumer of New York, chairman of the Democratic Senatorial Campaign Committee, and U.S. Representative Rahm Emanuel, the former chairman of the Democratic Congressional Campaign Committee and current chairman of the House Democratic Caucus. In the excruciatingly close Obama-Clinton duel, the superdelegates would likely hold the balance of power in choosing the party's nominee, especially if the campaign were to drag on to the party convention in Denver in late August. Although technically unpledged and able to switch their vote at any time, many superdelegates declared their support for candidates early in the primaries. By Super Tuesday, Hillary Clinton had already gathered the backing of about 200 superdelegates compared with Obama's estimated 110, an unsurprising figure given her senior party status. Therefore in a process similar to how the Electoral College works, a Democratic Party candidate could get the most popular votes in the primaries and still lose the nomination.

As former Senator Gary Hart explained to journalist Ari Berman, "Many of the superdelegates were in and out of the Clinton White House, invited to dinners, [and] have received contributions from Clinton allies." Hart, whose own insurgent candidacy for president in 1984 was opposed by the Democratic Party establishment, noted with some understatement that "there will be pressure brought to bear to cash in those chips."

Even before the rise of Barack Obama, Hillary Clinton was courting future superdelegates with cash. Since she took office in 2001, Hill PAC has given $887,000 to 121 superdelegates who would vote on the eventual presidential nominee at the 2008 convention. Barack Obama, however, was a quick study, and he tried hard to match Clinton with the political action committee he founded in 2005, called Hopefund. Despite Hillary's four-year head start in the Senate, he was able to give $715,000 to 107 superdelegates. Most superdelegates received contributions from Clinton and Obama in the range of $5,000 to the maximum legal donation of $10,000 per election cycle. To be sure, popular votes cast by ordinary people still mattered greatly to the candidates, since these voters would elect the majority of delegates. But in Democratic Party politics, to borrow from George Orwell, some voters are more equal than others—with superdelegates the most equal of all.[5]

Beyond the superdelegates, Hill PAC and Hopefund maintained an important interest in the general welfare of their party. As of Super Tuesday, Clinton's organization had given $493,000 to Democratic Party campaign committees through the 2006 midterm election, but none thereafter. Hopefund spread $265,000 over the 2006 and 2008 campaign cycles, with $120,000 going entirely to local and state party committees in Iowa and New Hampshire for the 2008 campaign. Hopefund also gave separate donations to 13 candidates for state office in New Hampshire and another early pri-

---

5 In such a topsy-turvy world, a Clinton loyalist and Democratic National Committee member from Washington, D.C., Harold Ickes Jr., could argue without irony that superdelegates actually deserved their "automatic" appointed status because "they do have a sense of what it takes to get elected," and "they are closely in touch with the issues and ideas of the jurisdiction they represent and they are as much or more in touch than delegates won or recruited by presidential campaigns." Certainly they were more in touch with the ideas and issues that concerned Hillary Clinton and the party leadership.

mary state, South Carolina, usually in the range of $1,000 each. The beneficiaries of Obama's patronage included John Shea and Beverly Hollingsworth, two candidates for New Hampshire's Executive Council, a kind of super-cabinet that advises and checks the governor. Thus, contributors to Hopefund who thought they were aiding the national party might have been surprised to learn that they were also helping Obama recruit potential allies in three critical primary contests. According to Scott E. Thomas, the former chairman of the Federal Election Commission, [Obama] was "clearly pushing the envelope [of legality], no doubt. I would clearly recommend the commission take another look at this to see if there is some reasonable line that can be drawn so presidential campaigns aren't directing donations from the PAC a few months before the primaries."

Obama's tactics worked. Neck and neck with the Clintons among the wealthy and corporately connected, his 11 straight primary victories following Super Tuesday proved his vote-getting prowess as well as his fund-raising acumen. When the Clinton campaign began to run short of money, and Hillary was forced in January 2008 to lend it $5 million from her personal funds, Obama still hadn't reached his full fund-raising potential. Having borrowed from Howard Dean's 2004 Internet expertise to raise large amounts of money in small contributions, Obama was better positioned than Clinton for a drawn-out primary battle. In January alone, he raised $28 million from the Internet, 90 percent of which came from contributions of $100 or less each. Through the end of January 2008, 47 percent of the total dollar amount Clinton raised from individuals came from people giving the maximum of $2,300, compared with only 29 percent of Obama's total. During the same period, just 20 percent of Clinton's total came from individuals who gave $500 or less, compared with 42 percent of Obama's. According to Michael J. Malbin, executive director of The Campaign Finance Institute, Obama had three times as many small donors, giving $200 or less, as Clinton. Hillary was now becoming hampered by what was once considered one of her greatest strengths. Having already given the maximum, Hillary's wealthier contributors could not be solicited again during the primary campaign. Obama, on the other hand, could go back to his devoted $100 contributors and ask for another small donation, or even two or three.

Obama's prowess in soliciting small contributions forced Clinton to follow suit: beginning the week of Super Tuesday, she appealed more aggressively to her supporters to donate through her website. In February, Clinton had dramatically increased the amount of money coming from donors contributing $200 or less to more than $17 million, up from $4.5 million in January. Obama's February total from small donors, $30.5 million, still dwarfed Clinton's.[6] However, these staggering small-donor figures were somewhat misleading. Obama's success was fueled by a marriage of traditional big-money fund-raising with Dean's more populist tactics. Even with all the small sums coming into the two campaigns, both Clinton and Obama were pseudo-populists compared with Dean. During the 2004 Democratic primary season, 60 percent of the total money Dean raised came from individuals giving $200 or less; only 8 percent came from those donating the maximum (then $2,000). Through February 2008, Obama's comparable proportions were 41 percent from small donors and 23 percent from individuals giving the maximum; Clinton's were 26 percent and 38 percent.

But money isn't everything in American politics, any more than votes are. Clinton fought back to win the popular votes in the Ohio,

---

6 Through the end of April, Obama had raised $120.9 million from those contributing $200 or less, for 47 percent of his total collected, compared with Clinton's $56.4 million from small donors, for 33 percent of her total. According to Michael Malbin's rough estimate, Obama's campaign had more than twice as many small donors as the Clinton campaign. Assuming an average of $75 per contribution, Obama would have 1.6 million small donors compared with 750,000 for Clinton.

Texas, and Rhode Island primaries on March 4, in part thanks to her status as a party elder. Loyal Democrats, especially older, less educated, working-class whites and Latinos, tended to vote for the more established candidate, Clinton; whereas blacks, better educated whites, and students tended to support Obama in greater numbers. This was paradoxical, since President Clinton's trade policy with Mexico, Canada, and China had cost so many blue-collar Americans their jobs. Although the candidates' generally pro-free-trade positions were essentially the same, Obama exploited the issue in industrialized and heavily unionized Ohio by highlighting Mrs. Clinton's support for NAFTA, her husband's first big legislative initiative as president and an enduring symbol of the Clintons' disregard for factory workers. But Hillary Clinton was able to turn the tables on Obama when a Canadian government memo surfaced showing that one of Obama's economic advisers, University of Chicago economist Austan Goolsbee, had told a Canadian official not to take Obama's criticism of NAFTA too seriously—that it was "more about political positioning than a clear articulation of policy plans." Obama's denial and then his awkward admission that the meeting did occur put him on the defensive. For the first time in the campaign, Clinton was able to characterize her opponent as dishonest, though her own newfound distaste for NAFTA was at least as dishonest, and cynical, as Obama's fairly mild critique. Indeed, the same Canadian news story that revealed Obama's hypocrisy on NAFTA also cited sources saying that representatives from the Clinton campaign had given similar reassurances to the Canadian government not to take her statements about NAFTA at face value.

Meanwhile, Clinton's harsher, more negative advertising took a toll. And the corruption trial of a Chicago businessman and Obama supporter, Antoin "Tony" Rezko (who had once helped Obama buy his home and expand his lot by purchasing an adjacent property), tarnished the fresh-faced, above-the-fray innocence of the newcomer from Illinois. On March 10 the delegate count was, according to CBS News, 1,570 for Obama, 1,461 for Clinton, with declared superdelegates still favoring Clinton by 44. But Clinton and the machine politicians who supported her were emboldened by her three simultaneous primary victories, even though they didn't significantly reduce Obama's delegate lead. On the night of the Ohio and Texas primaries, Pennsylvania Governor Ed Rendell, the state's Democratic leader and a "Hillraiser" (a fund-raiser who has collected at least $100,000 for Hillary Clinton), was grinning ear to ear during his interview with Chris Matthews of MSNBC, exuding confidence in a candidate only recently said to be on the verge of defeat. Anticipating the three major Clinton victories that evening, Rendell proposed a scenario in which the former first lady would win the April 22 primary in Pennsylvania, as well as the possible reruns of the Florida and Michigan primaries in June: "I think if she does all that, she'll probably be less than a percentage point behind in delegates. And then the superdelegates do have a role. We always have a role. And I think we should have a role, and that is to determine who, going into the convention, is our strongest candidate for the fall. . . . I think, right now, Hillary Clinton's the best standard-bearer for the states that we have to carry in the fall."[7] With exquisite condescension, Rendell undermined a key rationale for nominating Obama; namely, his broad national appeal, including in states

---

7 Democratic National Committee Chairman Howard Dean had given state party officials two options that might permit reinstatement of the Michigan and Florida delegations: one was to appeal to the party's rules committee; the second was for the state parties to submit plans for holding new primaries in June. Since attempts to hold new primaries failed, the rules committee met on May 31 to decide the fates of the two state delegations. This was important not only for delegate-counting purposes but because of Clinton's insistence that she led in the overall popular vote, if Florida and Michigan were counted. The Clinton campaign consistently failed to note that her popular vote totals would have been different if Obama's name had been on the ballot in Michigan and if he had enjoyed the opportunity to campaign in Florida.

previously conceded to the Republicans. "We've got to nominate the candidate who can win the blue states and the purple states. Barack Obama's a great candidate, but he's not winning Wyoming [in the general election]. He's not winning Utah. He's not winning Idaho."

Rendell was too smart to play the role of party boss on national television. When Matthews asked him if he planned to pressure U.S. Representative Bob Brady (Philadelphia party chairman and a superdelegate) to endorse Clinton, Rendell (a superdelegate as well and the former mayor of Philadelphia) demurred: "No, I wouldn't do that . . . because we've got to respect our African-American ward leaders." Ironically, Rendell had been criticized for allegedly disrespecting Pennsylvania African Americans. In an interview with the editorial board of the *Pittsburgh Post-Gazette* in February 2008, he said: "You've got conservative whites here . . . who are not ready to vote for an African American candidate. I believe, looking at the returns in my election, that had Lynn Swann been the identical candidate that he was—well-spoken, charismatic, good-looking but white instead of black—that instead of winning by 22 points, I would have won by 17 or so." Clinton carried Pennsylvania by a comfortable margin, 55 to 45 percent, not the blowout that Rendell might have hoped for but enough to implant the issue of race, so adroitly papered over by Obama during most of the campaign.

And the Clintons made the most of it. Before Pennsylvania, when the cable news networks had begun playing excerpts of sermons by Obama's fiery longtime black pastor, Rev. Jeremiah Wright, Obama was put on the defensive. His thoughtful and widely praised speech disavowing Wright's most inflammatory rhetoric, as well as his ultimate break with Wright, did much to control the damage. But the seed was sown in the minds of many voters that Obama was the sectarian candidate of "black" voters, and even the unwitting ally of the Nation of Islam leader Rev. Louis Farrakhan. Pundits might scold the Clintons for race-baiting, but the former first couple could sit back and let guilt by association take its toll. Every time CNN showed Wright saying that the September 11 attacks were "America's chickens . . . coming home to roost" (borrowing a phrase the Black Muslim radical Malcolm X used in response to the assassination of President Kennedy), another nervous white voter questioned Obama's background.[8] Every time they played the following segment of Wright angrily contrasting Obama's supposedly more difficult upbringing with Clinton's more privileged one, a white woman somewhere was very likely offended:

> Hillary never had a cab whiz past her and not pick her
> up because her skin was the wrong color. Hillary never
> had to worry about being pulled over in her car as a black
> man driving in the wrong [neighborhood]. I am sick of
> Negroes who just don't get it. Hillary was not a black
> boy raised in a single-parent home—Barack was. Barack
> knows what it means to be a black man living in a country
> and a culture that is controlled by rich white people.
> Hillary can never know that. Hillary ain't never been

---

8 The news reports and video excerpts of Wright's "America's chickens" comment consistently failed to include how he prefaced his use of the phrase in front of his mostly black parishioners at Chicago's Trinity United Church of Christ. "I heard Ambassador Peck on an interview yesterday," Wright said in his sermon, referring to Edward Peck—President Carter's ambassador to Iraq and deputy director of the White House Task Force on Terrorism in the Reagan Administration. "He was on Fox News. This is a white man and he was upsetting the Fox News commentators to no end. He pointed out, a white man, an ambassador, that what Malcolm X said when he got silenced by Elijah Muhammad was in fact true: America's chickens are coming home to roost." Wright might have been paraphrasing Peck who, in two separate interviews on Fox October 10 and 11, did not employ Malcolm X's celebrated declaration. Rather, Peck laid out some of the reasons (the death of children caused by the American economic embargo against Iraq, for example) that might have given Osama bin Laden and Saddam Hussein a motive to harm the United States. Peck was clear, however, that he doubted any complicity by Saddam in the attacks on the World Trade Center.

called a nigger. Hillary has never had her people defined as non-persons.[9]

Without perhaps intending it, the Clinton campaign had found its own Willie Horton with which to beat down its rival.[10]

The political consequences were not fatal to Obama, but there is little question that Wright and race helped Clinton to keep her campaign alive. Obama could brag of his "big state" win in North Carolina, and his near tie in Indiana on May 6, but it seemed increasingly clear that Clinton's campaign was surviving on the support of white working-class voters who might well vote against Obama in the general election. This was made abundantly clear when Clinton scored overwhelming victories in West Virginia on May 13 and in Kentucky on May 20. As Clinton herself put it, in an interview with *USA Today* published in early May, "I have a much broader base to build a winning coalition on. . . . Sen. Obama among working, hard-working Americans, white Americans, is weakening again" and "whites . . . who had not completed college were supporting me. There's a pattern emerging here."

---

9 The Clinton campaign repeatedly complained that Hillary was a victim of sexism. Geraldine Ferraro—former New York congresswoman, vice-presidential running mate, and one-time fund-raising-committee member on Hillary's campaign—went so far as to call Obama "sexist" and claim he wouldn't have enjoyed such success if he were a woman. The campaign's complaints against her press treatment, especially from MSNBC host Chris Matthews, at times seemed justified. But there was no clear evidence that Obama's campaign slighted Clinton on the basis of gender.

10 The first President Bush, during his 1988 campaign for president against Democratic challenger Michael Dukakis, ran television advertisements critical of Dukakis's weekend furlough program for prison inmates when he was governor of Massachusetts. One such prisoner, Willie Horton, a convicted murderer, escaped while on such a furlough and committed a rape. Horton, a black man then age 35, was shown repeatedly in a commercial that came to symbolize the racially charged political tactics associated with Bush advisers Lee Atwater and Roger Ailes, the current head of Rupert Murdoch's Fox News channel.

Indeed, there was. Hillary Clinton and her husband seemed bent not only on winning the nomination at any cost but also on destroying Obama's chances of beating McCain in November. "So why is Hillary still running so hard?" asked former Bill Clinton adviser Dick Morris and his wife, Eileen McGann, in a FoxNews.com article in late April, when Hillary's chances were fast evaporating. "Does Hillary want to beat up Obama so that he can't win the general election in November, assuring McCain of the presidency so that she has a clear field to run again in 2012? . . . Every day that she stays in the race and punches Barack Obama, she must realize that she is decreasing his chances of getting elected. . . ." Given the Clinton couple's track record in the last presidential campaign, the answer seemed to be yes. "In 2004, it is pretty obvious that Hillary did nothing to help John Kerry beyond giving a speech at the convention and waging a token campaign on his behalf. Bill did even less. Their goal was obvious: they wanted Kerry to lose to Bush so that Hillary could run in 2008. Is she playing the same game now?"

Clearly Morris was onto something. When Hillary easily won the Puerto Rico primary, her victory could be dismissed as hollow, since Puerto Ricans cannot vote in the presidential election. Nevertheless, Clinton campaign chairman Terry McAuliffe seized the occasion to declare that "[Obama] has a problem with the Latino community." But more telling evidence of the damage inflicted on Obama came two days later, on June 3, as the Clinton campaign entered its final phase. As predicted, Obama easily won the Montana primary with 57 percent of the vote. But in South Dakota, where Obama enjoyed the support of two home state and national party icons, George McGovern and former Senate Majority Leader Tom Daschle, Hillary beat Obama with 55 percent of the vote. As recently as April 16, a South Dakota Wesleyan University poll had found Obama leading Clinton 46 percent to 34 percent.

Perhaps the clearest foreshadowing of what might come in November had already been shouted out loud and clear at the meeting of the Democratic National Committee rules committee on May 31, were Hillary lost her fight to give full voting status to the Michigan and Florida delegations in accordance with the ambiguous vote totals in the two states' primaries. After nearly 10 hours of deliberations, the committee voted 19 to 8 to award half-vote status to the delegations and a 69-59 split of Michigan's delegates for Clinton—a compromise offered by the Michigan Democratic Party that gave Clinton four fewer than she claimed she had earned. Her outraged supporters jeered the result. One woman in the back of the room chanted, "McCain in '08."

A week later, in a speech that often sounded more like a campaign launch than a concession, Clinton announced that she would "suspend" her fight for the presidency. Before a cheering throng at the National Building Museum in Washington, D.C.—just 10 blocks away from the White House—she was at pains to remind her audience "that I was proud to be running as a woman, but I was running because I thought I'd be the best president." While Clinton plainly endorsed Obama, each time she called on her supporters to back her rival, her remarks were met with a mixture of boos and cheers. It seemed clear that Hillary Clinton's ambition to become president had been delayed but not defeated.

While Clinton and Obama were battling over money, votes, and favors, the Republicans were conducting their own intraparty war. Less obvious than Hillary's and Barack's attempts to buy influence with the superdelegates were the reasons underlying the resurgence of Republican Senator John McCain. This erstwhile reformer and "straight talk" candidate had pointedly criticized his party's future leader, George W. Bush, as well as the powerful Christian Right, during the bitter 2000 presidential campaign. Since the ugliness of the South Carolina primary eight years earlier, McCain had done a lot less straight talking about his rivals for power inside the Republican establishment. In March 2000, McCain, outraged at the attacks on his character and record by Bush and his surrogates, had called on his opponent to "get out of the gutter." Obviously referring to Bush, McCain had told reporters, "When you wrestle with a pig, you both get dirty and the pig likes it." Similarly forthright about the militant wing of the Christian evangelical movement, McCain had once gone so far as to upbraid politicians for "pandering to the outer reaches of American politics and agents of intolerance" found within the Christian Coalition and the Moral Majority. More tellingly, perhaps, he had accused powerful media televangelists such as Pat Robertson and Jerry Falwell (who died in 2007) of turning "good causes into businesses." As it turned out, McCain had never been so "moral" himself, especially not in his dealings with corporate lobbyists and rich contributors. As chairman of the Senate Commerce Committee in the late 1990s, the straight talker from Arizona had done a great deal to help a telecommunications lobbyist named Vicki Iseman and her broadcast television clients by intervening with the Federal Communications Commission to bring attention to their special interests. Iseman and her clients had in turn done a great deal for McCain, by providing free plane trips and making donations to McCain's campaign funds.

By 2008, McCain's presidential ambition had turned the one-time "maverick" into a man clearly prepared to accommodate himself to the exigencies of party politics, not just the needs of big business. The Arizona senator tried to repair relations with the Bush family, most notably through his vociferous support of the President's troop escalation and continued occupation of Iraq. And he openly courted the Christian Right, beginning in May 2006 with his commencement speech at Falwell's Liberty University in Lynchburg, Virginia. Even if the Bushes didn't like McCain and his displays of moral superiority, there wasn't much they could do to prevent his nomination. By 2008, the Bush family's position as the Republican Party's dominant powerbrokers was greatly diminished. In the 2006 midterm elections, the lame-duck President had lost his congressional majority because of voters' disenchantment with Iraq. To make matters worse, George W.'s younger brother Jeb, former governor of Florida and the next in line in the family political succession, had left elective politics, unable under Florida law to seek reelection to a third term as governor. Despite the President's assertion that his younger sibling would make "a great president," Jeb did not seek his party's nomination in 2008, and no serious draft-Jeb movement materialized.

For the time being it seemed that dynastic politics would be left to the Clinton family. And other than Senator Clinton's 2002 vote to authorize Bush to invade Iraq (and her persistent refusal to apologize for it), nothing seemed to hinder the early front-runner more than the idea of her husband returning to the White House as prince consort. As much as some Democrats said they craved a Clinton restoration, an equal number seemed to be saying that they found such an eventuality to be less than ideal—something akin to a Latin American family succession, like Argentina's, where the Perons famously succeeded each other, or where, more recently, Cristina Fernandez de Kirchner replaced her husband, Nestor Kirchner, as president. Every time Obama declared himself an agent of "change," the not so subtle message was: "God forbid that we have eight more years of the Clintons."

But what exactly did Obama mean by change? Apart from his early opposition to the invasion of Iraq (while an Illinois state senator), his gender, and the color of his skin, there was very little to distinguish the Illinois junior senator from the New York junior senator on the pressing issues confronting the nation. Obama's plan for national health insurance was somewhat more conservative than Clinton's, but both proposals leaned heavily on private insurance companies to provide coverage. As Harvard University medical Professor Steffie Woolhandler explained,

> Hillary's individual mandates would, as Obama charges, financially punish uninsured families [because they would be forced to buy health insurance]. Obama's plan contains no individual mandate, but would, as Hillary charges, fail to cover 15 million or more Americans.... Hillary's [and] Obama's ... mandate model health plans leave the private insurance industry in charge. Hence, the plans will continue to waste nearly one of every three health dollars on the overhead and paperwork that private insurers generate.

Such like-minded devotion to private-sector participation in public policy was unsurprising given the financial and political support to be had from the insurance and health-care businesses. Through the end of April 2008, Clinton's presidential campaign had received nearly $1.2 million from the insurance industry, with Obama getting $947,000. Overall, though, the bigger money was to be gotten from the companies that are paid directly or reimbursed by private insurance companies and public health programs such as Medicare and Medicaid—particularly pharmaceutical companies, health maintenance organizations (HMOs), and nursing homes. From the "health sector" Clinton collected more than $6.1 million, and Obama got almost $6.6 million.

On financial regulation and tax fairness, Clinton and Obama were once again more similar than they were different. In July 2007, the two leading candidates, prodded by John Edwards, had called on hedge-fund and leveraged-buyout-firm managers to have their profits taxed as regular income, at a top rate of 35 percent, instead of as capital gains, at a rate of 15 percent. But as of this writing, no such legislation had passed the Democrat-controlled Congress, and the issue of whether to tax billionaire fund managers like everyone else had disappeared from the campaign debate. One reason for this was Edwards's withdrawal from the race. Another might have been the fact that Clinton and Obama continued to reap big contributions from hedge-fund and "private equity" managers. As of May 1, both candidates had received $1.6 million from hedge funds and private equity firms. As impressive as these sums were, they were dwarfed by contributions from more traditional Wall Street powerhouses: for the same period, securities and investment firms had given Obama just over $7.9 million; Clinton, more than $7.1 million.

With all this money coming from financial sources, what had become of the Democratic Party's reputation as the party of the working man and woman—of blue-collar America? Gone, it was safe to say, with the Clinton Administration's embrace of "free trade" in the 1990s, reinforced by trade agreements that guaranteed the loss of at least 1.3 million lower-skilled and unionized jobs to countries like Mexico and China that offered cheap labor unrepresented by authentic unions. In keeping with their weakened status within both American society and the supposedly working-class party, labor unions had donated $267,000 to Clinton (as of May 1) for her 2008 campaign and just $95,000 to Obama. In the same period, three of Clinton's top five donors were investment banks or bank holding companies whose PACs and bundled contributions from employees each dwarfed labor's: Goldman Sachs, $448,000; Citigroup, $425,000; Morgan Stanley, $407,000. Obama's funding base was similar: four of his top five donors were Goldman Sachs, $571,000; UBS AG, $365,000; JPMorgan Chase, $362,000; and Citigroup, $358,000. Clinton's top donor, at $508,000, was DLA Piper, an international law firm. Obama's sixth-largest contributor, at $321,000, was National Amusements, Inc., the parent company of media mogul Sumner Redstone's Viacom and the CBS entertainment/television/radio empire (National Amusements donated $251,000 to Clinton). Among the heavy hitters of high finance were wealthy individuals who were spreading their bets: for example, billionaire investor Warren Buffett held fund-raisers for both Clinton and Obama in 2007, and he donated the maximum amount of $4,600 (for the primary and general election) to the two leading Democratic candidates. The even more cautious Lehman Brothers chairman, Richard Fuld, was another Wall Street mogul who wasn't taking any chances: he, along with 63 others, gave the maximum legal donations to Obama, Clinton, *and* John McCain for the primary campaign. No one hedged his bets more assiduously than Rupert Murdoch. On January 30, six days before Super Tuesday, his rabidly right-wing *New York Post* endorsed Obama over Clinton in the New York Democratic primary. However, by the end of April, Murdoch's News Corporation had risen to twentieth on Clinton's list of major donors, pitching in $154,000.

Big money's interest in Democratic presidential candidates and their party was just business, so to speak. With the shift in House and Senate control to the Democrats in 2006, the money followed the power: for the 2006 election cycle, the Republican Party and its candidates for federal office received 54 percent of all contributions from the financial, insurance, and real estate sector (FIRE), or $141 million of the total $259 million donated (in donations of $200 or more). For the 2008 cycle, the proportions had shifted the same way: the re-empowered Democratic Party and its candidates for national office have received 54 percent of FIRE's political largesse so far, which totaled $133 million of the $248 million sum donated through March 2008, with much more money to come.

Meanwhile, anyone hoping for reform of Washington's corrupt lobby system could contemplate three other disturbing numbers. According to the Center for Responsive Politics, through May 1, 2008, lawyers and lobbyists had given $17.6 million to Clinton and $17.5 million to Obama, who criticized a Congress in which "lobbyists write check after check" and "lobbyists set the agenda." While Obama could honestly state that he didn't take money from registered federal lobbyists; he was anything but reluctant to accept donations from in-house corporate lobbyists and from the first cousins of registered lobbyists; namely, lawyers who not only litigate but lobby government agencies and politicians less formally. In October 2007, according to *Newsday*'s Tom Brune, the "anti-lobbyist" Obama traveled to the Miami law offices of Greenberg Traurig, where he raised about $60,000 in a video conference-call to other offices around the country (and about $125,000 through March 2008). Obama was evidently unfazed by raising money at the firm that once employed Jack Abramoff as a lobbyist. Trailing far behind was Republican John McCain, the soon-to-be nominee of the party of business, with the not inconsiderable sum of $5.7 million. McCain hadn't neglected to prospect at Greenberg Traurig, either. Despite his anti-lobbyist platform, the lawyer-lobbying firm was, as of May 1, the "straight talker's" fourth-largest contributor, donating $157,0000. Appearances still mattered, however, and McCain was nevertheless forced in one mid-May week to remove five members from his campaign when their unseemly lobbyist roles were revealed. They included Thomas Loeffler, the campaign's national co-chair, whose lobbying firm worked on behalf of Saudi Arabia; Doug Davenport, regional campaign manager for the Mid-Atlantic states and founder of the DCI Group lobbying firm; and Doug Goodyear, the campaign's hand-picked director for the Republican National Convention and former CEO of DCI Group, which represented Burma's military junta in 2002. And at the end of the month, it was revealed that former Senator Phil Gramm, McCain's economic adviser, was a registered lobbyist for UBS bank while advising the candidate on his subprime-mortgage-bailout policy. Far from cutting ties to lobbyists, McCain's campaign seemed to recruit its staff from that industry more than any other.

On the war/occupation in Iraq there seemed to be a much sharper difference between the candidates—at least, if their rhetoric is taken at face value. In a speech delivered on October 2, 2002, when he was still just a state senator, Obama addressed an antiwar rally in Chicago. While saying he wasn't "against all wars," Obama was clear, eloquent, and prescient in his denunciation of not only the planned invasion of Iraq but also of its ancillary propaganda purposes.

> What I am opposed to is a dumb war. What I am opposed to is a rash war. What I am opposed to is the cynical attempt by Richard Perle and Paul Wolfowitz and other armchair, weekend warriors in this Administration to shove their own ideological agendas down our throats, irrespective of the costs in lives lost and in hardships borne.
>
> What I am opposed to is the attempt by political hacks like Karl Rove to distract us from a rise in the uninsured, a rise in the poverty rate, a drop in the median income—to distract us from corporate scandals and a stock market that has just gone through the worst month since the Great Depression. . . . Now let me be clear—I suffer no illusions about Saddam Hussein. He is a brutal man. A ruthless man. A man who butchers his own people to secure his own power. He has repeatedly defied U.N. resolutions, thwarted U.N. inspection teams, developed chemical and biological weapons, and coveted nuclear capacity. He's a bad guy. The world, and the Iraqi people, would be better off without him.

But I also know that Saddam poses no imminent
and direct threat to the United States, or to his
neighbors, that the Iraq economy is in shambles, that
the Iraqi military [is] a fraction of its former strength,
and that in concert with the international community
he can be contained until, in the way of all petty
dictators, he falls away into the dustbin of history.
I know that even a successful war against Iraq will
require a U.S. occupation of undetermined length, at
undetermined cost, with undetermined consequences. I
know that an invasion of Iraq without a clear rationale
and without strong international support will only fan
the flames of the Middle East, and encourage the worst,
rather than the best, impulses of the Arab world and
strengthen the recruitment arm of Al Qaeda.

By contrast, Hillary Clinton's convoluted October 10 speech on the
Senate floor in support of authorizing the Iraq War might have given a 2008 Democratic primary voter the impression that he or she
had a real choice between candidates.

President Bush's speech in Cincinnati [on October 7,
2002] and the changes in policy that have come forth
since the Administration began broaching this issue
some weeks ago have made my vote easier. Even though
the resolution before the Senate is not as strong as I
would like in requiring the diplomatic route first and
placing highest priority on a simple, clear requirement
for unlimited inspections, I will take the President at
his word that he will try hard to pass a U.N. resolution
and will seek to avoid war, if at all possible. . . :

This is a very difficult vote. This is probably the hardest decision I have ever had to make—any vote that may lead to war should be hard—but I cast it with conviction.

And perhaps my decision is influenced by my eight years of experience on the other end of Pennsylvania Avenue in the White House watching my husband deal with serious challenges to our nation. I want this President, or any future President, to be in the strongest possible position to lead our country in the United Nations or in war. Secondly, I want to ensure that Saddam Hussein makes no mistake about our national unity and support for the President's efforts to wage America's war against terrorists and weapons of mass destruction. . . .

My vote is not, however, a vote for any new doctrine of pre-emption, or for unilateralism, or for the arrogance of American power or purpose—all of which carry grave dangers for our nation, for the rule of international law, and for the peace and security of people throughout the world.

Having gotten pretty much everything wrong in her war speech, Hillary Clinton did make one very astute observation: "[Dissent] is central to our freedom and to our progress, for on more than one occasion, history has proven our great dissenters to be right." And since Obama the dissenter had gotten Iraq so right, then why had Senator Clinton refused so steadfastly during their contentious campaign to admit her mistake. More to the point, why hadn't Obama, once elected to the Senate, been more aggressive about righting the wrongs of Bush's Iraq policy?

In June 2006, when Democratic Senators John Kerry and Russ Feingold introduced an amendment to the annual defense appropriations bill that would have required the "redeployment" of most U.S. troops from Iraq within a year, Obama and Clinton voted against it. They preferred a second amendment, introduced by Senators Carl Levin and Jack Reed, that requested the President to start pulling out troops but without any strict requirements or deadlines. Both amendments failed to pass, and Clinton and Obama nevertheless voted for the overall defense bill, which continued funding for combat and other troops in Iraq. Without exception, on all subsequent votes concerning Iraq, Obama and Clinton had identical records. Only once did they buck their party's majority position—on the May 2007 supplemental military appropriation for Iraq, when they both voted no. The appropriation passed 80–14, so there was little risk for the two future presidential candidates as they jockeyed for position with antiwar voters.

This caution on military funding extended to the President's executive powers under the Constitution. While generally decrying President Bush's excessive use of "signing statements" intended to ignore the will of Congress, Obama (who once taught constitutional law) and Clinton were remarkably equivocal when asked whether they would issue signing statements as president. The subject had come to the fore when Bush issued a signing statement in January 2008, saying that, among other things, he had the power to bypass Congress's prohibition against using federal funds to establish permanent U.S. military bases in Iraq. Responding to a *Boston Globe* questionnaire on the issue, both senators criticized Bush for abusing signing statements but defended them in principle. "No one doubts that it is appropriate to use signing statements to protect a president's constitutional prerogatives," said Obama. Clinton was also ambivalent: "I would only use signing statements in very rare instances to note and clarify confusing or contradictory provisions, including provisions that contradict the Constitution. . . . My approach would be to work with Congress to eliminate or correct unconstitutional provisions before legislation is sent to my desk." Only John McCain, the Republican, said he would "never" attach signing statements to legislation passed by Congress: "If I disagree with a law that passed, I'll veto it."

Without a doubt, Obama injected new life into the Democratic Party, if only by challenging Hillary Clinton and thus driving millions more people to vote in the primaries. Despite his enormous financial support from high finance and big business, Obama's large number of small contributions gathered on the Internet demonstrated, like Howard Dean before him, that a good many Americans were hungry for a role in their own government.

But too often in his short political career, the title of Obama's 2006 political autobiography, *The Audacity of Hope*, didn't quite square with his actual political conduct. In 2000, it is true, when he was still just a state senator, Obama had done something indeed audacious—by running a hopeless primary challenge against an entrenched incumbent Democratic congressman, Bobby L. Rush, on Chicago's South Side. But he did so, according to the *Washington Post*'s David Ignatius, at the prodding of Mayor Richard M. Daley, who was likely seeking to punish Rush for having challenged him in the mayoral primary in early 1999.[11] With Daley publicly neutral in the congressional race, Obama lost badly, by more than a two-to-one margin. Perhaps, however, the upstart Obama gained valuable political experience—and credit—from losing. Henceforth it seemed that tactical caution, reinforced by his immense ambition to be president—and not audacity—was Obama's driving force. Just four years later he ran successfully for an open U.S. Senate seat with the help of Daley's crack political consultant David Axelrod and Daley's former chief of staff John Schmidt.

---

11 President Bill Clinton endorsed Rush in the race.

Another clue to understanding Obama as cautious and politically calculating was revealed in 2006, when the insurgent antiwar candidate Ned Lamont upset the incumbent Joseph Lieberman for the Democratic nomination for Senate in Connecticut. Before the primary, Obama had endorsed Lieberman, and his Hopefund contributed $4,200 to the ferociously pro-war incumbent's campaign; after the primary he endorsed Lamont, the primary winner, but with a marked lack of enthusiasm. Despite a $5,000 contribution to Lamont from the Hopefund, Obama seemed reluctant to oppose Lieberman openly. The Lamont campaign had wanted the party's hot young celebrity to appear at a pep rally in Connecticut on October 18 alongside Lamont, three Democratic House candidates facing tight races, and Senator Chris Dodd, a Democratic incumbent not up for reelection who would later declare himself a candidate for president. But despite personal appeals to Obama by Lamont's campaign, Obama simply dodged the request, according to a prominent party fund-raiser who asked not to be named. "Barack was exceedingly nervous about [appearing with Lamont]," the fund-raiser recalled in an interview. "The American Israel Public Affairs Committee was very, very forthright in asking him and others not to support Lamont." Even the appearance of the four other major state Democrats—recruited for the event at Obama's request in order to give Obama political cover—wasn't enough to allay the young senator's fears. "Barack was essentially not . . . closing the agreement with me," the fund-raiser told me. He said that he was informed by someone close to Obama, "Well, he's just going to duck you." The fund-raiser was annoyed, since he said Obama had committed to helping Lamont as much as he had helped Lieberman before the primary. When he encountered an "uncomfortable" Obama at a separate event in New York City for U.S. Representative and Tennessee Senate candidate Harold Ford Jr., the fund-raiser said Obama told him, "Well, you and I got to talk." But the conversation never took place. "He kind of . . . ran out of the exit and didn't talk to me after promising to talk with me."[12]

In the end, Obama's speech on behalf of Lieberman in the pre-primary days of March 2006 (when Lieberman was far ahead of Lamont in the polls) was the more telling "conversation" between Obama and a Connecticut party split between pro-war regulars and antiwar insurgents. Speaking to an audience of 1,700 at the state party's Jefferson-Jackson-Bailey fund-raising dinner in Hartford, the Obama who had once called the idea of invading Iraq "dumb," "rash," and "cynical" now promoted Bush's most prominent Democratic supporter on the war. "I know that some in the party have differences with Joe," Obama declared. "It's the elephant in the room. Joe and I don't agree on everything. But what I know is, Joe Lieberman's a man with a good heart, with a keen intellect, who cares about the working families of America." To a crescendo of applause, he added, "I am absolutely certain that Connecticut's going to have the good sense to send Joe Lieberman back to the United States Senate."

Obama was right, and not just about the eventual winner of the Senate race. The next day, Lieberman gently chided Obama for his use of an elephant metaphor, since the elephant is the symbol of the Republican Party. As it turned out, however, Lieberman *was* the elephant in the room. Although he hadn't switched parties as of this writing, he had endorsed John McCain, the presumptive Republican nominee, for president, calling the super hawk McCain "the strongest candidate on security." As punishment, the Democratic Party

---

12 The Lamont campaign had to settle for a bland email message from Obama, delivered on October 26, encouraging others to help: "Please join me in supporting Ned Lamont with your hard work on-the-ground in these closing weeks of the campaign. . . . A majority of Connecticut Democrats supported Ned Lamont in the August primary. I hope they will see this impressive movement through to the end by volunteering their time with Ned in these next two weeks."

stripped Lieberman of his superdelegate status. However, the Senate Democratic caucus did not dare strip Lieberman of his chairmanship of the Homeland Security and Governmental Affairs Committee, for such a move might hasten the "independent" Democrat's conversion to the Republican caucus, which would throw the Senate majority back to the Republicans. With a 51–49 majority, the loss of one Democratic member would cause an even split between the two parties, leaving Republican Vice President Dick Cheney, in his role as president of the Senate, to determine the balance of power. With Cheney casting the deciding vote in all ties, every Senate committee could convert to Republican control. We can't know for sure what Obama means by "change," but his two-faced dealings with Lieberman and Lamont sounded like more of the same.

While political donations and commentary cascaded down on the presidential primaries, American democracy bumped along its uncertain path in other locales, far from the roar of campaign rallies. In Portsmouth, Rhode Island, Conni Harding kept up her fight to stop big-box stores from ruining her neighborhood. But by the new year, the political terrain had gotten even tougher since the triumphant days of summer 2007. With the big-box-store moratorium set to expire on February 1, the Portsmouth Town Council met to debate a permanent limit on the size of retail stores. The January 7 meeting at the packed Town Hall council chamber was tense, for Preserve Portsmouth and major property owners were still very much at odds. During his testimony against what he termed an "arbitrary" limit on large-size establishments, the developer Allen Shers found himself heckled by audience members. According to Conni, when Shers extolled the "approximately" 150 jobs provided by the Home Depot in Middletown, an audience member called out that he had lost his job at a local lumber yard, forcing Council President Dennis

Canario to intervene and quiet the crowd. "All citizens have rights; all property owners have rights," Shers insisted, visibly annoyed. To drive home his point about the "rights" of the six landowners "that would be affected primarily" by a building cap, Shers evoked the famous revolutionary war slogan "No Taxation Without Representation": "I've heard the good for the many against the good for the few. This sounds like the preamble of confiscation without remuneration, which I believe is still against the law." Suddenly, however, Shers went silent. As Conni described it, "Literally, it was a Hollywood grab the heart, groan, and fall," as Shers collapsed to the floor.

With Shers taken to the critical-care unit of a Fall River, Massachusetts, hospital, the council cut short its discussion and extended the moratorium to March 1. Reconvening on February 4, the debate finally got down to questions of hard limits and hard money. First, the council unanimously passed a Planned Unit Development (PUD) resolution, which would subject all proposed buildings over 25,000 square feet to additional constraints and a special review process. Next, the "hard cap" resolution passed easily, 6–1. Then came the difficult part. Karen Gleason, the council radical, had suggested a 25,000-square-foot limit on new buildings, but those dimensions were even smaller than Clements' Market, and her idea was dismissed without a vote. Preserve Portsmouth and Councilman Huck Little wanted a 35,000-square-foot cap, big enough to allow the 32,000-foot Clements' to expand modestly if necessary, but Canario opposed this cap, saying it would make expansion for the store impossible, and the proposal failed by a 4–3 vote. The four nays—Canario, William West, James Seveney, and Leonard Katzman—then moved to adopt a 45,000-foot cap, and this measure passed 4–3. The minority tried to fight back with an amendment to reduce the cap to 40,000 feet, but this proposal, supported by Gleason, Little, and Peter McIntyre, failed by a 4–3 margin.

Conni declared herself "fairly pleased" with the outcome, in part because "it could have been much worse." After all, the temporary moratorium had capped the size of stores at only 55,000 square feet. There then arose, however, the possibility of a Wal-Mart "neighborhood market," at 40,000 square feet, moving into Jack Egan's empty lot. "I fully expect we're going to see one of those ['neighborhood' Wal-Marts]," said Gary Crosby, Portsmouth's assistant town planner and zoning enforcement officer, in an interview.

Now the ball was in Jack Egan's court. After our first encounter in Portsmouth when the first moratorium was passed, in August 2007 (during the Town Council meeting at which Egan not so subtly insulted Conni's husband, Luke), the developer called me to chat. He sounded conciliatory and even seemed to take seriously my suggestion that he and his very wealthy venture-capitalist younger brother consider donating the land to the Aquidneck Land Trust, a favorite charity of the Egans. Target's withdrawal was obviously going to cost Egan some money, but the deal's collapse, he said, "didn't change my life." By February of the following year, the developer was clearly unhappy with the new building cap, but he still planned to develop the site: "It won't be as acceptable a business deal," he said in an interview, "but you do what you can do." For now, Egan said, he had no firm plans, only "prospects. . . . We'll develop it, but obviously not with a big box. Any number of small retailers could go in there." Including, the savvy Egan surely knew, a "neighborhood" Wal-Mart.

In Chicago, meanwhile, the big-box lobby was faring much better. As of this writing, Alderman Joe Moore, opponent of Wal-Mart's poverty wages and would-be tamer of the retail giant's immense power, had still not reintroduced his defeated big-box minimum wage bill in the Chicago City Council. "Right now we have no immediate plans to reintroduce" the bill, Moore said in an interview in early February 2008. "We are tackling other, less polarizing issues at this time." To take on Daley and Wal-Mart yet again, Moore said he needed the full attention of his union allies, as well as a "more progressive caucus" in the Chicago City Council. For now, however, everyone in Democratic politics was preoccupied with the presidential campaign. Indeed, Moore himself was planning to go to Wisconsin to help the Obama campaign before the primary vote there on February 19.

It sounded like Moore wasn't quite up for another round of combat with the Daley machine. But he also might have been wary of the power of the retail industry, which contributed $840,000 to Obama and $1.1 million to Clinton (as of May 1). The big-box lobby might just be too big for a group of mere aldermen to fight.[1] Then again, maybe Joe Moore was just being realistic. Industrialized, unionized, high-wage America was fast fading from the political scene, increasingly supplanted by something we might call Free Trade World, where vast numbers of non-union retail employees worked long hours for low wages and no health insurance. When I visited Utica again in August 2007 (not long after attending the Portsmouth Town Council meeting), the older, upwardly mobile America of pre-Reagan days seemed even more beleaguered and depressed. On August 18, the lead story on the front page of the *Utica Observer-Dispatch* was about the annual reunion of former employees of the Chicago Pneumatic Tool Co., which had closed its plant in Frankfort, just over the Utica city line, in 1997 and moved its manufacturing operations to the lower wage, anti-union environment of South Carolina. The 430 people who lost their mostly

---

1 In November 2005, Hillary Clinton had ostentatiously returned a $5,000 contribution from Wal-Mart's political action committee in order to demonstrate her independence from the company on whose board she had served from 1986 to 1992. But she nevertheless accepted $20,000 in contributions from Wal-Mart executives and lobbyists.

unionized jobs were the remnants of the thousands who once worked at the Bleecker Street factory, and some of them still enjoyed getting together to re-experience what one man described as a feeling of "one big family" at the plant. From reading the story, it seemed that many ex-Chicago Pneumatic employees still didn't know what had hit them, for globalization, free trade, and neo-liberal economics were not concepts in everyday use at the plant. What Utica resident Steve Calenzo, 64, did recall was hearing from fellow managers that workers needed to shed their "Utica mentality." According to the *Observer-Dispatch*, Calenzo "wasn't sure exactly what they meant," but "he disagreed" with this assessment. "We used to tell them it was the Utica mentality that kept this place going for fifty years," Calenzo said.

When the Frankfort plant shut down, Calenzo, a production-planning manager, was one of 65 non-union workers who accepted jobs at the new non-union plant in Rock Hill, South Carolina. But three years later he was laid off again, so he moved back to Utica and retired. Calenzo explained in a separate interview that the company, hoping to reduce production and labor costs by moving south, wasn't able to manufacture tools as cheaply as it had hoped, so it shut down the factory in Rock Hill and shifted production elsewhere in the United States as well as outside the country, including to Mexico. A subsidiary of the Swedish multinational Atlas Copco Group, Chicago Pneumatic apparently had more ambitious plans at an even lower wage scale: in 2004 the company entered into a joint venture with a Chinese tool manufacturer, Qingdao Qianshao Precision Machinery Corporation, to make air tools in China under the Chicago Pneumatic brand name.

As for Utica's brand new Disaster Preparedness Training Center, the project had so far flopped. According to the *Observer-Dispatch*, the center employed only 10 people through January 2008, and would expect to employ only 10 more, or 40 fewer people than state officials originally predicted. Moreover, just 1,100 personnel trained at the facility in 2007—less than 5 percent of initial projections. State Homeland Security spokesmen were vague about the reasons for such low participation from New York's "first-responder community." But it seemed that not even the post-9/11 homeland-security boom could save Utica's economy.

With the exception of Varick Street, with its busy bar and restaurant scene, Utica's West Side, formerly dominated by Polish-Americans, appears run-down and poor. So poor, in fact, that along Court Street, I came across an unusual American vista: black and white families living next to each other, fully integrated in their poverty. On the more prosperous (and whiter) East Side, I did find some bright spots, however, including one of the hottest places in town: a lively, very good Italian restaurant and bar called Dominique's Chesterfield, which is almost catty-corner to the long defunct General Electric radio plant on Bleecker Street and only a couple of miles from the site of Chicago Pneumatic. The old GE building has a sign on it saying "Northeastern Unwoven," but I couldn't find any signs of business life in the building or its adjacent parking lot. Dominique's owner, Sal Borruso, told me that Utica's East Side, largely Italian in its industrial heyday, was now increasingly populated by recent immigrants from Russia and, of all places, the former killing fields of Bosnia. Ninety percent of the Bosnians were Muslim refugees from the Krajna region, and the remaining 10 percent were Catholic Croats and Orthodox Christian Serbs. Borruso liked the Bosnians, he said, because "they maintain their houses" and work hard. I asked if Muslim and Christian Bosnians got along better in Utica than they did during the Bosnian civil war and Borruso smiled: "Once they get a fast car and a good-looking girl it's like, 'Where am I from?'" And where did the Bosnians find work? "Wal-Mart or the prison," Borruso replied. "We've got three [Wal-Marts]."

And Utica's Bosnians weren't just distinguishing themselves by driving fast cars and maintaining a good work ethic. A former Bosnian soldier, Agan Hajric, blinded in a land-mine explosion during the civil war, had won the New York State chess championship in 2002, playing against opponents who could see, and placed eleventh in the national championship later that year. In 2007, he came in second in the United States Chess Federation's Blind Chess Championship. Hajric didn't work as a sales associate at Wal-Mart or in a prison: he was employed by Utica's Central Industries, a manufacturing division of the Central Association for the Blind and Visually Impaired.

I didn't leave Utica feeling very optimistic about American democracy—not even with Barack Obama's soaring talk of change and national unity. As Obama surged to the lead in his race against Hillary Clinton, I was struck by what seemed to me a contradiction. The populist Conni Harding had said that she was leaning toward voting for Obama in the March 4 Rhode Island primary, which I had expected, given the Illinois senator's studied attempts to cast himself as a man of the people. What was surprising, though, was that Conni's wealthy opponent, Jack Egan, declared his firm intention to vote for Obama in both the primary and, if possible, the general election.

That Harding and Egan favored the same candidate spoke to the paradox and poverty of American democracy. Obama was, it was true, a "black" candidate (though his mother was white), and his possible ascension to the White House was welcome news to those who hoped for an opening in the system—well-meaning people who thought Americans too racist to allow such a thing to happen. Citizens eager for change and suspicious of family and political dynasties—Bush or Clinton, Republican or Democrat—could rejoice in Obama's success. But they also tended to make the young senator into almost anything they wanted: reformer of the lobby system, friend of the poor in Chicago, opponent of special interests in Washington. And Obama was certainly forceful in his expressions of hope for America.

But you didn't need to look very far to understand one of the crucial reasons for Obama's nomination: an evidently brilliant sense of how not to frighten the American political and financial establishment at the same time as he assured voters of his independence. To accomplish this balancing act, Obama moved early in his Senate career to poach directly on the Clintons' turf—the milieu of rich and well-connected people who can finance political campaigns. As Obama himself writes in *The Audacity of Hope*, "Money can't guarantee victory—it can't buy passion, charisma, or the ability to tell a story. But without money, and the television ads that consume all the money, you are pretty much guaranteed to lose." Obama candidly describes the process: "Absent great personal wealth, there is basically one way of raising the kind of money involved in a U.S. Senate race. You have to ask rich people for it." And all that fund-raising can change a fellow: "Increasingly I found myself spending time with people of means—law firm partners and investment bankers, hedge fund managers and venture capitalists. As a rule, they were smart, interesting people, knowledgeable about public policy, liberal in their politics, expecting nothing more than a hearing of their opinions in exchange for their checks. But they reflected, almost uniformly, the perspectives of their class."

Despite Obama's "avoiding certain topics during conversations with them," it was getting harder to be a genuine democrat: "I know that as a consequence of my fund-raising I became more like the wealthy donors I met, in the very particular sense that I spent more and more of my time above the fray, outside the world of immediate hunger, disappointment, fear, irrationality, and frequent hardship of the other 99 percent of the population—that is, the people I'd entered public life to serve."

So what's a conflicted populist to do?

> Perhaps as the next race approaches, a voice within
> tells you that you don't want to have to go through all
> the misery of raising all that money in small increments
> all over again. . . . The path of least resistance—of fund-
> raisers organized by the special interests, the corporate
> PACs, and the top lobbying shops—starts to look
> awfully tempting, and if the opinions of these
> insiders don't quite jibe with those you once held, you
> learn to rationalize the changes as a matter of
> realism, of compromise, of learning the ropes. The
> problems of ordinary people, the voices of the Rust Belt
> town or the dwindling heartland, become a distant
> echo rather than a palpable reality, abstractions to
> be managed rather than battles to be fought.

I hope I'm wrong, but I think that for Obama, even the distant echo of the people's voices has been mostly drowned out by the thunderous cheers of his rallies and the whispered advice of his "smart, interesting" new friends on Wall Street and K Street. Like the Clintons before him, Obama recognized that the route to power runs at least as much through high finance and the Business Roundtable as through the humble living rooms of Iowa and New Hampshire. Perhaps Obama had even out-Clintoned the Clintons. In *The Audacity of Hope*, published before he announced his candidacy for president, Obama described his conversations with Robert Rubin, one of President Clinton's treasury secretaries and a great promoter of "free trade" and economic liberalization: "It would be hard to find a Democrat more closely identified with globalization than Rubin— not only had he been one of Wall Street's most influential bankers for decades, but for much of the nineties he had helped chart the course of world finance." Now the former community organizer in the public-housing projects of Chicago's South Side was turning to a Wall Street titan for guidance. Was this what Obama meant when he wrote, "I worry that there was also another change at work" inside him?

> [Rubin] also happens to be one of the more thoughtful and unassuming people I know. So I asked him whether at least some of the fears I'd heard from Maytag workers in Galesburg [Illinois, who lost their unionized jobs making washing machines when production moved to Mexico in 2004] were well founded—that there was no way to avoid a long-term decline in U.S. living standards if we opened ourselves up entirely to competition with much cheaper labor around the world. "That's a complicated question," Rubin replied.

And an even more complicated question for Obama, given Rubin's critically important executive post at Citigroup, the third-largest bank contributor to the Illinois senator's presidential campaign. According to the very attentive Obama, Rubin dispensed the usual orthodoxies about "the pace of technological change" and "the size of the countries we're competing against," such that "I suppose it's possible that even if we do everything right, we still could face some challenges." But Obama is not too worried.

> Most economists will tell you that there's no inherent limit to the number of good new jobs that the U.S. economy can generate, because there's no limit to human ingenuity. . . . I tend to be cautiously optimistic that if we get our fiscal house in order and improve our educational system, [the] children [of laid-off factory

workers] will do just fine. Anyway, there's one thing
that I would tell the people in Galesburg *is* certain. Any
efforts at protectionism will be counterproductive—and
it will make their children worse off in the bargain.

Oh, the complexity of politics and money! "I appreciated Rubin's
acknowledgement that American workers might have legitimate
cause for concern when it came to globalization," observed Obama
with exquisite condescension for the laid-off workers of Maytag.

> In my experience, most labor leaders have thought
> deeply about the issue and can't be dismissed as
> kneejerk protectionists. Still, it was hard to deny Rubin's
> basic insight: We can try to slow globalization,
> but we can't stop it.

Was Obama reading any literature on trade and economics that argued another point than those made by Milton Friedman, Jagdish
Bhagwati, and Jeffery Sachs?[2] Had he heard of the British writer
John Gray, or even of his fellow Senator Sherrod Brown of Ohio?
Was he aware of contrary examples of successful economies with
substantial import barriers such as Japan, South Korea, and Germany? Did he know that the argument about "globalization" and trade
wasn't a new one, or that the United States once had a booming,
growing economy with high tariffs, or that his role model Abraham

---

2 In fact, Bhagwati, the reigning high priest of pro-free-trade economists, praised
Obama in the *Financial Times* on March 4, 2008, as "a less disturbing prospect" than
Hillary Clinton. When Obama and Clinton sparred over NAFTA before the March 4
Ohio primary, both candidates tried to portray themselves as critics of past "free-
trade" agreements. Bhagwati was confident that Obama, advised on economics by
Austan Goolsbee of the University of Chicago Graduate School of Business, would
not turn protectionist once elected president.

Lincoln was a protectionist? Could it be that Obama's published thoughts were the authentic expressions of a thoroughly pedestrian mind? Or were they simply the hedging propaganda of an ambitious politician who learned long ago that he couldn't beat the system—that at best he could only join it and perhaps co-opt it.

Or maybe Obama was nothing more than the leader of a faction that aimed to seize control of the Democratic Party from the Clintons and their friends. Even before Hillary endorsed her opponent on June 7, Obama was swooping down on her top campaign donors in New York City's ritziest zip codes. His first major post-victory fund-raiser took place on the evening of June 4 at the Park Avenue home of Richard Reiss, an investment manager for Georgia Advisors. Reiss had initially donated the maximum amount of $4,600 to the Clinton campaign in October 2007. But by late February, the winds were shifting and he donated $2,300 to Obama. Headliners at Reiss's $2,300-a-plate fund-raiser included *Sex in the City* star Sarah Jessica Parker, Caroline Kennedy, the daughter of John F. Kennedy, and Ted Sorensen, a close aide to the late president. The Obama campaign had already reached out for new sources of cash by offering former Clinton fund-raisers a spot on its national finance committee if they could each raise $250,000. The negotiations between the two fund-raising operations resembled nothing so much as a merger discussion between two corporations, with Hassan Nemazee, Clinton's finance chairman, holding out for the best offer. "It would be important how much Senator Obama and his top advisers in Chicago reached out, and how welcome our people felt," Nemazee told the *New York Times*. One top Clinton fund-raiser who remained unimpressed by Obama's advances was Lady Lynn Forester de Rothschild. She told the *Times* she would even consider backing McCain: "I love my country more than I love my party . . . I can't just fall in line." However attractive the Clinton money pool appeared, such aggressive solicitation of wealthy donors seemed to some to be at odds with Obama's reputation as a small donor, "people's" candidate. As Michael Malbin, executive director of the Campaign Finance Institute, put it, "If [Obama] were to suddenly look like Hillary Clinton in the early months, where he would go only after high-dollar donors, it could turn off people ringing doorbells for him."

The same might be said of an Obama-Clinton ticket. While such an alliance was widely discussed, the downsides for both Obama and Clinton were manifest. Obama would risk having his authority undermined by the very party bosses that he had bested. As former Carter National Security Adviser Zbigniew Brzezinski put it, the Clintons residing in the vice-presidential mansion would function as a "government-in-exile." As for Clinton, it was difficult to see how a subordinate position would appeal to her. "It's hard to imagine that after spending her whole life playing second-fiddle to a superstar pol, Hillary wants to do it again," *New York Times* columnist Maureen Dowd wrote. "She's been vice president." Whatever the popular logic of an Obama-Clinton ticket, internal party politics suggested that such a thing could never be: if Obama was the leader of a new faction seeking to dethrone the Clintons, what rationale could there be for inviting them to sit at court?

In early February, the nationally syndicated comic strip *Doonesbury* acknowledged Obama's charisma, as well as his endorsement by Senator Edward Kennedy and Kennedy's niece Caroline by calling him "the first black Kennedy."[3] This was half a joke, a reference to the novelist Toni Morrison's questionable description of Bill Clinton

---

3 Obama actually might be the first black Reagan. Certainly there was a passing resemblance in their sunny dispositions. In January 2008, Obama expressed what sounded like admiration for the late Republican president. In an interview with the *Reno Gazette-Journal*, he said, "I don't want to present myself as some sort of singular figure. I think part of what's different are the times. . . . I think Ronald Reagan changed the trajectory of America in a way that Richard Nixon did not and in a way

as "the first black president." But there was a serious critique inside the bon mot: *Doonesbury*'s creator, Gary Trudeau, was old enough to remember John F. Kennedy's soaring but often empty rhetoric. And he certainly knew that Kennedy was a man consumed by ambition, whose family grabbed control of the Democratic Party in 1960 in a primary campaign notable for its raw displays of political muscle, money, and organizing power.

As Gideon Rachman wrote in the *Financial Times*,

> [Obama's] most famous phrases are vacuous. The "audacity of hope"? It would be genuinely audacious to run for the White House on a platform of despair. . . . "The fierce urgency of now"? It is hard to see what Mr. Obama means when he says this—other than that some inner voice has told him to run for president.

Acknowledging Obama's intelligence and good education, while mocking his supposedly brilliant rhetoric, Rachman observed, ironically, "Just because Mr. Obama gives lousy, empty speeches, it does not mean that he will be a lousy, empty president."

I agree, but I'm not hopeful about an Obama presidency. Obama's campaign had attracted great numbers of antiwar Dem-

---

that Bill Clinton did not. He put us on a fundamentally different path, because the country was ready for it. I think [Americans] felt like with all the excesses of the '60s and '70s—and government had grown and grown but there wasn't much sense of accountability in terms of how it was operating. I think . . . he just tapped into what people were already feeling, which was, 'We want clarity, we want optimism, we want a return to that sense of dynamism and entrepreneurship that had been missing.'" Reagan's "optimism" and "dynamism" were captured by his 1984 campaign slogan "It's morning in America."

ocrats with his proposal to withdraw all combat forces from Iraq within 16 months of his inauguration as president. But there were signs that Obama's utterly conventional foreign-policy entourage—led by Bill Clinton's national security adviser, Anthony Lake—didn't really believe their candidate's declarations on Iraq. A former Latin American foreign minister who knows Lake told me privately, "If Obama is elected you're not leaving Iraq. He'll draw big crowds in the Third World, like Kennedy in Berlin, which will be good for America's image abroad. But you're not getting out of Iraq." Indeed, Samantha Power, a foreign-policy adviser to Obama (before she resigned from the campaign, shortly after calling Hillary Clinton "a monster" in a March 2008 newspaper interview with *The Scotsman*), seemed to support the former foreign minister's skeptical assessment of Obama's commitment to leave Iraq when she told the BBC, "You can't make a commitment in whatever month we're in now [March 2008] . . . about what circumstances [in Iraq] are going to be like in January 2009. He will not obviously rely on a plan that he crafted as a presidential candidate or as a U.S. senator." Power called Obama's plan for U.S. withdrawal from Iraq a "best-case scenario."

Audacity had so far been outweighed by caution in Obama's relations with the money interests. Why would it be any different in his relations with the Wilsonian interventionists who dominated the leadership of both parties? Looking toward reelection in 2012, and fearing a backlash if he looked "cowardly" in Iraq, Obama could well abandon the popular will and keep up the American occupation. Similarly, if Hillary Clinton ever became president, the Democratic hawks, of which she was one, would remain ascendant. John McCain was promising a hundred years of occupation if necessary, so the hopes of a sovereign people, desperate for peace and attention to problems at home, were likely to be dashed. Absent a third party with a Lincoln at the head of it, or an authentic populist revolt from within the Democratic Party, it was hard to see a prompt end to the Iraq catastrophe and its anti-democratic effects, not to mention its immense cost in money and lives.[4] If there was a will of the people—a spirit of self-governing sovereignty—it remained buried alive.[5]

---

4 As of March 2008, more than 4,000 American soldiers had died and more than 29,000 had been wounded in combat. At least 100,000 Iraqi civilians had lost their lives during the invasion and occupation of their country. The refugee count was equally grim: 2.5 million Iraqis have been displaced within Iraq since the arrival of U.S. troops, and another 2.5 million have left the country. An estimated $500 billion had been spent so far by the American people to support an invasion that was predicated on a lie, as well as a "democratic" nation-building project that had been imposed on a largely unwilling populace. According to a controversial book by Nobel prize–winning economist Joseph Stiglitz and Harvard professor Linda Bilmes, the Iraq War will ultimately cost $3 trillion.

5 It seemed unlikely as of this writing that Ralph Nader's third try for the presidency or Bob Barr's Libertarian candidacy would have much impact on the general election.

ACKNOWLEDGEMENTS

Although made in America, this book was conceived in France, so I must first thank my French publisher, Laurent Beccaria, whose idea it was for me to "explain" U.S. democracy to a foreign audience. However, this Franco-American collaboration would never have been possible were it not for my French mother, Christiane, who not only kept her native culture and language alive in me but also turned me into a passionate reader of French and American literature. My interest in politics, injustice, and a good story derive directly from books my mother recommended to me when I was growing up: works like Edith Hamilton's *Mythology*, Alexander Dumas's *The Count of Monte Cristo*, and John Dos Passos's *U.S.A.* trilogy.

This is the first book I've begun writing without knowing a major part of the ending; the 2008 election remains very much up for grabs. As such, I've needed research and fact-checking help above and beyond the ordinary. David Johnson did the heaviest lifting—in part I mean that literally—since he soldiered on with barely a complaint during a very painful three-month struggle with a herniated disc. Given my tight deadlines in two languages and the constantly shifting political landscape, I was often tempted to feel sorry for myself. At times working horizontally from home, David made me feel ashamed that I permitted myself even a hint of self-pity. Despite his back problems (now happily resolved), he provided unfailingly good editorial judgment and advice. Moreover, to be fact-checked by a Ph.D. in philosophy is a challenge and privilege that few writers will ever enjoy. David's doctorate argues better than anything else the benefits of advanced, non-journalism degrees for journalists.

David picked up where my first talented researcher, Paul Gleason, left off. Paul is a literary man with a keen eye for the salient quote, and he did his own heavy lifting through a labyrinth of texts, government reports, and statistical tables that were essential to the completion of this enterprise. Ellen Rosenbush edited the manuscript with the same care and skill that she brings every month to *Harper's Magazine*. Since the death of my first book editor, Sara Blackburn, Ellen is the person I turn to without thinking twice.

At *Harper's Magazine*, there are many lively and spirited editors and contributors to lean on in times of need—too many to name here. However, I must single out Roger Hodge for getting me to read Joseph Schumpeter seriously, and David Mamet for introducing me to the cynical wisdom of George Horace Lorimer.

Four newspaper editors (but they are all far more than that) have helped me in this task with specific advice and inspiration: Robert Whitcomb, Keith Burris, Bernard Descôteaux, and the late Val Ross. As always, my wife, Renee, and my daughters, Sophie and Emme, provided me with inestimable moral support—even keeping me company in our Sag Harbor, Long Island, studio when it just got too lonely at the keyboard.

I'm a journalist, of course, but I never forget than I'm a publisher, too. In my book-writing career I've been privileged to be published by two of the great independent publishers of the twentieth century,

Arthur J. Rosenthal and Roger W. Straus Jr. Now, I'm lucky enough to be published by one of the great independent publishers of the twenty-first century, Dennis Johnson. To Dennis, his wife and co-publisher, Valerie, and their able assistant Kelly Burdick, I offer my deepest gratitude.

Finally, I want to thank Alfred Flarsheim, someone who helped me a great deal when I was a child. I wish he were alive to read this book.

States' Rights Democratic Party, *see*
 Democratic Party
Stephanson, Anders, 195–196, 203,
 208–209
Stevenson, Adlai, 51
Stewart, Rod, 148
Stiglitz, Joseph, 260
Stone, I. F., 25
Strauss, Bob, 66
Strobel, Warren, 186
Sulzberger, Arthur Ochs Jr., 181
superdelegates, *see* Democratic Party
Supreme Court, 41, 42, 60, 129, 161,
 162, 165–166, 197
Swann, Lynn, 226

Taft, William Howard, 53
Target, 106–107, 110–118, 120–121,
 123–124, 128, 136, 174, 182, 247
Taubman, Philip, 180–181
taxes, 73, 74, 83, 85, 105, 111, 114,
 117, 151
 and education, 109–110, 161,
 163
 and equality, 147, 152–153
 and estates, 152–153
 and hedge funds, 233–234
Taylor, Zachary, 209, 213
Teamsters, 54
terrorism, 10, 24, 31, 33, 95, 96–97,
 123, 134–135, 182, 185, 204,

206–207, 239
 also see Al Qaeda
Thatcher, Margaret, 68
Thernstrom, Stephan, 145
37th Ward Pastors Alliance, 131
Thomas, Scott E., 222
Thrasher, Max Bennett, 142
Thurmond, Strom, 53, 191–192
Tilden, Samuel, 42
Time, 215–216
Time Warner, 148
de Tocqueville, Alexis, 18–21, 30,
 103, 105, 164, 170–171
 and American exceptionalism, 18
 and American lack of freedom of
 opinion, 178–179
 and American social mobility,
 145–147
 and the legal aristocracy, 37–38
 and skepticism about American
 democracy, 18–21
Toledo Blade, 184
Torricelli, Robert, 71
Trippi, Joe, 74
Treaty of Versailles, *see* Woodrow
 Wilson
Trinity United Church of Christ
 (Chicago), 227
Trudeau, Gary, 258
Truman, Harry, 53, 70, 191–192, 202,
 207